HERMETICA

Published in Great Britain by
SOLOS PRESS.
First printing 1992
Second printing 1993

UK Distribution:
Ashgrove Distribution,
4 Brassmill Centre, Brassmill Lane,
Bath, Avon, BA1 3JN.

US Distribution:
Atrium Publishers Group,
11270 Clayton Creek Road,
P.O. Box 108,
Lower Lake,
CA 95457.

ISBN 1 873616 02 3

Set in 10.5 on 12 point Palatino
Printed and bound in Great Britain by
Cromwell Press Ltd., Broughton Gifford,
Melksham, Wiltshire.

HERMETICA

THE ANCIENT GREEK AND LATIN WRITINGS WHICH CONTAIN RELIGIOUS OR PHILOSOPHIC TEACHINGS ASCRIBED TO

HERMES TRISMEGISTUS

ENGLISH TRANSLATION, INTRODUCTION

AND APPENDIX BY

WALTER SCOTT

FOREWORD BY A. G. GILBERT

SOLOS PRESS

Contents

FOREWORD

THE *Hermetica* presented in this volume have had a long and chequered career. Western attitudes towards these 'Ancient Greek and Latin writings which contain religious or philosophic teachings ascribed to Hermes Trismegistus', (The subtitle of the original 1924 edition of Walter Scott's translation), have alternated between the extremes of enthusiasm for a lost source of knowledge to scholarly disdain.

The first response is exemplified by the decree of Cosimo de Medici who, knowing that he had only a short time to live, ordered Marsilio Ficino to put aside the works of Plato and get on with translating the *Corpus Hermeticum*, which had just come into his possession. The ideas contained in the *Hermetica* had a profound effect upon such Renaissance scholars as Pico della Mirandola, Ramon Lull and Giordano Bruno. They regarded Hermes as the Egyptian Moses and therefore treated his writings with the same sort of veneration normally reserved for the bible. The Hermetic philosophy brought a much needed breath of fresh air into the stagnant atmosphere of late medieval Europe. It provided a justification for studying astrology and this in due course led inevitably to the discovery that the Sun and not the Earth lies at the centre of the solar system. It is no exaggeration to say that the *Corpus Hermeticum*, most especially *Libellus* I, The Pimander, was the manifesto which shocked Europe out of the Middle Ages, paving the way for the Renaissance and the Enlightenment which was to follow two centuries later in the late 1600s.

The second approach, that of critical scholarship, begins with the publication in 1614 of a volume entitled *De rebus sacris et ecclesiasticis exercitationes XVI* by Isaac Casaubon, a protestant and one of the greatest Greek scholars of his time. Using his extensive knowledge of Greek texts and of the language as it had evolved over the centuries, he was able to prove that the texts of the *Hermetica* were not as ancient as had been imagined, that they dated from the post Christian era, using a late vocabulary. He found that they contained echoes of Plato, (particularly the Timaeus), of the Book of Genesis and of St. John's Gospel. He also concluded that because they make mention of Phidias and the Pythian games, that they were not translations of works by some mythical personage called Hermes but relatively modern writings by pagan authors responding to the challenges of Judaism and Christianity.

This is very much the stance taken by Walter Scott, the translator and editor of the texts included in this volume. As his introduction makes clear, he regards the texts as coming from the early centuries AD at a time when Egypt was under Roman domination but not yet Christian and still some centuries before the birth of Mohammed. He concurs with Casaubon that the texts borrow heavily from Plato, Genesis and St. John's Gospel and concludes that they were written by men of Egyptian blood but Greek education for the benefit of small circles of interested students. The adoption of the names Hermes, Tat, Asclepius, Ammon etc. as the characters in the dialogues he sees as a spurious, literary device to add a touch of Egyptian authenticity to what are in essence second-rate, NeoPlatonic texts. He does, however, concede that there is a special 'tone of feeling' to the *Hermetica* that is authentically Egyptian and quite unlike the Greek dialogues of Plato. He also dismisses Casaubon's theory that they are Christian forgeries.

There is indeed a strong sense of religiosity about the *Hermetica* that is somewhat reminiscent of the Indian Upanishads. Clearly the *Hermetica* were written by men who were concerned not just with Philosophy for its own sake but as a means to religious ends.

Given that such expert Greek scholars as Casaubon and Scott have come to the conclusion that these texts are of late authorship and contain very little that is not to be found in Plato or other classical sources, is there any sense in which they can be of use to us today? Alternatively is there any way in which these scholars could be wrong? To consider these question we have to bear in mind that even scholars have their prejudices.

Casaubon was not a disinterested party. When he wrote his book debunking the *Hermetica*, he was in the employ of James I. During the previous reign of Elizabeth I there had been a flowering of occultism including the magic of Dr Dee. This was anathema to the new king and his rather stiff-necked, presbyterian court. By discrediting the *Hermetica*, Casaubon was taking the axe to what he saw as a tree of delusion. The study of Astrology, Cabbala & Spiritualism was all justified by reference to the writings of Hermes. Dismiss these as forgeries and the whole edifice of Renaissance Mysticism would come tumbling down, leaving the field clear for a re-emergence of pure, protestant Christianity.

Scott, though clearly an admirer of the *Hermetica* for their poetic quality if not the ideas they contain, brought to them that British love for all things Greek that so characterised the age of Byron. Wearing the glasses of a classical scholar he approaches the *Hermetica* with all the prejudice of a Greek. Granted that Alexandria was founded by Alexander the Great, that the Ptolemies were of Greek extraction and that with the death of Cleopatra, Egypt passed into Roman dominion but does this really mean that all things Egyptian had been forgotten by the time the Greek *Hermetica* were written? Scott, like so many of his generation, seems to idolise the Greek philosophers of the classical period especially Plato. Yet if we read Plato we discover that the Classical Greeks regarded Egypt as the repository of the most ancient knowledge. Many of the greatest Greek philosophers made the journey to Egypt for initiation into secret rites. For them the hippy trail led not to Katmandu but to Sais in Egypt. It was the priesthood of Sais who, according to Plato, instructed Solon (c. 638-558 BC), in the mysteries and who told to him the story of Atlantis that Plato was later to repeat in the Timaeus. Plutarch (AD 46-120) the Greek biographer and miscellaneous writer, certainly visited Egypt and based his Greek account of Isis and Osiris on what he was taught by the priests there. Pythagoras, the father of all Greek philosophy was also an initiate of the Egyptian schools, and no doubt it was there that he developed his interest in geometry, a subject which they invented. He probably even learnt the theorem which carries his name from the Egyptians!

That the Egyptians were keen on writing down all forms of knowledge is not just hearsay. Alexandria housed the greatest library of the ancient world until it was burnt down by the Romans in an act of vandalism worthy of Mao Tse Tung's red guards. Contained in the library were texts from all over the known world and of course thousands from Egypt itself. Could it not be possible that rather than the Egyptian writers of the *Hermetica* plagiarising Plato that it was the other way round? That Plato (or rather his teacher Socrates) learnt much of what he puts down in the Timaeus from Egyptian sources? This is not to say that the *Hermetica* necessarily predate Plato but rather that they both draw on a common source, a secret teaching handed down by Egyptian initiates.

Is there anything else about the *Hermetica* that would give us cause to believe they are more than what Scott says they are, late writings derived from Greek proto-types? Well there is, though in places it seems he has almost deliberately obscured this from our eyes in his, probably subconscious, desire to maintain the supremacy of the Greek schools. In the first place there are certain words which he either translates literally without reference to context or doesn't translate at all, leaving them in the Greek. The most obvious example is his translation of the words *"Kore Kosmu"*, the name given to Excerpt XXIII of the Stobaeus. In a foot note to the original edition he gives the meaning of this as "the Eye-pupil of the universe". Yet, as any student of mythology would know, *Kore* also means virgin, most especially the virgin daughter of Demeter, mother nature. The story of Demeter's search for her daughter Kore after the latter was carried off by Hades formed the basis of the Eleusinian mysteries. The exoteric teaching of the myth concerns the mystery of life and death, the re-emergence of vegetation in spring and its death in autumn. The virgin daughter of Demeter (nature) spends six months of the year underground, that is hidden from sight and six months in full expression as leaf, flower and fruit. It is the mystery of life-force and the alternation of nature between summer and winter. The esoteric teaching concerns the soul and its equivalent cycles of life and death. This is what was taught in the cult centres of Eleusis and elsewhere, the meaning of life and death. The *Kore Kosmu* concerns the creation of the universe, the birth of souls and the fall of man. Very likely it draws upon some hidden teachings that have their origins in the mystery schools. We should more properly call this chapter "the daughter of the universe", this daughter being planet Earth.

Another name which is also not translated is that of Agathodaimon. In the original Greek text this is given as two words and has the meaning of "good spirit". In the fragments where this name occurs it is clear that the author is conversing with what we would perhaps call his "spirit guide". This title *agatho daimon* most properly belongs to Osiris, the hidden lord of the underworld. If so then we have the sense that for the ancient Egyptians Osiris was not just the king of the dead but also the good spirit, someone to whom they prayed for guidance.

Other problems arise from the translation of words from one language to another, where the concepts conveyed by the words used do not properly correspond. The most important example of this is the Greek *logos*, which we translate literally as "word". Yet we know, even in English, that this is an inadequate translation. The word *logos* is the root of such words as logic and legal. It is also the suffix to all those subject words that end in -ology. *Logos* does not just mean "word", it means something more like law or decree, the way things are written, the way things are ordered, the truth about something. All of these things were summed up for the ancient Egyptian in one word *Maat*, which was translated into Greek as *logos*. Yet for them this was an entirely inadequate translation of what was for them probably the most important concept in their religion.

Maat signifies the law, yet it is not just any old law but the truth. *Maat* was personified as a goddess with the hieroglyph of an ostrich feather. The favourite theme for Egyptian paintings and one which turns up again and again in tomb murals and on papyri is the scene of the judgement of the soul after death. It was believed by the Egyptians that after death the soul leaves the body and is taken to a hall of judgement. Here the heart — that is the person's essential nature — is weighed in the balances against the feather of *Maat*. If it passes this test, then it is free to go on into the court of Osiris, if it fails then it is cast to a terrible monster, the original crocodile under the bed! The feather symbolises both the light, abstract quality of truth and also the

plume pen with which the deeds of the individual soul are
recorded in the book of life. It therefore symbolises abstract
justice, the law which cannot be cheated because it is what it is.

Trying to find a Greek word which would properly translate
the concept of *Maat* was impossible, and as a consequence a
number of different words are used depending on context. Thus
we can see that sophia (wisdom) is really the perception of
Maat, that *logos* (word) is the written law as edict and perhaps
gnosis (knowledge) is the state of comprehending *Maat*.

We, in studying an English translation of the *Hermetica*, are
in a doubly difficult situation in trying to understand Egyptian
concepts at third hand. Yet we should beware of automatically
assuming there is an identity of intent between Greek and
Egyptian philosophy. In the first place, for the Greeks philosophy was always a process of unravelling truth by a process of
argument. Logic is a process of deductive reasoning, a working
through of ideas by means of lively debate, either real or imagined. To the Ancient Egyptians truth was something which had
been revealed long ago in the past. The work of philosophy,
indeed of the whole society was to keep alive that truth, to
preserve teachings unchanged. *Maat* expressed itself on every
level as the correct way of doing things. Thus there was a correct
way of making statues, of painting murals, of dressing and of
worship. The Egyptians were not only highly religious people,
they were also ultra-conservative. This is why their culture
remained almost unchanged for millennia.

The tension between new ideas and old established tradi-
tions is something common to all ages and all peoples. In our
own times it is expressed, for example, in the architectural
debate between those who seek to preserve classical styles and
those who are all the time seeking new ways of building using
new materials. It is always difficult to resolve such debates and
often it boils down to the authority of the proponents of one
view or the other. Ultimately the authority of the church, for
example, lies in its credentials as the custodian of the teachings
of Jesus Christ and the acceptance by a large part of mankind
that he was (or is) the embodiment of God.

For the Egyptians living at the time when the *Hermetica* in
the form that we have them were probably written, it was a time
of considerable upset. The Romans had suzerainty over the

land, there were no more pharaohs and their religious beliefs were under attack from all sides. As so often happens, out of this turmoil emerged men of strong belief who had the ability to take the old teachings and make them into something suitable for their time. These men were the writers of our *Hermetica*, which were no doubt circulated as a means of attracting pupils to their schools. Scott is rather dismissive of their use of names such as Hermes, Asclepius and so on, yet he makes no mention of the fact that Plato all the time puts words into the mouth of Socrates and his former pupils. It is clear that the Egyptian masters, if such we should call them, were well aware of the necessity of delineating their own line of succession. If the Platonic school ultimately drew its authority from its father Socrates, then the Egyptian school, not to be outdone traced its lineage back to Hermes. A cynic might say this was a cheap ploy to gain more credibility, yet if these masters were in possession of certain teachings handed down from remote times, teachings which were in fact the practical aspect of the philosophy advertised in the Hermetic pamphlets, then they had every right to tag their pamphlets with the name of the father of their school.

Who then is Hermes Trismegistus and did he really exist? There is obviously no certain answer to this question but we can at least explore the possibility and see where it takes us. To the Ancient Egyptians he was not known as Hermes but as Thoth, the god depicted with an Ibis head who officiated at the ceremony of the weighing of the heart. Thoth was credited with the invention of writing, with the setting out of the calendar, with the possession of great magical powers and above all with wisdom. It is unfortunate that in English we have only the one word god to translate a whole range of different words available in languages such as Egyptian. The gods or *neteru* of the Egyptians were not to be confused with the great creator of the universe or God (capital G). They were viewed as being more like a 'communion of saints', that is people of especial merit who had 'gone over' and been granted immortality. Thoth (Hermes) would appear to fall into this category.

In the Hebrew tradition Hermes is identified with the biblical Enoch, who gets only a very brief mention in the fifth chapter of Genesis where it says cryptically "Enoch walked with God; and he was not, for God took him". A rather more expanded version of the life of Enoch is available in the Apocryphal *Ethiopian Book of Enoch*. Enoch emerges as a formidable prophet, able to converse with God and witness to the fall of the angels. Much of the book is given over to Apocalyptic visions but Enoch teaches mankind the necessary arts and sciences to survive in the material world. To the Arabs Hermes is identified with Set, and Agatha Daimon, (that is Osiris), with Idris the companion of the prophet. These correspondences are rather meagre and hardly represent biographical proof for the existence of either Hermes or Osiris, so where else can we look for evidence? The answer to this is perhaps rather surprising, or at least it is to someone who requires scholarly research, we have to look to the psyche.

The Evidence of Edgar Cayce.

One of the most remarkable people of our century was the psychic Edgar Cayce. Born of humble origins in 1877 on a farm in Kentucky he was to become the most famous clairvoyant of modern times. At the age of 21 he lost his voice through laryngitis and when all medication had failed hypnosis was tried. Whilst in a sleeping trance state he was able to diagnose his own condition and it was rectified. Soon after it was discovered that not only could he describe his own physical state but that of others as well. In a sleeping trance state he was able to diagnose the ailments of people who were many thousands of miles away and prescribe for them often quite unorthodox remedies. In the waking state he couldn't remember anything of what he had said and was certainly unable to exhibit the same powers of diagnosis.

This however, was not to be the end of the matter. In due course it was discovered that he could not only describe and diagnose ailments but whilst in his sleeping trance state he was able to reach into the personal and collective 'records' of souls and give 'past-life' readings. He did this for over 2500 people, the readings being carefully noted down by an assistant. From this was developed a most extraordinary library. One could dismiss the readings as just so much more 'channelled' nonsense if it were not for their remarkable consistency. Taken together the readings provide the basis of a cohesive set of teachings and fill in many missing chapters of history, not least the early history of Egypt.

According to Cayce, Egypt was originally inhabited by people of the black race who established tribal rule in the area of the Upper Nile near what was later to become the valley of the kings. At around 11000 BC there was reigning a king called Raai, who was later to be deified as the god Re. At this time there was an invasion of Egypt by white men from the Caucusus led by a king called Arart and guided by a priest called Ra-Ta (an earlier incarnation of Cayce himself). Raai surrendered almost immediately rather have blood shed. After a period of tension stirred up by a native scribe, peace was established when Arart stepped down in favour of his son Araaraat. He also adopted the trouble-making scribe into his own family with the name Aarart. Power was then shared by a triumvirate of Araaraat, Arart (the native scribe) and Ra-Ta the high priest.

As if this weren't enough, according to Cayce there was a further influx of peoples into Egypt from the then sinking continent of Atlantis. These people, who were of the red race, brought with them advanced knowledge of science and technology as well as historical and other records from Atlantis. It was then that the Great Pyramid was constructed, taking a hundred years to build from BC 10,490 to 10,390. This was not a tomb but rather a hall of initiates for what is referred to as "The Great White Brotherhood" and Hermes is mentioned by name as being involved in this project, along with Re the old king. Nearby, somewhere between the Great Pyramid and the Sphinx (also built at that time) was constructed a smaller pyramid to house a hall of records from Atlantis. This, apparently, will be discovered before the end of the century.

What are we to make of all this? Certainly at first sight it seems pretty fanciful. Here we have an ordinary man Cayce, a Southern State, Sunday School teacher, who never read anything except the Bible, yet would regularly go into a deep sleep and talk about Egypt and Atlantis - not to mention a hundred other topics! Was he a fool, a mad-man, a complete fraud or a prophet? Whatever, we may think of him (and there are dozens of books in print based on his readings for those who wish to study the matter further), on the subject of Ancient Egypt he provided some startling insights.

If we look to Egyptian Mythology we find parallels to the Cayce story in the legend of Horus and Set. According to the myth, Osiris, the god of the dead, was once king of Egypt. He was overthrown by a usurper - Set (his brother), who claimed the throne for himself. In this he was challenged by Isis, the wife of Osiris, who said her son Horus should now become king. Set challenged Horus to combat and the matter was brought to the attention of Re, the Sun god. He favoured Set as the most senior claimant but most of the other gods, favoured Horus. Eventually after a long struggle, the gods appealed to Osiris himself who declared Horus the rightful heir, though Set retained some power as the god of winds and storms. This in outline is the story, though it has many elaborations with mythological elements relating to the fertility cult of Osiris and the practices of mummification.

If we compare this with the Cayce story we can see that his king Arart is to be identified with Osiris, (in fact the name Osiris is the Greek version of Ås-År, not so very different from Arart). The usurper in the Cayce story is the Set of the myth. According to Cayce he was a native Egyptian, which might explain Re's support for him. The Egyptians regarded Set as being an Ethiopian, that is black, which would again fit well with Cayce. Yet in the myth he is the brother of Osiris, Horus' uncle. How could this be if they were of different race? The answer to this is given by Cayce, Set was adopted into the royal family to put an end to the rebellion and re-establish unity between the peoples.

There is further evidence for Cayce's early history of Egypt to be found in the crowns worn by the gods. The first god, Re, is usually depicted as wearing a crown with two long ostrich feathers. As we have seen earlier, the ostrich feather was a symbol for *Maat*, meaning justice, truth and the rule of law; and *Maat* was the daughter of Re. One is reminded here of the Greek goddess Athena, who stood for wisdom and insight and who also was born out of the head of Zeus, the chief God. Osiris, when he became king in Re's place, adopted the *Atef* crown, which is a combination of the white crown of upper Egypt and the two feathers of Re. In Myth and Symbol in Ancient Egypt by R.T. Rundle Clark, there is an interesting passage from the Book of the Dead concerning the *Atef* crown.

'There was a cry of acclamation in Henen/nesu [a cry] of joy in Naref, when Osiris appeared [as king] in the place of Re; he had inherited his throne and was ruling the Two Lands and all the people...

The company of the gods was well content thereat but Set was in great despair:

"[I] would that you give me the panoply of the Universal Lord," said Osiris to Re, "for then Set would respect me when he saw my appearance as yours and there would come to me all people, commoners, citizens, noblemen--all--who would see how you have established my respect and created my authority."

Now it seemed good to Re to do all that he had said, whereupon Set came and he cast his face upon the ground when he saw what Re had done for Osiris,

and the blood flowed from his nose

—and that is how agriculture began

But on the very first day that he wore it

Osiris had very much suffering in his head from the heat of the *Atef* Crown

which [he wore] that men and gods should respect him.

And when Re returned in the evening to see Osiris in Henen/nesu

he found him sitting in his house with his head angry from the *Atef* Crown.

Then Re proceeded to let out the pus and the blood

and Re said to Osiris "Behold you are freed from the blood and the pus which were hurting your head."

—and that is how the majestic pool came into existence in the temple of Henen/nesu.'

This passage again confirms the Cayce story that Re stood down in favour of Osiris, that the *Atef* crown was a symbol of the unity between two different peoples (the white invaders from Carpathia and the black indigenous population) and that all except Set accepted the new situation that prevailed. It is also interesting that only Osiris is shown as wearing the *Atef* crown, other gods are shown as wearing either the double crown *pschent* of the two lands or either of the two single crowns of upper and lower Egypt. The crown of Lower Egypt was the red *deshret* that of Upper Egypt not the two feathers of Re but a white crown, the *hedjet*. The *pschent* was a combination of these two. Could it be that the red crown signified the red people, the invaders from Atlantis spoken of by Cayce?

Interestingly, our earliest known mention of Atlantis is in the writings of Plato. In the Critias he narrates the story of Solon's visit to Sais in Egypt. In this delta region of Egypt he says the locals are very friendly towards the Greeks and claim some kinship to them. The Egyptians evidently had preserved in their temples records from the earliest times of events from all over the world which had come to their ears. One such story concerns Atlantis. At a period 9000 years before (that is about 9,600 BC) an arrogant power, Atlantis, swept over Europe as far as the Tyrrenian Sea and Africa as far as the border of Libya and Egypt. The aim of the Atlanteans was to enslave both Greece and Egypt and all the peoples within the Mediterranean area. The Greeks, notably the Athenians, fought back and defeated the Atlanteans, freeing the peoples of both Europe and Africa. Later in a great earthquake Atlantis, an island larger than Libya and Asia (presumably Turkey) combined was swallowed up by the sea.

There are remarkable correspondences between this account and Cayce's. First of all the time period is the same, roughly 10,000 BC. Secondly there is the belief that the Greeks are somehow related to the Delta Egyptians, who as we have seen would have been largely composed of the earlier white invaders led by Arart or Osiris. If these invaders had only recently come from the Caucusus, it is not unreasonable to assume that they would still have had a strong sense of kinship with other Caucasians who had moved into the Levant and into Greece and that they would indeed have received aid from the Greeks in their struggle against Atlantis. In the Isis and Osiris story, there is a long elaboration of how the grieving Isis went to Syria to recover the body of her lost husband, how she brought him back to life and of how she and Horus had to hide amongst the reeds of the Delta marshes till Horus was strong enough to take on Set. The association of the Delta region of Egypt with the Osiris/Horus dynasty is clear, whilst Set is both associated with the old dynasty of Re (who almost perversely accepts his claim) and with the desert regions to the west of the Nile valley. Could Set's backers be the Atlanteans, the red race who were at that time pressing in from the west?

According to the Cayce records, many of the Atlanteans were good people intent on bringing their knowledge to Egypt for safe keeping before their land finally sank beneath the waves. However, there were others who were intent on making slaves out of the earlier Egyptians, both black and white. Their's was the opposite of the rule of law or *Maat* which disappeared from the land for a short period with Seth's supremacy. Egyptian mythology makes much of how Horus (Araaraat) re-established *Maat* as the basis of life and this was never again forgotten. This then led to a golden age of unity in Egypt.

In all of this Thoth (Hermes) has a prominent place as the vizier of Re and protector of Osiris. He is usually depicted with an Ibis head, which suggests that he comes originally from the Delta region (the fifteenth lower Egyptian Nome has the Ibis as its emblem). According to the legends it was Thoth who persuaded the two warring factions of Horus and Set to submit to the arbitration of the gods. The role of Thoth as peacemaker is shown most movingly in a hymn contained in Chapter 183 of The Book of the Dead:

'I have come before you [Osiris], O son of Nut, O Prince of
  Eternity!
I am a follower of Thoth, rejoicing in all that he has done:
he brought the sweet air for your nose,
life and vigour to gladden your face
and the North Wind that comes from Atum for your nostrils.
O Lord of the Sacred Land!
He made the light shine on your inert body,
for you he illumined the dark ways,
for you he dispelled the weakness in your limbs through his potent
  spell,
for you he reconciled the Two Lands,
for you he put an end to storm and confusion,
for you he pacified the Two Lands
so that they are at peace together,
putting away the anger in their hearts
so that they fraternise together.'

Thoth/Hermes then was the wise teacher and peace-maker who not only invented writing and attended the judgement of souls, but also brought to an end the civil war between Upper and Lower Egypt, the supporters of Set and Horus and persuaded Re to judge in favour of Horus, whilst still leaving room at court for Set. It is perhaps worth noting that the Great Pyramid of Giza was built at the head of the Nile Delta, at the point where Upper and Lower Egypt meet. In Excerpt XXIV of the Stobaeus (Isis to Horus) we read that Egypt is the country which lies at the centre of the world, that it corresponds with the heart in the human body. Clearly then the Pyramid was built at a point which is the heart of the heart. Since the heart was believed to be the seat of the soul, the Pyramid must also be seen as in a special way the seat of the soul, emphasising its role in spiritual initiation.

Why one may ask is it that such historical figures as Osiris, Horus, Set and Thoth became venerated as gods rather that merely remembered as patriarchs? The answer to this would seem to be that in the eyes of their contemporaries they were already larger than life characters and it was a simple step for them to be transformed in the popular consciousness from men to demi-gods and then later to appropriate the full weight of archetypal projection. With the passage of centuries, the real people—the kings Re, Osiris, Horus and the other important personages Isis, Thoth and Set— lose their humanity and accumulate layers of myth. They gradually lose their sense of history and become identified with archetypal patterns of human behaviour and the powers behind nature. Thus it is that Re becomes the Sun God, Osiris the god of the underworld and also of rebirth, Isis is the Great Goddess able to transform herself with her spells, Set is the god of storms and chaos and Horus the divine hero the son who avenges his father and re-establishes the rule of Law. The civil war which seems to have occurred around 10,400 BC ceases to be a local affair and becomes a battle between titanic forces, Gods and Demons struggling for not just the land of Egypt but creation itself.

The Egypt that emerges from the Edgar Cayce readings is one of a new nation born out of a disintegrating world. It was a multi-racial society, with all the stresses and strains that that brings and also one coping with planetary changes, with earthquakes and sinking continents, with the movement of the poles and great floods. If there was ever a time for a great philosopher to appear and bring to mankind important teachings for the future, this was it—and his name was Hermes.

Why then do we not read in the extant Pyramid texts and coffin texts and other inscriptions of the Pharaohs, works equivalent to our Greek *Hermetica*? The answer is probably that what we have so far found is only the public face of the religion of Ancient Egypt. The Book of the Dead, whilst based on a philosophy and belief in the afterlife, is largely a collection of hymns to be sung over the dead body, somewhat like the text of a modern day funeral service. One would scarcely expect to find a detailed philosophy enumerated in such texts which are essentially ritualistic in character. Trying to understand the world of Ancient Egypt by excavating the Valley of the Kings gives a distorted view of reality. It is like trying to form an accurate view of Britain by excavating Highgate Cemetery. For the vast majority of Egyptians, like Christians today, religion was about piety and the observance of due ritual. They were not concerned about the finer points of philosophy, only with making sure that when the fateful day came they could ensure a good 'weighing of the heart'. The priesthood ministering to them gave them what they wanted, lots of pious texts and pictures showing them worthy of entry into heaven, to a place in the court of Osiris. Those who wanted more than this went to special schools associated with the temples.

Whilst each temple had its own seminary for training priests and priestesses to serve the cult of whichever god who was their own special concern, there must have been places of a more esoteric nature where initiates sought the "real thing", that is *gnosis*. If the Cayce readings are to be believed, then the Great Pyramid was such a place. It seems likely that the city of Hermopolis, the centre of the cult of Thoth/Hermes also housed such a school. Human nature being what it is and in particular Pharaohs being what they were, it would not be surprising if such schools went underground, distancing themselves from day to day politics.

Another problem remains and that is the vexed question of dates. According to the text books, Egypt as a unified kingdom was brought about by the conquest of the North (the Delta) by

King Narmer of the south in 3100 BC. However, to quote Wallis Budge (former keeper of Egyptian and Assyrian antiquities at The British Museum) in his book The Mummy:

'The chronology of Egypt has been and must be for some time yet, a subject of difficulty and of variety of opinion. The fixed points in Egyptian history are so few and the gaps between them so great, that it is quite impossible to establish an accurate system of chronology: approximate dates are all that can be hoped for at present....The system of chronology by Brugsch, which is based on the calculation of three generations to a century, is generally used throughout this book [The Mummy]'. Quite!

Most textbooks on Egypt take Mena or Menes as the first historical king of Egypt, quoting the Egyptian historian Manetho (3rd century BC) in evidence and give him a date of anywhere between 4400 and 3100 BC. However, this is to be economical with the truth. Unfortunately we don't have an original version of Manetho's history, we only have quotes from later writers, most of whom were more concerned to tie in Manetho's chronology with their own conceptions of biblical history than to render us a reliable text. The Armenian version of Eusebius' Manetho's History of Egypt, written about 326 AD begins:

'The first man (or god) in Egypt is Hephaestos [Ptah], who is renowned among the Egyptians as the discoverer of fire. His son, Helios [Re] was succeeded by Sosis [Shu]: then follow in turn Cronos [Geb], Osiris, Typhon [Set], brother of Typhon, and lastly Orus [Horus], son of Osiris and Isis. These were the first to hold sway in Egypt. Thereafter, the kingship passed from one to another in unbroken succession down to Bydis through 13,900 years. The year I take, however, to be a lunar one, consisting of 30 days: what we now call a month the Egyptians used to style a year'.

There is a note in the Loeb edition from which this is taken that says:

'there is no evidence that the Egyptian year was ever equal to a month: there were short years (each of 360 days) and long years of 365 days.

Following Horus there are then the reigns of Demigods and Spirits of the Dead. In all he ends up with 24,900 years, which he happily compresses to 2206 years by assuming he is dealing with months of thirty days. We can see why Eusebius was perplexed, how do you fit 24,900 years into the accepted Biblical chronology which placed the creation of the world at only 4004 BC?

In another version from the Latina Barbari we get:

'In the Kingdom of Egypt we have the oldest of all kingdoms, and are minded to record its beginning, as it is given by Manetho. First, I shall put down the reigns of the gods, as recorded by the Egyptians. Some say that the god Hephaestus reigned in Egypt for 680 years; after him Sol [Re], son of Hephaestos, for 77 years; next Sosinosiris [Sosis and Osiris] for 320 years; then Orus the ruler, for 28 years; and after him, Typhon for 45 years. Total for the reigns of the gods, 1550 years.' [The actual total is 1150 years].

It can be seen from these two quotations, both apparently drawing from the same source, just how difficult it is to arrive at a satisfactory chronology for the earliest Egyptian kingdoms, assuming that is that the "gods" were really men, albeit very special men, who lived a very long time ago. Most modern commentators are content to consign the gods, demigods and spirits of the dead to the twilight world of mythology and like Eusebius to press on with what they term the first dynasty beginning with Menes. To quote from Syncelus according to Eusebius:

'In succession to the Spirits of the Dead and the Demigods, the Egyptians reckon the First Dynasty to consist of eight kings. Among these was Menes, whose rule in Egypt was illustrious.'

The Armenian version goes like this:

'In succession to the Spirits of the Dead and the Demigods, the Egyptians reckon the First Dynasty to consist of eight kings. The first of these was Menes, who won high renown in the government of his kingdom.'

One possible answer to the problem of dates and dynasties is that people, particularly the early kings of Egypt, used to live a lot longer than we do today. Indeed Cayce claimed that Re's rule covered 199 years. Araaraat (Horus) he says ruled for 84 years. If we accept the Biblical Enoch as being the same person as the Egyptian Hermes, then he lived (according to the Bible) for 365 years. His son, Methuselah of the Bible —Tat in The *Hermetica* lived for nine hundred and sixty nine years! Little wonder then these people were regarded as gods.

Modern writers, despairing of the earlier history of Gods and Spirits of the Dead, have latched onto Menes as the true founding father of Egypt and have, for no real reason, assumed it was he and his descendants who unified the two Egypts. It is not until the third dynasty, under King Zoser that it is believed pyramids were built, again a reference to Manetho, who is quoted in the account of Africanus:

'...Tosorthros, [Zoser] for 29 years. <In his reign lived Imuthes [Imhotep]>, who because of his medical skill has the reputation of Asclepius among the Egyptians, and who was the inventor of the art of building with stone. He also devoted attention to writing.'

There is a note in the Loeb edition that says:

'If the emendation in the text be not accepted, the statement would surely be too inaccurate to be attributed to Manetho. The Egyptian Asclepius was Imouth or Imhotep of Memphis, physician and architect to King Zoser, afterwards deified: on Philae Ptolemy II, Philadelphus built a little temple to Imhotep.'

In other words, it would seem that it was not Zoser who was the inventor of the art of building with stone, but his vizier Imhotep, who was also the famous physician Asclepius. This brings us back to The *Hermetica*, for one of the principle characters in the dialogues is Asclepius. Could then the school of Imhotep be a continuation of a more ancient school founded by Thoth/Hermes in the, by then, legendary time of Ra, Osiris and Isis?

According to Manetho, in his various versions, it was not until the Fourth Dynasty that the Great Pyramid was constructed. In the Africanus version we read:

'The Fourth Dynasty comprised eight kings of Memphis, belonging to a different line:

1. Soris, for 29 years
2. Suphis [I] for 63 years. He reared the Great Pyramid, which Herodotus says was built by Cheops. Suphis conceived a contempt for the gods: he also composed the Sacred Book which I acquired in my visit to Egypt because of its high renown.'

(Africanus went from Palestine to Alexandria, attracted by the renown of the philosopher Heraclas, Bishop of Alexandria). The question of dating the construction of the Great Pyramid has been of concern to Egyptologists throughout the ages. Most agree that it was built by Khufu (or Cheops) as a monumental tomb. Yet why should we assume that pyramids were only built as tombs, even those which contained mummies? We know full well from our own days that the rich and powerful love to be buried within sacred structures but that does not mean that sacred structures are necessarily built specifically as mausolea. How many kings and queens are buried in the great cathedrals of England, yet no-one would claim that these were built for the sole purpose of providing a grand tomb. We are entitled to believe that such important structures as pyramids served a greater purpose than merely satisfying the whims of the pharaohs. After all most pharaohs continued to be buried in the valley of the kings, as they had done for centuries before Cheops.

The existence of the cartouche showing the name Khufu both within the structure of the pyramid and at the quarries where the stones were gathered would seem to suggest that it was indeed built in the reign of this king. Yet we cannot be certain that this was so, he may merely have adapted the pyramid or made some repairs. Also we don't know for sure that the words contained in cartouches are always proper names and not attributes or generic titles. Whatever the case, there is a clear discrepancy between the accepted academic view that the Great Pyramid was built sometime around 2600 BC and the Cayce readings that state it was built much earlier around 10,000 BC. Perhaps the pyramid that we see is a later structure built on the site of an earlier one.

Bringing together these strands of Egyptian history and pre-history, what can they tell us about The *Hermetica*? Well, first we begin to see that the Ancient Egyptian state was probably very much older than is generally supposed. Rather like the modern United States it would seem to have been a multi-racial state, bringing together men and women from the white, the red and the black races. After some early difficulties, they do seem to have been successful in pulling together to build a society that was to last not just a few decades but for millennia. It would seem that the kingdom was founded by some legendary figures, known to us as the 'gods' Re, Osiris and Horus. Amongst these was Hermes, who taught the Egyptians how to read and write as well as much other secret knowledge.

We may suppose that if there were such a person as this Hermes, then he would have taken steps to set up schools to pass on this knowledge for the benefit of future generations. If he was the 'god' who taught reading and writing, then it is safe to assume that he would have left 'Books of Hermes', presumably in the form of papyri. Some of these may have been liturgical in character, the fore-runners of the Books of the Dead, others would have been of a more philosophical nature.

At or around the time of King Zoser there was a renaissance of learning under the guiding influence of Imhotep, known to the Greeks as Asclepius. The writings of Hermes, if they still existed, would have been added to and probably elaborated upon. If they didn't exist, then they may have been created at this time as a vehicle for the philosophy being put forward by Imhotep.

This philosophy, or variants of it, may have continued in one form or another throughout the intervening centuries alongside a knowledge of ancient history preserved at Sais. By the time Solon visited Egypt around 600 BC, all memory of Atlantis had been lost except for the records kept by the Egyptian priests. Other knowledge of a more philosophical nature could have been passed on to certain initiated Greeks, notably Pythagoras, Socrates and Plato, forming the starting point for Greek Philosophy. In the meantime Books of Hermes were still being discussed amongst esoteric circles of Egyptians, probably being added to along the way. These in due course were translated into Greek to form the basis of our *Hermetica*.

This interpretation stands at variance with the conclusions of Scott and others, who see in The *Hermetica* nothing much more than Egyptian-spiced Platonism, yet there is other evidence for the existence of a continuing thread of Egyptian mysticism right up to our present day.

A modern Mephisto

If Cayce, known as the 'sleeping prophet', was this century's most famous medium, then its most enigmatic guru has to be Gurdjieff. Born of Armenian-Greek parents in the border regions of Russia and Turkey, he devoted his early life to the 'quest for enlightenment'. Being fluent in Turkish, Russian, Greek, Armenian and probably a few other languages and dialects, he was better placed than most to seek out whatever secret knowledge was still preserved in the Middle East at the turn of the century. By his own claims he made long journeys through much of Asiatic Russia, Tibet, Iraq, Iran, Turkey, Egypt, Abyssinia and probably India and Indonesia. In his writings he claims that he was one of a group of like-minded people. They apparently pooled their researches to build up a corpus of knowledge and religious techniques from all over the ancient world. Out of this he built his "system" (a loosely structured programme of philosophical discourses, techniques for meditation and sacred dances) which he taught first in Russia and then, after the Bolshevik revolution, in the West. His teachings caused quite a stir amongst the literati and 'new age' fraternity of the early twenties but after a serious car accident he closed down his institute and concentrated on writing.

One might dismiss him as yet another charlatan wise-man (and certainly he cultivated this image) if it weren't for the quality and penetrating insight of the ideas he put forward. He drew to himself a number of men and women of outstanding calibre in their chosen fields, some of whom were to form 'schools' and circles of their own. Many of his former students (and indeed their students) have written books either about the great man himself or elaborating on the ideas he taught. Indeed a whole *Corpus Gurdjiefficum* has grown up, enough to fill a small library.

The obvious question posed by the advent of Gurdjieff's system in the west is where exactly did he get it from? He never claimed to have invented the system himself, merely to have collaborated with others in putting it together from various esoteric teachings he and they had received on their visits to inaccessible monasteries and other places where these things were preserved. The great flaw of Gurdjieff's system, or so it would seem to most outside commentators, is that it is incomplete. Whilst his original intention from perhaps 1916-23 had been to establish a network of schools and study groups through which he would channel his "Ideas" in their entirety, he abandoned this scheme after the car accident and put his main effort into his writings. Even his best known student, P. D. Ouspensky who had worked with Gurdjieff from 1916 to 1920 and himself spent the rest of his life teaching the system, was forced to conclude that it was incomplete. His own journal of his time with Gurdjieff and of the teachings he received was first entitled *Fragments of an Unknown Teaching* before this was changed to *In Search of the Miraculous*, the earlier title being downgraded to a subtitle. At best it seems then that Gurdjieff was no more than a 'Herald of Coming Good', the title he gave to his own coming-out pamphlet that he was later to hastily withdraw from open circulation.

The students he left behind when he died in 1950 were stuck with a paradox. If Gurdjieff were an initiate with the sort of knowledge and powers they believed him to possess, then he must have been sent to the west by the school which instructed him. He himself claimed to have discovered a secret society called the Sarmoun Brotherhood living in an inaccessible valley, who taught him the most important elements of his system. Consensus agreement was reached between the different groups of former students, who had by this time factionalised, that this brotherhood, if it existed at all, was to be found in the Islamic world in the remote regions of Southern Russia. In fact, it was concluded, in the area of those cities with such romantic names (Bukhara, Samarkand, Tashkent) that lay on the old Silk Road and where life was pretty much as it had been for thousands of years. That being so, then it was logical that the 'Masters of Wisdom', the people who instructed Gurdjieff and sent him to the west, must practice an esoteric form of Islam, which means of course Sufism. The question then was not whether or not Gurdjieff was a Sufi, but into which order he was initiated.

Following these deliberations J. G. Bennett, his best known English student and a man of great intellectual acumen himself, made a number of fairly fruitless journeys to Turkey and Armenia in search Gurdjieff's teachers. It was of no surprise to him when eventually a Sufi teacher turned up and asked him to surrender the title deeds on a very large house in Kingston-upon-Thames, so that he could start a Sufi school in place of Bennett's own Gurdjieff group. Bennett did as he was asked but may have been somewhat shocked when this new teacher, instead of using the property as a school, sold it for demolition!

Be that as it may, he continued to believe that there were Masters of Wisdom living in the area of Bukhara and that when the time was right, there would be a 'second-coming' of a master in the tradition of Gurdjieff.

All this and much more besides obscured the reality of Gurdjieff's discoveries and indeed of his own obsessions. The Sufi theory, attractive as it might be from a geographical point of view, was at variance with one simple fact: Gurdjieff was an Armenian-Greek. Even for a man like Gurdjieff, who undoubtedly had a wide and eclectic taste for all things mysterious and esoteric, to become a Moslem would have gone against the grain. Without a full and sincere commitment to Islam it is extremely unlikely that any Sufi sheikh would have initiated him into even the most rudimentary of degrees of his society let alone taken him into the most Holy of Holies. Then as now the Armenians and Greeks were enemies of the Turks and Azeris, who they regarded as oppressors. It seems unlikely that Gurdjieff could have so overcome the conditioning of his early life as to abandon the cause of his own people and embrace in its entirety the faith of Islam, the religion of their enemies. This should have been obvious to Bennett, for he himself ran up against this same brick wall. Though on his travels he was happy to mix with Sufis, to visit mosques and take part in prayers and even spoke fluent Turkish, he could never quite bring himself to embrace Islam. In fact though born a protestant, he ended his life as a Roman Catholic, a convert to the old faith.

If Gurdjieff was not a Sufi, what was he then? Well certainly his teachings show influences from the east. In particular much of his psychology would seem to be based on Taoist Yoga. The sort of Chinese Alchemy that is written of in such texts as *The Secret of the Golden Flower* was undoubtedly taught as a practical philosophy of self-transformation. It seems likely that he learnt techniques involving hypnotism and the use of 'subtle energies' in either China or Tibet. However, he himself claimed that his philosophy was 'Esoteric Christianity', it therefore seems reasonable to suppose, that the essence of his work was Christian. His writings also betray another deep and abiding interest, Ancient Egypt!

As an Armenian-Greek he was born into the Orthodox branch of Christianity, which differs significantly from Roman Catholicism and even more so from Western Protestantism. During the days of the Byzantine Empire, most of the Middle East was Orthodox if it was Christian. The Orthodox church was never as centralised as its western cousin and indeed it was the claims of the Roman popes to supremacy which led to the schism between Rome and Constantinople. Today we tend to think of Orthodoxy as a Russian or Greek phenomenon but before the days of Islam, there were related churches in many other countries, including Egypt. Today there are very few Coptic (meaning Egyptian) christians left in Egypt, yet in the early centuries AD it was one of the largest congregations. At the time of Christ there was a very large community of Jews in Alexandria including groups of Essenes. These people drew much of their inspiration from the Books of Enoch which were ruled out as non-canonical by later church councils, and are not even included in the Apocrypha of a modern bible. With the coming of Islam, the Coptic church gradually dwindled in Egypt but it continued to be the accepted religion in Ethiopia. Long after the Books of Enoch had disappeared from the west, one at least was still preserved in that country and it was only in 1793 that it, the so called *Ethiopic Book of Enoch,* was brought back to the West. A second book *The Book of the Secrets of Enoch* was also preserved in Russia and Serbia—both orthodox countries and is now again available in the west. Fragments of the Books of Enoch have been found amongst the Dead Sea Scrolls and it is now clear that these writings greatly influenced the early writers of the Gospels and Epistles.

Enoch is of course the Biblical equivalent of Hermes, so we are entitled to regard these writings really as Jewish *Hermetica.* We can only assume that the inspiration for writing these books, which are largely dated to the second and first centuries BC, was the same as for the *Hermetica* we have in this book. The Enochian material and the Hermetic material belong to the same Egyptian tradition traced back to Thoth/Hermes/Enoch. Gurdjieff, who could easily have come across *The Book of the Secrets of Enoch* in Russia and who would have been able to read The *Hermetica* in the original Greek, is quoted as saying he would like to end his life in Ethiopia, his favourite country. At

that time Ethiopia was still a little known backwater in the Horn
of Africa. It had succeeded in avoiding colonisation at the time
the rest of Africa was carved up by the Great Powers and it was
a Christian country with a king who claimed direct descent
from David. It was also the home of a lost tribe of black Jews,
known as Falashas, who are only now being accepted into
Israel. Ethiopia was ravaged by the Italian Fascists in the 1930s
and today is a sorry place of famines, wars and the naftermath
of a brutal communist regime but in the early part of the century
it was still something of a paradise, an island of tranquillity at
the head of the Nile. Perhaps this then was the valley home of
Gurdjieff's Sarmoun brotherhood and not Central Asia.

Is there any other evidence to support this contention? Yes
there is in a remarkable book published in the 1970s, *The Sirius
Mystery*. This book begins with an examination of a discovery
made in the 1940s by two French anthropologists, M. Griaule
and G. Dieterlen. During their work in Mali in what was the
French Sudan, they came across several Sudanese tribes who
preserved a secret teaching concerning the Sirius star system.
The essence of this teaching was that Sirius had a dark companion star and that from it came to Earth, at regular intervals a
being who instructs mankind.

Through careful and imaginative research, Robert Temple,
the author of *The Sirius Mystery* was able to construct a thesis
showing that whatever knowledge these people had, came in
the first place from Ancient Egypt. He also examined many
Egyptian myths and legends, going deeply into the Osiris story,
the orientation of temples and connected matters and was able
to demonstrate the existence of a secret tradition concerning
Egypt, Sirius and the coming of extra-terrestrials to Earth.
Though sensationalist in parts and extreme in others, the book
became a best-seller and was even well received by the scientific
establishment.

Now there is nothing new about doctrines concerning extra-
terrestrial visitations to Earth. The plight of the fallen angels,
the *Nephelim* of the Bible, is one of the major themes of the Books
of Enoch. What was different was the way Temple was able to
show a clear connection between the star system of Sirius, extra-

terrestrial visitation and the foundation of Egypt—and to link this with knowledge preserved by a few obscure Sudanese tribes to this very day.

Interestingly, Gurdjieff was also one for space myths. His magnum opus entitled *Beelzebub's Tales to his Grandson* is a fiction based on the supposed career of one such 'fallen angel', who for the sin of *hubris* in his youth, has been exiled to the outermost part of the galaxy, to the planetary system of our Sun. The Tales to his Grandson are a wonderful collection of anecdotes, morality tales, satires and adventures given by the now aged angel as he returns home on the starship *Karnac* at the end of his long sentence. Like any wise grandfather he is concerned for the education of his grandson and he weaves together his magic carpet of tales both to entertain the lad on a long journey and to instruct him bit by bit in the meaning of life. The subjects of Atlantis and Egypt are discussed at length (along with many other things) and his choice of the name *Karnac* for the spacecraft suggests he was hinting at an Egyptian source for his information. The structure of the discourses of Beelzebub is of course reminiscent of The *Hermetica*. When we examine the teachings themselves there is much that is strikingly familiar, from the constant use of the words *Kosmos* and *Logos* to the major theme of the book, the need for man to live life in accordance with conscience, a very deep understanding of *Maat*.

In the work of Gurdjieff and in *The Sirius Mystery* we have clear evidence that the Hermetic tradition, in one form or another, existed right up to modern times. Whether there are still true initiates 'after the order of Hermes' still alive today, when so much of Africa and Asia has been laid waste by war, famine and natural disasters, it is impossible to say but it is clear that The *Hermetica* we have here belong to that long tradition and are worthy of not only scholastic enquiry into provenance but careful study of their contents. Old Cosimo Medici was right, these books were worth translating first!

Notes to this edition.

The original 1924 edition of Scott's translation of the *Hermetica* consists of four volumes. Volume I contains the original Greek and Latin texts as well as the translations and notes included here. Volumes II and III provide extra commentaries on the

Corpus Hermeticum, the *Asclepius* and the *Stobaeus*. Volume IV provides *Testimonia* (many of which are only given in an untranslated form), as well as addenda to the notes on the earlier texts. The whole work is presented in a forbiddingly academic style, with copious footnotes and annotations that at times threaten to overwhelm the texts. Whilst of great interest no doubt to fellow scholars of Greek and Latin, whose interest is largely linguistic as opposed to esoteric, this approach does obscure the simple message of the *Hermetica* themselves. The *Hermetica* are too important as original, esoteric documents to be left buried under such mountains of extra verbiage. In this edition we have attempted a compromise. To maintain a free-flow we have incorporated into the texts themselves many of Scott's footnotes. Where these concerned uncertainties of translation we have printed them within [ ], where they were comments we have enclosed them in< >. Other footnotes in Greek or Latin, or those concerning particular MSS which he was working from, we have left out altogether.

The original Volume I begins with a very lengthy introduction , including introductions to each of the included texts. In the present volume we have kept the first and more general part of this introduction at the start of the book, whilst moving the rest of his more specific commentaries on individual texts to an Appendix. Again our reason for doing this has been to shift the emphasis away from commentary and back to the texts themselves. We leave it to the reader to make up his or her own mind as to the authenticity of the ideas they contain.

A. G. G. 1993

INTRODUCTION

The Hermetica dealt with in this book may be described as 'those Greek and Latin writings which contain religious or philosophic teachings ascribed to Hermes Trismegistus'. It does not much matter whether we say 'religious' or 'philosophic'; the writers in question taught philosophic doctrines, but valued those doctrines only as means or aids to religion.

There is, besides these, another class of documents, the contents of which are also ascribed to Hermes Trismegistus; namely, writings concerning astrology, magic, alchemy, and kindred forms of pseudo-science. But in the character of their contents these latter differ fundamentally from the former. The two classes of writers agreed in ascribing what they wrote to Hermes, but in nothing else. They had little or nothing to do with one another; they were of very different mental calibre; and it is in most cases easy to decide at a glance whether a given document is to be assigned to the one class or to the other. We are therefore justified in treating the 'religious' or 'philosophic' *Hermetica* as a class apart, and, for our present purpose, ignoring the masses of rubbish which fall under the other head.

By what sort of people, and in what circumstances, were our *Hermetica* written? That question may be answered as follows. There were in Egypt under the Roman Empire men who had received some instruction in Greek philosophy, and especially in the Platonism of the period, but were not content with merely accepting and repeating the cut and dried dogmas of the orthodox philosophic schools, and sought to build up, on a basis of Platonic doctrine, a philosophic religion that would better satisfy their needs. Ammonius Saccas, the Egyptian teacher of the Egyptian Plotinus, must have been a man of this type; and there

were others more or less like him. These men did not openly
compete with the established schools of philosophy, or try to
establish a new school of their own on similar lines; but here
and there one of these 'seekers after God' would quietly gather
round him a small group of disciples, and endeavour to com-
municate to them the truth in which he had found salvation for
himself. The teaching in these little groups must have been
mainly oral, and not based on written texts; it must have consisted of private and intimate talks of the teacher with a single
pupil at a time, or with two or three pupils at most. But now and
then the teacher would set down in writing the gist of a talk in
which some point of primary importance was explained; or
perhaps a pupil, after such a talk with his teacher, would write
down as much of it as he could remember; and when once
written, the writing would be passed from hand to hand within
the group, and from one group to another.

Specimens of such writings have come down to us, and these
are our *Hermetica*. The *Hermetica* are short records, most of them
not many pages in length, of talks such as I have described, or
similar talks imagined by the writer, and doubtless modelled
on those which actually took place.

But if that is what the *Hermetica* are, how is it that they have
been commonly thought to be something very different? That
has resulted from the fact that in these writings the names given
to teacher and pupils are fictitious. The teacher is, in most cases,
called Hermes Trismegistus, and the pupil, Tat or Asclepius or
Ammon.

What was the reason for that? Why did these writers prefer
to call the tractates which they wrote 'Discourses of Hermes
Trismegistus', and compose dialogues in which they made
Hermes speak as teacher, instead of writing in their own names,
and saying in their own persons whatever it was that they
wanted to say? The motive must have been similar to that
which made a Jew write a Book of Daniel, or a Book of Enoch,
instead of a book of his own. In the Hellenistic period, and
under the Roman Empire, that vigour of independent thought,
which showed itself so conspicuously among the Greeks of
earlier centuries, had dwindled away. There was an increasing
tendency to lean on the support of authority and tradition; and
among those who were interested in philosophy, the man who

was *'nullius addictus iurare in verba magistri'* became more and more exceptional. It is true that there was at the same time a strong tendency to syncretism; that is to say, men of different philosophic schools were very ready to borrow thoughts from one another; but that, for the most part, meant little more than that a man acknowledged the authority of two or more masters instead of only one, and made some attempt to blend or reconcile the teachings of those masters. The names of the great thinkers of earlier times —Plato, Pythagoras, and others —were held in almost superstitious veneration; and lists were drawn up in which the succession of pupils of those great teachers was set forth, and it was stated that A had learnt from B, and B from C, and so on. Every one must, it was thought, have learnt from some one else whatever wisdom he possessed; it hardly occurred to people that any one could possibly hit on a truth by thinking for himself. And the great masters themselves came to be dealt with in the same way. Plato was commonly held to have learnt from Pythagoras; and there arose a desire to get direct access to the sources from which Plato had drawn his philosophy. In Plato one got the wisdom of Pythagoras at second hand; it would be still better if one could get it at first hand. It must have been chiefly in response to this demand, that there were produced (mostly between 100 B. C. and 100 A. D.) large numbers of pseudonymous writings ascribed to this or that early Pythagorean —or in some cases even to Pythagoras himself, in spite of the recorded fact that Pythagoras has left nothing in writing.

But then again Pythagoras in turn must have learnt from some one else. From whom did *he* get his wisdom? An answer to this question was found by Greeks resident in Egypt, or men of Egyptian race who had acquired Greek culture. It had long been accepted as a known historical fact that both Pythagoras and Plato studied in Egypt. They must have studied in the schools of the Egyptian priests. And what was taught in those schools? No one, except the priests themselves, knew what was taught in them; the priests were careful to keep that knowledge to themselves. All that the outside public knew about it was that the priests had in their hands a collection of ancient books, which were said to have been written by the god Thoth, the scribe of the gods and inventor of the art of writing. Some of those books are known to us now —the 'Book of the Dead', for instance, and others of like character; and it may seem to us strange that any one should ever have imagined them to contain a profound philosophy. But in those times none but the priests had access to them; and a Greek, even if he had got access to them, could have made nothing of them, since they were written in a script and language unknown to him. That which was known to so few must, it was thought, be something very high and holy. From all this inferred that Pythagoras and Plato got their wisdom from the priests of Egypt, and the priests of Egypt got it from their sacred books which were the books of Thoth.

Greeks, from the time of Herodotus or earlier, had been accustomed to translate the Egyptian god-name Thoth by the name Hermes. At a later time they distinguished this Egyptian Hermes from the very different Hermes of Greece by tacking on to the name a translation of an epithet applied by Egyptians to their god Thoth, and meaning 'very great'; and thenceforward they called this personage (whether regarded by them as a god or as a man) Hermes Trismegistus and the Egyptian books ascribed to him 'the writings of Hermes Trismegistus '.

Hence it was that men such as I have spoken of, little known and almost solitary thinkers, came to choose Hermes Trismegistus as the name best suited for their purpose, and in their writings gave out as taught by Hermes what was really their own teaching. These men were teaching what they held to be the supreme and essential truth towards which Greek philosophy pointed; and it was taken as known that Greek philosophy was derived from the Egyptian books of Hermes, in which that essential truth was taught. Their own teachings therefore must necessarily coincide in substance, if not in words, with the unknown contents of those Egyptian books+ that is, with what Hermes himself had taught. That being so, that which they wrote might as well be ascribed to Hermes as to the actual authors; and if that were done, their writings would gain the prestige attached to that great name. A piece of writing to which little attention might be paid if it only bore the name of some obscure Ammonius, would carry more weight if it professed to reveal the secret teaching of Hermes Trismegistus.

Some one of the teachers of whom I have spoken must have been the first to hit on this device; others, into whose hands his writings passed, were urged by like motives to follow his example; and before long the Hermetic dialogue or discourse became, in certain circles in Egypt, the established form for writings on these subjects.

It is not necessarily to be assumed that the authors of the *Hermetica* intended to *deceive* their readers, any more than Plato did, when he wrote dialogues in which Socrates was made to say things that Socrates had never said. It may be that the writers, or some of them at least, did not mean or expect to deceive any one, and that, within the narrow circle of readers for which each of these writings was originally intended, no one was deceived. But when the document passed beyond the bounds of that circle, and got into the hands of others, those others at any rate were apt to take it at its face value, and think it to be a genuine and trustworthy record of things that had been said by an ancient sage named Hermes Trismegistus, or a translation into Greek of things that he had written in the Egyptian language. And that is what was commonly thought by people who knew of these writings, for about thirteen hundred years, from the time of Lactantius to that of Casaubon. There may, perhaps, be some who think so still.

What sort of person was this Hermes Trismegistus thought to be? Was he a god or a man? If one of the Hermetic writers had been asked that question, he would, I think, have answered in some such way as this: 'Hermes was a man like you and me —a man who lived in Egypt a very long time ago, in the time of King Ammon. But he was a man who attained to *gnosis* (that is to say, knowledge of God, but a kind of "knowledge" that involves union with God); and he was the first and greatest teacher of *gnosis*. He died, as other men die; and after death he became a god —just as you and I also, if we attain to *gnosis*, will become gods after *our* deaths. But in the dialogues which I and others like me write, and in which we make Hermes speak as teacher, we represent him as talking to his pupils at the time when he was living on earth; and at that time he was a man.'

Comparing the *Hermetica* with other writings of the period on the same subjects, we find that there are two things that are 'conspicuous by their absence' in these documents. In the first-place, the Hermetic writers recognize no inspired and infallible Scripture; and there is, for them, no written text with the words of which all that they say must be made to conform. They are therefore not obliged, as were the Jew Philo, and Christians such as Clement and Origen, to connect their teaching at every step with documents written in other times and for other purposes, and to maintain, as Jews and Christians were driven to do, that when the inspired writer said one thing he meant another. Hence each of the Hermetists was free to start afresh, and think things out for himself —free in a sense in which Jews and Christians were not free, and even the professional teachers of Pagan philosophy, much occupied in expounding and commenting on the writings of Plato or Aristotle or Chrysippus, made comparatively little use of such freedom as they had. Released from this subjection to the past, a Hermetist could go straight to the main point, unhampered by the accumulations of lumber by which others were impeded; and this made it possible for him to pack into the space of a few pages all that he found it needful to write. Hence there is in the *Hermetica* a directness and simplicity of statement such as is not to be found in other theological writings of the time, whether Pagan, Jewish, or Christian. I do not mean to say that there is much that is *original* in the doctrines taught in the *Hermetica*; the writers were ready enough to accept suggestions from others (mostly from the Platonists), and there is little in these documents that had not been thought of by some one else before. But if a Hermetist has adopted his beliefs from others, they are none the less *his own* beliefs; and his writing is not a mere repetition of traditional formulas. He may have accepted the thought from some one else, but he has thought it over afresh, and felt its truth in his own person. Some at least of the Hermetic writers felt themselves to 'be inspired by God.' They speak of the divine *nous* in much the same way that a Jew or Christian might have spoken of the Spirit of God. It is the divine *nous* which has entered into the man that tells him what he needs to know; and with that divine *nous* the man's true or highest self is identical or consubstantial. 'Think things out for yourself', says a Hermetist, 'and you will not go astray.'

And a second thing to be noted is the absence of *theurgia* —*that* is, of ritualism, or sacramentalism. The notion of the efficacy of sacramental rites, which filled so large a place both in the religion of the Christians and in that of the adherents of the Pagan mystery cults, is (with quite insignificant exceptions) absent throughout these *Hermetica*. The writer of *Corp. XI.* (ii), for instance, says, 'Everywhere God will come to meet you'. He does not say that God will come to meet a man in initiation rites like those of Isis or Mithras, or in the water of baptism, or the bread and wine of the Christian Eucharist; what he does say is, 'God will come to meet you *everywhere*', in all you see, and in all you do.

At what dates were the *Hermetica* written? The external evidence (collected in the *Testimonia)* proves that in A. D. 207-13 some *Hermetica* of the same character as ours were already in existence and accessible to Christian readers; and that in or about A.D. 310 most, if not all, of the extant *Hermetica* were in existence, as well as many others that have perished. From internal evidence I have been able to assign a definite date to one document only. If I am not mistaken, the Greek original of *Ascl. Lat.* III was written within a year or two of A. D. 270.

With respect to all the other *Hermetica*, we have nothing to go upon except the character of the doctrines taught in them. What can be inferred from that?

There was no one system of Hermetic philosophy or theology, no one body of fixed dogmas; each of these numerous writers had his own manner of thinking, and looked at things from his own point of view; and there are wide differences between the teaching of one *Libellus* and that of another. But underlying all these differences there is a certain general similarity, such as would naturally result from similar training and a common environment.

In the first place, the influence of Plato —and of the *Timaeus* more than any of Plato's other dialogues —is manifest in almost every page. Most of the Hermetists were probably not much given to reading (that would seem to follow from the fact that they relied on talk much more than on books in their teaching), and it may be that some of them had never read a line of Plato's own writings; but somehow or other, whether by attendance at the public lectures of professional teachers of philosophy, or by private talk with men who knew about these things, they had imbibed the fundamental doctrines of that kind of Platonism which was current in their time.

But this prevailing Platonism is modified, in various degrees, by the infusion of a Stoic ingredient. Terms and conceptions derived from Stoic physics or cosmology are to be found in most of the *Libelli*. Now Platonism modified by Stoic influence —the sort of syncretic Platonism that we find in Philo, for instance —was not and cannot have been anywhere in existence much before the first century B.C.. There can have been no such blending of doctrines during the period of scepticism in the Platonic school, when Academics such as Carneades were waging war against the dogmatism of the Stoics. It was not until that feud had died down, that the scepticism of the Academy was replaced by a more positive form of Platonic teaching; and it was only then that Platonists began to Stoicize, and Stoics to Platonize. This new departure may be dated, roughly speaking, at about 100 B. C. Among the Stoics who Platonized, the most prominent name is that of Posidonius, who wrote between 100 B. C. and 50 B. C.; and in some of the *Hermetica* the influence of Posidonius can be clearly seen. Any proposal to put the date of the *Hermetica* before 100 B.C. may therefore be disregarded. It is not merely probable, but certain, that the true date is later than that.

But how much later? If we want an answer to that question, we must not be content with talking about the *Hermetica* in general; we must examine the *Libelli* one by one, and try to find out, with regard to each of them in turn, what date is indicated by the details of doctrinal statement that we find in that particular document. That is what I have tried to do. Inferences drawn from *data* of this kind must inevitably be somewhat vague; but the conclusion towards which I have found myself led is this —that the *Hermetica* which have come down to us were most of them, if not all, written in the third century after Christ. Some of them may have been written before the end of the second century; but probably none so early as the first century. And this conclusion, drawn from the doctrinal contents of the documents, agrees with the date A.D. 270, which is indicated by the prophecy in *Ascl. Lat.* III, and does not disagree with the external evidence.

So far, I have spoken only of doctrines derived from Greek philosophy. That includes nearly all that these documents contain; but not quite all. There are, in some of the *Libelli*, things that may or must have come from some other source. But these are of quite subordinate importance.

In the first place, it may be asked whether there is anything in the *Hermetica* that is derived from the indigenous religion of Egypt. As far as definite statements of doctrine are concerned, there is very little. With the exception of the mere framework and setting of the dialogues —the names Hermes Trismegistus, Ammon, &c., and mentions of a few supposed facts that are connected with those names —there is hardly anything of which it can be asserted without doubt that it is of native Egyptian origin. Here and there one comes on a form of expression, or a way of putting things, which is not quite that to which we are accustomed in Greek philosophic writings; and in some of these cases it seems *possible* that what the writer says was suggested to him by phrases that were in use in the Egyptian cults. For instance, we find it stated in some of the *Hermetica* that God is self-generated; that God is hidden; that God is nameless; and yet innumerably-named; that God is bisexual; that God is life, and the source or author of all life; and so on. Parallels to these statements can be found in native Egyptian documents; and in each of these cases it is possible that the writer got the notion from an Egyptian source; but then it is also possible that it came to him from some other quarter. And even if on such points we give Egypt the benefit of the doubt, the Egyptian ingredient in Hermetic doctrine still remains comparatively small in amount; the main bulk of it is unquestionably derived from Greek philosophy.

Egyptian influence may, however, have worked more strongly in another way; it may have affected the spirit or temper of the writers. These men were, some of them certainly, and probably almost all, Egyptians by race, though Greek by education; and there is in some of their writings a fervour and intensity of religious emotion, culminating in a sense of complete union with God, or absorption into God, such as is hardly to be found in Greek philosophic writings, until we come down to Plotinus, who was himself an Egyptian by birth and bringing up. It is true that in Plato himself there was something of 'mysticism ', if this mood or state of feeling may be so named; but in him there was so much else beside, that the passages in his writings in which it finds expression are comparatively few and far between. And something of the same sort may be said also of most of the followers of Plato in later times (until we come to Plotinus) —such men as Plutarch for instance. Numenius (who was a Syrian) may have been more like the Hermetists; but of him we have only short fragments. There may have been something more nearly analogous to the religious fervour of the Hermetic writers in some of the Greek mystery-cults, and still more in foreign mystery-cults adopted by the Greeks, especially that of Isis (which again was of Egyptian origin). But the votaries of those cults stood, for the most part, on a far lower intellectual level than the Hermetists, and their devotion to the gods they worshiped was inextricably intermixed with sacramental rites and quasi-magical operations from which the Hermetic teachers held aloof. And when we compare the Hermetists with the Greek writers on philosophy from whom they got their doctrines, we find that it is just this greater intensity of religious fervour that marks them off as different. I am inclined to think then that it is this tone of feeling that is the distinctively Egyptian element in the *Hermetica*. What we have in them is the effect that was produced by Greek philosophy when it was adopted by men of Egyptian temperament.

Secondly, is there anything of Jewish origin? There is, undoubtedly, something of this; but not much. In *Corp. I* (the *Poimandres*), and in the short piece *Corp.* III, knowledge of the beginning of the Book of Genesis is clearly shown. Moreover, *Corp.* I contains a doctrine derived from Jewish speculations about Adam, and shows, in some respects, close resemblances to Philo. The writer of that one document was certainly affected by Jewish influence. But that *libellus* differs widely from the rest of the *Hermetica*; there is no reason to suppose that most of the Hermetists had ever seen or heard of it; and I do not think it was ascribed to Hermes by its author.

In the rest of the *Hermetica* we find hardly more than an isolated term or phrase here and there that seems to be of Jewish origin; hardly more, that is, than any Pagan might have picked up in occasional talks with Jews, or by reading the first chapter of *Genesis*, which was probably known to many Pagans of the time as an interesting specimen of a barbarian cosmogony. Thirdly and lastly, is there any borrowing from Christians? To this my answer is that I have failed to find anything in the doctrines taught that is of Christian origin —with the possible exception of the doctrine of rebirth in *Corp.* XIII. That is the only extant *libellus* in which the notion of rebirth occurs; and its author (or the author of an earlier *Hermeticum* to which he refers) *may* have got it from a Christian source; but it cannot be said to be certain that he did.

Setting that aside, I can find nothing in the doctrines taught that is derived from Christianity. The Hermetists have no Christ, and no equivalent for Christ.' Hermes is nothing of the sort; he is merely a man and a teacher, and differs from other human teachers only in degree. Some of the Hermetists speak of a 'second God', and apply to him phrases resembling some of those applied by Christian theologians to the second Person of the (Christian Trinity. But this 'second God' of the Hermetists is the Kosmos (or, in some few cases, Helios); and when Hermetic writers call the Kosmos 'son of God' and 'image of God', they are following a tradition derived from Plato's *Timaeus*, and not from the New Testament. (There are also a *few* Hermetic passages in which a hypostatized *logos* of God occurs; but in those cases the source is Jewish, not Christian.) The 'second God' of the Hermetists differs fundamentally from the Christ of the Christians in this, that he is not a Saviour of mankind. There is in the *Hermetica* no trace of a 'Saviour' in the Christian sense —that is, of a divine or supra-cosmic Person, who has come down to earth to redeem men, has returned to the world above, and will take up his followers to dwell there with him. Hermetists might speak of salvation; it was salvation that they sought, and held that they had found; but they did not speak of a Saviour such as was worshipped by the Christians. According to their doctrine, it is by the operation of the divine *nous* in a man that the man is saved; and the divine *nous* was never incarnated upon earth.

The Hermetic writers must, of course, have known very well that Christianity was there. Some of them may have known little about its inner meaning, and may perhaps have thought of

Christians merely as one of the various kinds of people included under the general term *asebeis* or *atheoi* but whether they knew much or little about Christianity, they ignored it in their writings. There is, indeed, one Hermetic document, *Ascl. Lat.* III, the writer of which does speak of Christianity (without naming it); but he speaks of it as of a deadly enemy, and foresees its coming victory over the Pagan cults with intense distress and horror. There is also, in *Corp. IX*, a passing remark which probably refers to Christians, and likewise implies that they are enemies. But these two instances are exceptional; and the Hermetists in general appear to have considered Christianity either a thing too hateful to be spoken of, or a thing too contemptible to be worth mention.

It would almost seem then that, if any borrowing took place, it must have been the other way about. Did Christians borrow anything from Hermetists? But 'borrowing' is hardly the right word. It is not to be supposed that the Christian Church took over this or that theological dogma ready made from Hermetists, or from any other Pagans. And yet the Christian Church took over a good deal; for it took over the men themselves. If not the very men by whom our *Hermetica* were written, at any rate most of their sons or grandsons or great-grandsons, and most of their pupils, or the pupils of their pupils, must have turned Christians, as most Pagans did at about that time. Some few of them may have held out, and stuck to Paganism; and the results towards which the teaching of such men tended may be seen in Plotinus and his Neoplatonic successors. But most of them must have turned Christians. And what did that mean? In some respects the change would not be a large one. The Hermetist, when he became a Christian, would not have so very much to unlearn. If one were to try to sum up the Hermetic teaching in one sentence, I can think of none that would serve the purpose better than the sentence 'Blessed are the pure in heart, for they shall see God'. To that extent at least the Hermetist had nothing new to learn from the Christian catechist. He had been accustomed to aspire towards union with God, and to hold that 'to hate one's body' is the first step on the way to the fulfilment of that aspiration; and when we come upon him, a little later on, transformed into a Christian hermit in the Egyptian desert, we find that he is still of the same opinion. On the other hand, the convert would have to accept, *in addition to* the doctrines which he already held, some others that were new and strange to him; he would be told that he must henceforth believe in a Saviour who had 'become flesh'; and he would have to admit the efficacy of certain sacramental rites, and the infallibility of certain writings, and so on.

But we have to consider not only what conversion to Christianity meant for the Hermetists themselves, but also what were the effects produced by their conversion in the body of Christians into which they were incorporated. And it is here, if anywhere, that the influence of the Hermetic teaching on Christianity is to be looked for. However much these men may have been 'born again' in Christian baptism, they must have retained, under altered forms, much of their ingrained ways of thinking and feeling, and must have impressed something of this on those who were henceforth their fellow-Christians. So far as their influence extended, there would be a tendency to emphasize those sides or aspects of Christian doctrine and of Christian life which were most nearly in accord with the Hermetic teaching. And though the Hermetic teachers and their adherents must have been few in number in comparison with the mass of Egyptian Christians, their influence may have been far more than in proportion to their number; for they were the men who had been most in earnest about religion as Pagans, and they would be much in earnest still. Men of the stamp of these Hermetic teachers must have been prominent among those who set the tone in the Christian monasteries which sprang up in Egypt in the fourth century, and took the lead in debates on questions of Christian theology in Alexandria. And in that sense it might be said that in the *Hermetica* we get a glimpse into one of the many workshops in which Christianity was fashioned.

The extant *Hermetica* are:

(1) The *libelli* of the *Corpus Hermeticum*.
(2) The Latin *Asclepius* mistakenly attributed to Apuleius.
(3) The Hermetic excerpts in the *Anthologium* of Stobaeus.
(4) Fragments quoted by Lactantius, Cyril, and other writers.

CORPUS HERMETICUM

LIBELLUS I

The Poimandres [of Hermes Trismegistus].

ONCE ON A TIME, when I had begun to think about the things that are, and my thoughts had soared high aloft, while my bodily senses had been put under restraint by sleep, yet not such sleep as that of men weighed down by fullness of food or by bodily weariness, methought there came to me a Being of vast and boundless magnitude, who called me by my name, and said to me,

'What do you wish to hear and see, and to learn and come to know by thought?' 'Who are you?' I said. 'I,' said he, 'am Poimandres, the Mind of the Sovereignty.' 'I would fain learn,' said I, 'the things that are, and understand their nature, and get knowledge of God. These,' I said, 'are the things of which I wish to hear.' He answered, 'I know what you wish, for indeed I am with you everywhere; keep in mind all that you desire to learn, and I will teach you.'

When he had thus spoken, forthwith all things changed in aspect before me, and were opened out in a moment. And I beheld a boundless view; all was changed into light, a mild and joyous light; and I marvelled when I saw it. And in a little while, there had come to be in one part a downward-tending darkness, terrible and grim. And thereafter I saw the darkness changing into a watery substance, which was unspeakably tossed about, and gave forth smoke as from fire; and I heard it making an indescribable sound of lamentation; for there was sent forth

from it an inarticulate cry. But from the Light there came forth
a holy Word, which took its stand upon the watery substance;
and methought this Word was the voice of the Light.

And Poimandres spoke for me to hear, and said to me, 'Do
you understand the meaning of what you have seen?' 'Tell me
its meaning,' I said, 'and I shall know.' 'That Light,' he said, 'is
I, even Mind, the first God, who was before the watery substance which appeared out of the darkness; and the Word
which came forth from the Light is son of God.' 'How so?' said
I. 'Learn my meaning,' said he, 'by looking at what you yourself
have in you; for in you too, the word is son, and the mind is
father of the word. They are not separate one from the other; for
life is the union of word and mind.' Said I, 'For this I thank you.'

'Now fix your thought upon the Light,' he said, 'and learn to
know it.' And when he had thus spoken, he gazed long upon
me, eye to eye, so that I trembled at his aspect. And when I
raised my head again, I saw in my mind that the Light consisted
of innumerable Powers, and had come to be an ordered world,
but a world without bounds.' This I perceived in thought,
seeing it by reason of the word which Poimandres had spoken
to me. And when I was amazed, he spoke again, and said to me,
'You have seen in your mind the archetypal form, which is prior
to the beginning of things, and is limitless.' Thus spoke
Poimandres to me.

'But tell me,' said I, 'whence did the elements of nature
come into being?' He answered, 'They issued from God's Purpose, which beheld that beauteous world and copied it. The
watery substance, having received the Word, was fashioned
into an ordered world, the elements being separated out from
it; and from the elements came forth the brood of living creatures. Fire unmixed leapt forth from the watery substance, and
rose up aloft; the fire was light and keen, and active. And
therewith the air too, being light, followed the fire, and mounted
up till it reached the fire, parting from earth and water; so that
it seemed that the air was suspended from the fire. And the fire
was encompassed by a mighty power, and was held fast, and
stood firm. But earth and water remained in their own place,
mingled together, so as not to be separated; but they were kept
in motion, by reason of the pneumatic Word which moved
upon the face of the water.

And the first Mind, that Mind which is Life and Light, being bisexual, gave birth to another Mind, a Maker of things; and this second Mind made out of fire and air seven Administrators, who encompass with their orbits the world perceived by sense; and their administration is called Destiny.

And forthwith the Word of God leapt up from the downward-tending elements of nature to the pure body which had been made, and was united with Mind the Maker; for the Word was of one substance with that Mind. And the downward tending elements of nature were left devoid of reason, so as to be mere matter.

And Mind the Maker worked together with the Word, and encompassing the orbits of the Administrators, and whirling them round with a rushing movement, set circling the bodies he had made, and let them revolve, travelling from no fixed starting point to no determined goal; for their revolution begins where it ends.

And Nature, even as Mind the Maker willed, brought forth from the downward-tending elements animals devoid of reason; for she no longer had with her the Word. The air brought forth birds, and the water, fishes, earth and water had by this time been separated from one another, and the earth brought forth four-footed creatures and creeping things, beasts wild and tame.

But Mind the Father of all, he who is Life and Light, l gave birth to Man, a Being like to Himself And He took delight in Man, as being His own offspring; for Man was very goodly to look on, bearing the likeness of his Father. With good reason then did God take delight in Man; for it was God's own form that God took delight in. And God delivered over to Man all things that had been made.

And Man took station in the Maker's sphere, and observed the things made by his brother, who was set over the region of fire; and having observed the Maker's creation in the region of fire, he willed to make things for his own part also; and his Father gave permission, having in himself all the working of the Administrators; and the Administrators took delight in him, and each of them gave him a share of his own nature.

And having learnt to know the being of the Administrators, and received a share of their nature, he willed to break through the bounding circle of their orbits; and he looked down through the structure of the heavens, having broken through the sphere and showed to downward-tending Nature the beautiful form of God. And Nature, seeing the beauty of the form of God, smiled with insatiate love of Man, showing the reflection of that most beautiful form in the water, and its shadow on the earth. And he, seeing this form, a form like to his own, in earth and water, loved it, and willed to dwell there. And the deed followed close on the design; and he took up his abode in matter devoid of reason. And Nature, when she had got him with whom she was in love, wrapped him in her clasp, and they were mingled in one; for they were in love with one another.

And that is why man, unlike all other living creatures upon earth, is twofold. He is mortal by reason of his body; he is immortal by reason of the Man of eternal substance. He is immortal, and has all things in his power; yet he suffers the lot of a mortal, being subject to Destiny. He is exalted above the structure of the heavens; yet he is born a slave of Destiny. He is bisexual, as his Father is bisexual, and sleepless, as his Father is sleepless; yet he is mastered by carnal desire and by oblivion.'

Thereafter I said, 'Tell me the rest, O Mind; for I too am mastered by desire to hear your teaching.' And Poimandres said, 'This is the secret which has been kept hidden until this day. Nature, mingled in marriage with Man, brought forth a marvel most marvellous. Inasmuch as Man had got from the structure of the heavens the character of the seven Administrators, who were made, as I told you, of fire and air, Nature tarried not, but forthwith gave birth to seven Men, according to the characters of the seven Administrators; and these seven Men were bisexual and .' And thereupon I said, 'Now indeed, Poimandres, my desire is strong, and I long to hear; do not swerve aside.' 'Nay, be silent,' said Poimandres; 'I have not yet finished explaining this first thing.' 'See, I am silent,' said I. 'These seven Men then,' said he, 'were generated in this wise. Nature brought forth their bodies; earth was the female element, and water the male element; and from the aether they received their vital spirit. (But their incorporeal part was made after the form of Man; and the Man in them changed from Life and Light into soul and mind, soul from Life, and mind from Light. And all things remained so until the end of a period. And now I will tell you that which you have been longing to hear. When the period was completed, the bond by which all things were held together was loosed, by God's design; all living creatures, having till then been bisexual, were parted asunder, and man with the rest; and so there came to be males on the one part, and likewise females on the other part. And thereon God spoke thus in holy speech: Increase and multiply abundantly, all ye that have been created and made. And let the man that has mind in him recognise that he is immortal, and that the cause of death is carnal desire. And he who has recognised himself enters into the Good. And when God had thus spoken, his Providence, by means of Destiny and the structure of the heavens, brought about the unions of male and female, and set the births going; and all creatures multiplied after theirkinds. And he who has recognised himself has entered into that Good which is above all being; but he who, being led astray by carnal desire, has set his affection on the body, continues wandering in the darkness of the sense-world, suffering the lot of death.'

'But what great sin,' said I, 'do those who are in ignorance commit, that they should be deprived of immortality?' 'O man,' said he, 'it seems you have not heeded what you heard. Did I not bid you mark my words?' 'I do so,' said I, 'and I keep in memory what you have told me, and moreover I am thankful for it.' 'If then you have marked my words,' said he, 'tell me why those who are in ignorance deserve death.' I answered, 'It is because the source from which the material body has issued is that grim darkness, whence came the watery substance of which the body is composed; (and therefore those who have set their affection on the body are deservedly held captive) in the sensible world, from which is drawn the draught of death.' 'O man,' said he, 'you have understood aright. But why is it that he who has recognised himself enters into the Good, as it was said in God's speech?' I answered, 'It is because the Father of all consists of Light and Life, and from him Man has sprung.' 'You are right,' said he 'If then, being made of Life and Light, you learn to know that you are made of them, you will go back into Life and Light.' Thus spoke Poimandres.

'But tell me this too,' said I. 'God said, Let the man who has mind in him recognise himself; but have not all men mind?' 'O man,' said Mind to me, 'speak not so. I, even Mind, come to those men who are holy and good and pure and merciful; and my coming is a succour to them, and forthwith they recognise all things, and win the Father's grace by loving worship, and give thanks to him, praising and hymning him with hearts uplifted to him in filial affection. And before they give up the body to the death which is proper to it, they loathe the bodily senses, knowing what manner of work the senses do. Nay, rather I myself, even Mind, will not suffer the workings of the body by which they are assailed to take effect; I will keep guard at the gates, and bar the entrance of the base and evil workings of the senses, cutting off all thoughts of them. But from men that are foolish and evil and wicked and envious and covetous and murderous and impious I keep far aloof, and give place to the avenging daemon. And he brings to bear on such a man the fierce heat of fire, and tortures him, tossing him about in the tumult of the senses; and he equips the man more fully for his lawless deeds, that so he may incur the greater punishment. And that man ceases not to struggle blindly; he gives way to boundless appetites, his desire being insatiable; and so by his own doing he makes the fire yet hotter for his torment.'

'Full well have you taught me all, O Mind,' said I, 'even as I wished. But tell me furthermore of the ascent by which men mount; tell me how I shall enter into Life.' Poimandres answered, 'At the dissolution of your material body, you first yield up the body itself to be changed, and the visible form you bore is no longer seen. And your vital spirit you yield up to the atmosphere so that it no longer works in you; and the bodily senses go backto their own sources, becoming parts of the universe, and entering into fresh combinations to do other work. And thereupon the man mounts upward through the structure of the heavens. And to the first zone of heaven he gives up the force which works increase and that which works decrease; to the second zone, the machinations of evil cunning; to the third zone, the lust whereby men are deceived; to the fourth zone, domineering arrogance; to the fifth zone, unholy daring and rash audacity; to the sixth zone, evil strivings after wealth; and to the seventh zone, the falsehood which lies in wait to work harm. And thereupon, having been stripped of all that was wrought upon him by the structure of the heavens, he ascends to the substance of the eighth sphere, being now possessed of his own proper power; and he sings, together with those who dwell there, hymning the Father; and they that are there rejoice with him at his coming. And being made like to those with whom he dwells, he hears the Powers, who are above the substance of the eighth sphere, singing praise to God with a voice that is theirs alone. And thereafter, each in his turn, they mount upward to the Father; they give themselves up to the Powers, and becoming Powers themselves, they enter into God. This is the Good; this is the consummation, for those who have got gnosis.

And now, why do you delay? Seeing that you have received all, why do you not make yourself a guide to those who are worthy of the boon, that so mankind may through you be saved by God?' And when Poimandres had thus spoken to me, he mingled with the Powers.

And I inscribed in my memory the benefaction of Poimandres; and I was exceeding glad, for I was fed full with that for which I craved. My bodily sleep had come to be sober wakefulness of soul; and the closing of my eyes, true vision; and my silence, pregnant with good; and my barrenness of speech, a brood of (holy thoughts). And this befell me, in that I received from Poimandres, that is, from the Mind of the Sovereignty, the teaching of (truth); whereby becoming God inspired, I attained to the abode of Truth.

Therefore with all my soul and with all my strength did I give praise to God the Father, saying:

'Holy is God the Father of all, who is before the first beginning; holy is God, whose purpose is accomplished by his several Powers; holy is God, who wills to be known, and is known by them that are his own.

Holy art Thou, who by thy word hast constructed all that is; holy art Thou, whose brightness nature has not darkened; holy art Thou, of whom all nature is an image.

Holy art Thou, who art stronger than all domination; holy art Thou, who art greater than all preeminence; holy art Thou, who surpassest all praises.

Accept pure offerings of speech from a soul and heart uplifted to thee, Thou of whom no words can tell, no tongue can speak, whom silence only can declare.

I pray that I may never fall away from that knowledge of thee which matches with our being; grant Thou this my prayer. And put power into me, that so, having obtained this boon, I may enlighten those of my race who are in ignorance, my brothers and thy sons.

Wherefore I believe and bear witness that I enter into Life and Light. Blessed art thou, Father; thy Man seeks to share thy holiness, even as Thou hast given him all authority.' And when I had given thanks and praise to the Father of all, I was sent forth by him, having had power given me, and having been taught the nature of all that is, and seen the supreme vision. And I began to preach to men the beauty of piety and of the knowledge of God, saying: 'Hearken, ye folk, men born of earth, who have given yourselves up to drunkenness and sleep in your ignorance of God; awake to soberness, cease to be sodden with strong drink and lulled in sleep devoid of reason.' And when they heard, they gathered round me with one accord. And I said, 'O men, why have you given yourselves up to death, when you have been granted power to partake of immortality? Repent, ye who have journeyed with Error, and joined company with Ignorance; rid yourselves of darkness, and lay hold on the Light; partake of immortality, forsaking corruption.' And some of them mocked at my words, and stood aloof; for they had given themselves up to the way of death. But others besought me that they might be taught, and cast themselves down at my feet. And I bade them stand up; and I made myself a guide to mankind, teaching them the doctrine, how and in what wise they might be saved. And I sowed in them the teachings of wisdom; and that which I sowed was watered with the water of immortal life. And when evening was come, and the light of the sun was beginning to go down, I bade them all with one accord give thanks to God. And when they had accomplished their thanksgiving, they betook them every man to his own bed.

LIBELLUS II

A discourse of Hermes Trismegistus to Asclepius.

Hermes. Is it not true of everything which is moved, Asclepius, that it is moved in something, and is moved by something? Asclepius. Assuredly. *Hermes.* And is not that in which the thing is moved necessarily greater than the thing moved? *Ascl.* Yes. *Hermes.* And that in which the thing is moved must be of opposite nature to the thing moved. *Ascl.* Certainly it must.

Hermes. Now this Kosmos is great; there is no body greater than the Kosmos. *Ascl.* Agreed. *Hermes.* And it is massive; for it is filled with many other great bodies, or rather, with all the bodies that exist. *Ascl.* It is so. *Hermes.* And the Kosmos is a body, is it not? *Ascl.* Yes. *Hermes.* And a thing that is moved? *Ascl.* Assuredly. *Hermes.* Of what magnitude then must be the space in which the Kosmos is moved? And of what nature? Must not that space be far greater, that it may be able to contain the continuous motion of the Kosmos, and that the thing moved may not be cramped through want of room, and cease to move? *Ascl.* Great indeed must be that space, Trismegistus. *Hermes.* And of what nature must it be, Asclepius? Must it not be of opposite nature to the Kosmos? And of opposite nature to body is the incorporeal. *Ascl.* Agreed. *Hermes.* That space then is incorporeal.

Now that which is incorporeal is either something that appertains to God, or else it is God himself. (By 'a thing that appertains to God' I mean, not a thing that comes into being, but a thing without beginning.) If then the incorporeal thing is something that appertains to God, it is of the nature of eternal substance; but if it is God himself, it must be distinct from substance. Space is an object of thought, but not in the same sense that God is; for God is an object of thought primarily to himself, but Space is an object of thought to us, not to itself. That which is an object of thought is such to him who contemplates it in thought; Space therefore is an object of thought, not to itself (for it is not contemplated by itself), but to us. And if Space is an object of thought, not as God is, but as the working of a power by which things are contained, then Space is something other than God.

Moreover, everything that is moved is moved, not in something that is itself moved, but in something that stands fast. And the mover too stands fast; it is impossible that that which moves a thing should be moved together with the thing it moves.

Ascl. How is it then, Trismegistus, that the things which in our world move other things are moved together with the things they move? For I have heard you say that the planet-spheres are moved by the sphere of the fixed stars; and surely that sphere is itself moved. *Hermes.* In that instance, Asclepius, the two things are not moved together. Their movements are contrary; for the sphere of the fixed stars is not moved in the same way as the planet-spheres, but in the opposite direction. And the contrariety of the two movements keeps the fulcrum stationary; for motion is stayed by resistance. The planet-spheres then, being moved in the opposite direction to the sphere of the fixed stars, . It cannot be otherwise. Look at the (Great Bear and the Little Bear. As you see, they neither set nor rise; are they moved, think; you, or do they stand fast? *Ascl.* They are moved, Trismegistus. *Hermes.* And of what kind is their movement? *Ascl.* It is a movement which circles round one point. *Hermes.* Yes, and their revolution round one point is a movement that is held fast by immobility. For revolution round one point prevents departure from the orbit; and the prevention of departure from the orbit results in revolution round one point. And even so it is that movement in contrary directions is steadfast and stable, being kept stationary by the contrariety. I will give an example which you can see with your own eyes. Take the case of some animal on earth; look at a man, for instance, swimming. The water flows; but the resistance made by the swimmer's hands and feet keeps him stationary, so that he is not borne away down stream. —*Ascl.* That example makes the matter clear, Trismegistus.

All movement then takes place within something that stands fast, and is caused by something that stands fast.

The movement of the Kosmos then, and of every living being that is material, is caused, not by things outside the body, but by things within it, which operate outwards from within; that is to say, either by soul or by something else that is incorporeal. For the body which contains a soul is not moved by a body; indeed, body cannot move body at all, even if the body moved be soulless. *Ascl.* What mean you, Trismegistus. When logs and stones and all other soulless things are moved, are they not moved by bodies? *Hermes.* Certainly not, Asclepius. That which is within the body, and which moves the soulless thing, is not a body; and that is what moves both the body of him who carries a thing and the body of the thing carried; for a soulless thing cannot of itself move anything. Thus it is that you see the soul distressed by the weight of its burden, when it bears two bodies at once.

I have now explained to you what is that by which things are moved, as well as what is that in which things are moved.

Ascl. But surely, Trismegistus, it must be in void that things are moved. *Hermes.* You ought not to say that, Asclepius. Nothing that is, is void; it is only that which is not, that is void. That which exists can never come to be void; (this is implied in the very meaning of the word 'existence';) and that which is could not be a thing which is, if it were not filled with something existent. *Ascl.* But what would you say, Trismegistus, of an empty jar, or pot, or trough, and the like? Are not such things void? *Hermes.* How far you are in error, Asclepius! Do you suppose these things to be void? The truth is rather that they are completely full. *Ascl.* What do you mean, Trismegistus? *Hermes.* Is not air a body? *Ascl.* Yes. *Hermes.* And does not that body permeate all things that are, and fill them by its permeation? And are not bodies composed of a mixture of the four elements? All things that you call void then are filled with air; and if with air, they are filled with all four elements. Thus we are led to a conclusion opposite to what you said; we must say that all those things which you call full are void of air, because the presence of other bodies in them leaves no space unoccupied, and so they have no room to admit the air. Hence the things which you call void ought to be called hollow, not void; for they are full of something that exists. *Ascl.* There is no gainsaying that, Trismegistus.

Hermes. Now what was it that we said of that Space in which the universe is moved? We said, Asclepius, that it is incorporeal. *Ascl.* What then is that incorporeal thing? *Hermes.* It is

Mind, entire and wholly self-encompassing, free from the erratic movement of things corporeal; it is imperturbable, intangible, standing firm-fixed in itself, containing all things, and maintaining in being all things that are; and it is the light whereby soul is illuminated.

Ascl. Tell me then, what is the Good? *Hermes.* The Good is the archetypal Light; and Mind and Truth are, so to speak, rays emitted by that Light.

Ascl. What then is God? *Hermes.* God is He that is neither Mind nor Truth, but is the cause to which Mind and Truth, and all things, and each several thing that is, owe their existence. Nothing is left over, except that which is not. And all things that come into being come out of things that are, not out of things that are not. For not such is the nature of things which are not, that they can come to be something; their nature is such that they cannot come to be anything. And not such is the nature of things which are, that they can ever cease to be. God is not Mind then, but the cause to which Mind owes its being.

And so, in our worship of God, we ought to call him by these two names; they belong to Him alone, and to none beside him. None of the other beings called 'gods', nor any man or daemon, can be good in any degree. God alone is good; all other things are incapable of containing such a thing as the Good. Neither body nor soul has room enough in it to contain the Good; for such is the greatness of the Good, that it is coextensive with the existence of all things that are, things corporeal and things incorporeal, objects of sense and objects of thought together. And God is the Good, and nothing but the Good. Call nothing else good then, nothing but God; it would be impious. And never call God anything but the Good; that also would be impious. All men speak of the good, but some do not understand what the Good is; and hence it is that some do not understand what God is. And in their ignorance they call the gods good, and they call certain men good; whereas gods and men can never be good, and cannot possibly become good.

For the Good is utterly alien to gods and men; but it is inseparable from God, for it is God himself. All the other gods are called good merely because men have sought to honour them by giving them a title which belongs to God; but God is called the Good not by way of honouring him, but because that is his nature; for the nature of God is one and the same with the nature of the Good. God then is the Good, and the Good is God.

And the other name of God is 'Father'. He is called the Father, because he is the maker or begetter of all things; for it is the part of a father to beget. And for this reason the begetting of children is held by those who think aright to be the most weighty concern in human life, and the most pious of deeds. That a man should depart from life and leave no child is a great misfortune, and a great sin; it is a thing accursed in the sight of the Sun. Such a one is punished by the daemons after death; and the punishment is this, that the soul of the man who has no child is condemned to enter a body that is neither that of a man nor that of a woman. Therefore, Asclepius, never be glad on behalf of any man that he is childless, but pity his misfortune, knowing what manner of punishment awaits him.

Let this suffice. What I have taught you today, Asclepius, is a beginning of knowledge of the nature of all things.

LIBELLUS III

A holy discourse of Hermes Trismegistus.
That God is the first of all things and the universe is
divine and nature is divine.

God is the source of all that is; He is the source of mind, and of nature, and of matter. To show forth his wisdom has He made all things; for He is the source of all. And nature is a force by which God works; nature operates in subjection to necessity, and her work is the extinction and renewal of things.

There was darkness in the deep, and water without form; and there was a subtle breath, intelligent, which permeated the things in Chaos with divine power. Then, when all was yet undistinguished and unwrought, there was shed forth holy light; and the elements came into being. All things were divided one from another, and the lighter things were parted off on high, the fire being suspended aloft, so that it rode upon the air;

and the heavier things sank down, and sand was deposited beneath the watery substance, and the dry land was separated out from the watery substance, and became solid.

And the fiery substance was articulated, with the gods therein; and heaven appeared, with its seven spheres, and the gods, visible in starry forms, with all their constellations. And heaven revolved, and began to run its circling course, riding upon the divine air.

And each god, by his several power, put forth that which he was bidden to put forth. And there came forth four-footed beasts and creeping things and fishes and winged birds, and grass and every flowering herb, all having seed in them according to their diverse natures; for they generated within themselves the seed by which their races should be renewed.

And God ordained the births of men, and bade mankind increase and multiply abundantly. And He implants each soul in flesh by means of the gods who circle in the heavens. And to this end did He make men, that they might contemplate heaven, and have dominion over all things under heaven, and that they might come to know God's power, and witness nature's workings, and that they might mark what things are good, and discern the diverse natures of things good and bad, and invent all manner of cunning arts.

And it is the lot of men to live their lives and pass away according to the destiny determined by the gods who circle in the heavens, and to be resolved into the elements. And some there are whose names will live on, because they have left upon the earth mighty memorials of their handiwork; but the names of the many time will hide in darkness. And every birth of living flesh, even as every growth of crop from seed, will be followed by destruction; but all that decays will be renewed by the measured courses of the gods who circle in the heaven. For the whole composition of the universe is dependent on God, being ever renewed by nature's working; for it is in God that nature has her being.

LIBELLUS IV

A discourse of Hermes to Tat.
The Basin.

Hermes. For the incorporeal is not a thing perceptible by touch or sight; it cannot be measured; it is not extended in space; it is like nothing else. God is not fire, nor water, nor air, nor breath; but all these things have been made by him. You must understand then that God is pre-existent, and ever-existent, and that He, and He alone, made all things, and created by his will the things that are. For inasmuch as He is good, He willed that all things should be good. And when the Creator had made the ordered universe, he willed to set in order the earth also; and so he sent down man, a mortal creature made in the image of an immortal being, to be an embellishment of the divine body. For it is man's function to contemplate the works of God; and for this purpose was he made, that he might view the universe with wondering awe, and come to know its Maker.

The Kosmos ...,b ut man has this advantage over all other living beings, that he possesses speech and mind. Now speech, my son, God imparted to all men; but mind he did not impart to all. Not that he grudged it to any; for the grudging temper does not start from heaven above, but comes into being here below, in the souls of those men who are devoid of mind. *Tat.* Tell me then, father, why did not God impart mind to all men? *Hermes.* It was his will, my son, that mind should be placed in the midst as a prize that human souls may win. *Tat.* And where did he place it? *Hermes.* He filled a great basin with mind, and sent it down to earth; and he appointed a herald, and bade him make proclamation to the hearts of men: 'Hearken, each human heart; dip yourself in this basin, if you can, recognising for what purpose you have been made, and believing that you shall ascend to Him who sent the basin down.' Now those who gave heed to the proclamation, and dipped themselves in the bath of mind, these men got a share of gnosis ; they received mind, and so became complete men. But those who failed to heed the proclamation, these are they who possess speech indeed, but have not received mind also. And these, inasmuch as they know not for what purpose they have been made, nor by whom they have been made, are held under constraint by anger and incontinence; they admire the things that are not worth looking at; they give heed only to their bodily pleasures and desires, and believe that man has been made for such things as these. But as many as have partaken of the gift which God has sent, these, my son, in comparison with the others, are as immortal gods to mortal men. They embrace in their own mind all things that are, the things on earth and the things in heaven, and even what is above heaven, if there is aught above heaven; and raising themselves to that height, they see the Good. And having seen the Good, they deem their sojourn here on earth a thing to be deplored; and scorning all things corporeal, they press on to reach that which alone is good. Such, my son, is the work that mind does; it throws open the a way to knowledge of things divine, and enables us to apprehend God. *Tat. I* too, father, would fain be dipped in that basin. *Hermes.* If you do not first hate your body, my son, you cannot love yourself; but if you love yourself, you will have mind; and having mind, you will partake of knowledge also. *Tat.* What mean you, father? *Hermes.* It is not possible, my son, to attach yourself both to things mortal and to things divine. There are two sorts of things, the corporeal and the incorporeal; that which is mortal is of the one sort, and that which is divine is of the other sort; and he who wills to make his choice is left free to choose the one or the other. It is not possible to take both; and when the one is slighted, then the working of the other becomes manifest. The choice of the better is glorious for the chooser; for it not only saves the man from perdition, but also shows him to be pious towards God. The choice of the worse is perdition to the man, and is likewise an offence against God; for as processions pass through the midst of the people, but can do nothing themselves, and obstruct the way for others, even so these men merely pass in procession in the Kosmos, led along by things corporeal. This being so, my son, God has done his part towards us, and will do it; it is for us to do our part accordingly, and not to fall short. For God is blameless; it is we that are to blame for our evils, if we choose the evils in preference to the goods.

You see, my son, through how many bodily things in succession we have to make our way, and through how many troops of daemons and courses of stars, that we may press on to the one and only God. For we can never reach the farther boundary of the Good; it is limitless, and without end; and in itself, it is without beginning, though to us it seems to begin when we get knowledge of it. For the thing to be known does not itself begin to be when we get knowledge of it; it is only for us that our knowledge makes it begin. Let us then lay hold on this beginning, and make our way thither with all speed; for it is hard for us to forsake the familiar things around us, and turn back to the old home whence we came. Things seen delight us, and things unseen give rise to disbelief. Now the things that are evil are more manifest to sight; but the Good cannot be seen by things manifest; for it has no form or shape. It is impossible that an incorporeal thing should be manifested to a thing that is corporeal; because the incorporeal is like to itself, but unlike to all else.

God is in all things, as their root and the source of their being. There is nothing that has not a source; but the source itself springs from nothing but itself, if it is the source of all else. God then is like the unit of number. For the unit, being the source of all numbers, and the root of them all, contains every number within itself, and is contained by none of them; it generates every number, and is generated by no other number. Now everything that is generated is incomplete, and divisible, and subject to increase and decrease; but that which is complete is subject to none of these things.

In these outlines, my son, I have drawn a likeness of God for you, so far as that is possible; and if you gaze upon this likeness with the eyes of your heart, then, my son, believe me, you will find the upward path; or rather, the sight itself will guide you on your way. For the   has a power peculiar to itself; it takes possession of those who have attained to the sight of it, and draws them upward, even as men say the lodestone draws the iron.

LIBELLUS V

A discourse of Hermes to his son Tat.
That God is hidden from sight, and yet is most manifest.

This doctrine also, Tat, I will expound to you, that you may not remain uninitiated in the mysteries of Him who is too mighty to be named God. Grasp the meaning of my words; for if you grasp it, that which seems to the many to be hidden will become most manifest to you. For all that is manifest has been brought into being; for it has been manifested. But that which is hidden is ever-existent; for it has no need to be manifested. ; for God is ever-existent; and He makes manifest all else, but He himself is hidden, because He is ever-existent. He manifests all things, but is not manifested; He is not himself brought into being in images presented through our senses, but He presents all things to us in such images. It is only things which are brought into being that are presented through sense; coming into being is nothing else than presentation through sense. It is evident then that He who alone has not come into being cannot be presented through sense; and that being so, He is hidden from our sight.

But He presents all things to us through our senses, and thereby manifests himself through all things, and in all things; and especially, to those to whom He wills to manifest himself. Begin then, my son Tat, with a prayer to the Lord and Father, who alone is good; pray that you may find favour with him, and that one ray of him, if only one, may flash into your mind, that so you may have power to grasp in thought that mighty Being. For thought alone can see that which is hidden, inasmuch as thought itself is hidden from sight; and if even the thought which is within you is hidden from your sight, how can He, being in himself, be manifested to you through your bodily eyes? But if you have power to see with the eyes of the mind, then, my son, He will manifest himself to you. For the Lord manifests himself ungrudgingly through all the universe; and you can behold God's image with your eyes, and lay hold on it with your hands.

If you wish to see Him, think on the Sun, think on the course of the Moon, think on the order of the stars. Who is it that maintains that order? The Sun is the greatest of the gods in heaven; to him, as to their king and overlord, all the gods of heaven yield place; and yet this mighty god, greater than earth and sea, submits to have smaller stars circling above him. Who is it then, my son, that he obeys with reverence and awe? Each of these stars too is confined by measured limits, and has an appointed space to range in. Why do not all the stars in heaven run like and equal courses? Who is it that has assigned to each its place, and marked out for each the extent of its course? The Bear, who revolves upon herself, and carries round with her the whole Kosmos, who is it that has imposed this task upon her? The air is the instrument by which life is conveyed to all creatures upon earth;) who is it that owns this instrument? Who is it that has confined the sea within its bounds, and fixed the earth firm in its seat? Some one there must be, my son, who is the Maker and the Master of all these; it could not be that place and limit and measure should be observed by all, if there were not one who has made them. For all order must have been made; it is only that which is out of place and out of measure that has not been made. And yet, my son, even that which is out of place and out of measure is not without a master. If there is aught that is in disorder, ...; for disorder also is subject to the Master, but he has not yet imposed order upon it.

Would that it were possible for you to grow wings, and soar into the air! Poised between earth and heaven, you might see the solid earth, the fluid sea and the streaming rivers, the wandering air, the penetrating fire, the courses of the stars, and the swiftness of the movement with which heaven encompasses all. What happiness were that, my son, to see all these borne along with one impulse, and to behold Him who is unmoved moving in all that moves, and Him who is hidden made manifest through his works!

Such is the order of the universe. But if you wish to see Him through mortal creatures also, both those on earth and those in the depths of the sea, Think, my son, how man is fashioned in the womb; investigate with care the skill shown in that work, and find out what craftsman it is that makes this fair and godlike image. Who is it that has traced the circles of the eyes, that has pierced the orifices of the nostrils and the ears, and made the opening of the mouth? Who is it that has stretched the sinews out and tied them fast, and dug out the channels of the veins? Who is it that has made the bones hard, and covered the flesh with skin? Who is it that has separated the fingers, and shaped the broad surface of the soles of the feet? Who is it that has bored the ducts? Who is it that has shaped the heart into a cone, and joined the sinews to it, that has made the liver broad, and the spleen long, and hollowed out the cavities of the lungs, and made the belly capacious? Who is it that has so fashioned the most honourable parts that all may see them, and concealed the parts that are unseemly? See how many crafts have been employed on one material, and how many works of art are enclosed within one compass! All are beautiful, all true to measure, yet all are diverse one from another. Who produced all these? What mother, or what father? Who but the hidden God, who has wrought all things by his own will? No one says that a statue or a portrait has come into being without a sculptor or a painter; and has such a work as this come into being without a Maker? How blind men are ! How impious, how obtuse! Never, my son, deprive the things made of their Maker; but rather...

For who else is the Father of all? Surely, He alone; and it is his work to be father. Nay, if I needs must speak with some boldness, I will even say that it is his very being to set all things in motion, and to make all things; and as it is impossible for anything to come into being without a maker, so too it needs must be that He does not exist, if he is not ever making all things, in heaven, in air, on earth, and in the deep, in every part of the Kosmos, in all that is and in all that is not. For in all this there is nothing that He is not. He is both the things that are and the things that are not; for the things that are He has made manifest, and the things that are not He contains within himself.

Such is He who is too great to be named God. He is hidden, yet most manifest. He is apprehensible by thought alone, yet we can see Him with our eyes. He is bodiless, and yet has many bodies, or rather, is embodied in all bodies. There is nothing that He is not; for all things that exist are even He. For this

reason all names are names of Him, because all things come
from Him, their one Father; and for this reason He has no name,
because He is the Father of all.

Who then can speak of Thee or to Thee, and tell Thy praise?
Whither shall I look when I praise Thee? Upward or downward, inward or outward? For Thou art the place in which all
things are contained; there is no other place beside Thee; all
things are in Thee. (And what offering shall I bring Thee? For)
all things are from Thee. Thou givest all, and receivest nothing;
for Thou hast all things, and there is nothing that Thou hast not.

And at what time shall I sing hymns to Thee? For it is
impossible to find a season or a space of time that is apart from
Thee.

And for what shall I praise Thee? For the things Thou hast
made, or for the things Thou hast not made? For the things
Thou hast made manifest, or for the things Thou hast concealed?

And wherewith shall I sing to Thee? Am I my own, or have
I anything of my own? Am I other than Thou? Thou art
whatsoever I am; Thou art whatsoever I do, and whatsoever I
say. Thou art all things, and there is nothing beside Thee nothing that Thou art not. Thou art all that has come into being, and
all that has not come into being. Thou art Mind in that Thou
thinkest; and Father, in that Thou createst; and God, in that
Thou workest; and Good in that Thou makest all things.

LIBELLUS VI

A discourse of Hermes Trismegistus.
That the Good is in God alone, and nowhere else.

The Good, Asclepius, must be a thing that is devoid of all
movement and all becoming, and has a motionless activity that
is centred in itself; a thing that lacks nothing, and is not assailed
by perturbations; a thing that is wholly filled with supplies (of
all that is desired). Everything that furnishes any sort of supply
is called good; but the Good is the one thing which is the source
of all things, and supplies all things at all times.

And this belongs to none save God alone. There is nothing that God lacks, so that he should desire to gain it, and should thereby become evil. There is nothing that God can lose, and at the loss of which he might be grieved. There is nothing stronger than God, to do him wrong, and so provoke him to quarrel. God has no consort, to excite in him the passion of love; no disobedient subject, to rouse anger in him; there is none wiser than God, to make him jealous. And since his being admits of none of these passions, what remains, save only the Good?

But as no evil can be found in such a being, even so the Good cannot be found in any other. In all other things all is evil, in things small and great alike, in each thing severally, and in the one living being that is greater than all, and mightiest of all. For all things that come into being are full of perturbations, seeing that the very process of coming into being involves perturbation. But wherever there is perturbation, there the Good cannot be, and wherever the Good is, there no perturbation at all can be; even as wherever day is, night cannot be, and wherever night is, day cannot be. Hence the Good cannot be in things that come into being, but only in that which is without beginning.

Yet as participation in all the ideal archetypes of things is distributed in the world of matter, so also participation in the Good. And in this way the Kosmos too is good, in that the Kosmos also makes all things and so, is good in respect of its function of making things. But in all other respects the Kosmos is not good; for it is subject to perturbation, and the things which it makes are subject to perturbation. It is impossible then for things in this world to be pure from evil; and that which is good in this world is that which has the smallest share of evil; for in this world the good becomes evil.

The Good then is in God alone. In man, that which is called good is so called in comparison with evil; for that which is not evil beyond measure is named good. Thus in men, Asclepius, it is only the name of the Good that is present; the thing itself is nowhere to be found. It is impossible; for there is not room for the Good in a material body, hemmed in and gripped as such a body is by evil, by pains and griefs, desires and angry passions, delusions and foolish thoughts. And what is worst of all, Asclepius, each of these things of which I have spoken is in this world believed to be the greatest good, whereas it is rather an evil than which none is greater. This error it is that leads the train of all the evils. And for my part, I thank God for this very thought that he has put into my mind, even the thought that the Good is absent, and that it is impossible for it to be present in the Kosmos. For the Kosmos is one mass of evil, even as God is one mass of good.

For we need not fear to say, Asclepius, that the very being of God, if 'being' can be ascribed to God, is the Beautiful and the Good. But it is not possible that the light of the Beautiful and the Good should shine on anything in the Kosmos. For all things which the eye can see are mere phantoms, and unsubstantial outlines; but the things which the eye cannot see are the realities, and above all, the ideal form of the Beautiful and the Good. And as the eye cannot see God, so it cannot see the Beautiful and the Good. For the Beautiful and the Good are parts of God; they are properties of God alone; they belong to God, and are inseparable from him; they are without blemish, and most lovely, and God himself is in love with them. If you are able to apprehend God, then you will apprehend the Beautiful and the Good, .' For that Beauty is incomparable, and that good in this world is that which has the smallest share of evil; for in this world the good becomes evil.

The Good then is in God alone. In man, that which is called good is so called in comparison with evil; for that which is not evil beyond measure is named good. Thus in men, Asclepius, it is only the name of the Good that is present; the thing itself is nowhere to be found. It is impossible; for there is not room for the Good in a material body, hemmed in and gripped as such a body is by evil, by pains and griefs, desires and angry passions, delusions and foolish thoughts. And what is worst of all, Asclepius, each of these things of which I have spoken is in this world believed to be the greatest good, whereas it is rather an evil than which none is greater. This error it is that leads the train of all the evils. And for my part, I thank God for this very thought that he has put into my mind, even the thought that the Good is absent, and that it is impossible for it to be present in the Kosmos. For the Kosmos is one mass of evil, even as God is one mass of good.

For we need not fear to say, Asclepius, that the very being of God, if 'being' can be ascribed to God, is the Beautiful and the Good. But it is not possible that the light of the Beautiful and the Good should shine on anything in the Kosmos. For all things which the eye can see are mere phantoms, and unsubstantial outlines; but the things which the eye cannot see are the realities and above all, the ideal form of the Beautiful and the Good. And as the eye cannot see God, so it cannot see the Beautiful and the Good. For the Beautiful and the Good are parts of God; they are properties of God alone; they belong to God, and are inseparable from him; they are without blemish, and most lovely, and God himself is in love with them. If you are able to apprehend God, then you will apprehend the Beautiful and the Good, . For that Beauty is incomparable, and that Good is inimitable,' even as God himself is. As then you apprehend God, even so you must apprehend the Beautiful and the Good. For they are incommunicable to all other things, because they are inseparable from God. If you seek knowledge of God, you are also seeking knowledge of the Beautiful. For there is one road alone that leads to the Beautiful, and that is piety joined with knowledge of God.

Hence those who have not that knowledge, and have not travelled on the road of piety, are not afraid to call a man 'beautiful and good'; and that, though the man has never even in dream seen anything that is good, but is encompassed by every kind of evil, and has come to believe that the evil is good, and in this belief, is insatiable in his dealings with evil, and fears to be deprived of it, and strives with all his might not only to keep it, but to increase it. Such, Asclepius, are the things which men deem good and beautiful. And we cannot shun these things nor hate them; for the hardest thing of all is this, that we have need of them, and cannot live without them.

LIBELLUS VII

That ignorance of God is the greatest evil in men.

O men, whither are you being swept away? You are drunken;
you have drunk up the strong drink of ignorance; it has over
powered you, and now you are even vomiting it forth. Stand
firm; turn sober; look upward with the eyes of the heart, if you
cannot all, yet those at least who can.

This evil of ignorance floods all the land; its current sweeps
along the soul which is penned up in the body, and prevents it
from coming to anchor in the havens of salvation. Suffer not
yourselves then to be borne along down stream by the strong
current, but avail yourselves of a backflow, those of you who
are able to reach the haven, and cast anchor there, and seek a
guide to lead you to the door of the House of Knowledge. There
you will find the bright light which is pure from darkness; there
none is drunken, but all are sober, and they look up and see
with the heart Him whose will it is that with the heart alone He
should be seen. For He cannot be known by hearing, nor made
known by speech; nor can He be seen with bodily eyes, but with
mind and heart alone.

But first you must tear off this garment which you wear, this
cloak of darkness, this web of ignorance, this (prop) of evil, this
bond of corruption, this living death, this conscious corpse, this
tomb you carry about with you, this robber in the house, this
enemy who hates the things you seek after, and grudges you the
things which you desire. Such is the garment in which you have
clothed yourself; and it grips you to itself and holds you down,
that you may not look upward and behold the beauty of the
Truth, and the Good that abides above, and hate the evil of this
thing, discovering its ill designs against you. For it makes sense
less what men deem to be their organs of sense, stuffing them
up with the gross mass of matter, and cramming them with
loathly pleasures, so that you may neither hear of the things you
ought to hear of, nor see the things you ought to see.

LIBELLUS VIII

A discourse of Hermes Trismegistus.
That nothing that exists perishes, but men are in error when
they call the changes which take place 'destructions' and
'deaths'.

Hermes. We have now to speak, my son, of soul and body; I must explain in what way the soul is immortal, and by the working of what sort of force of the composition and dissolution of a body.

For death has nothing to do with any of them. The word 'death' is a mere name, without any corresponding fact. For death means destruction; and nothing in the Kosmos is destroyed. For seeing that the Kosmos is the second God, and an immortal being, it is impossible that a part of that immortal being should die; and all things in the Kosmos are parts of the Kosmos.

First of all things, and in very truth eternal and without beginning, is God, who is the maker of the universe; and second is the Kosmos, which has been made by God in his image, and is kept in being and sustained by God. The Kosmos is everliving; for it is made immortal by the Father, who is eternal.' Ever- living is not the same as 'eternal'. The Father has not been made by another; if he has been made at all, he has been made by himself; but it ought rather to be said that he has never been made, but ever is. But the Kosmos is ever being made. For the cause of the existence of the universe is the Father; but the Father is the cause of his own existence. The Kosmos then has been made immortal by the Father, who is eternal.

The Father took all that part of matter which was subject to his will, and made it into a body, and gave it bulk, and fashioned it into a sphere. This quality the Father imposed on the matter; but matter is of itself immortal, and its materiality is eternal. Moreover, the Father implanted within this sphere the qualities of all kinds of living creatures, and shut them up in it, as in a cave; for he willed to embellish with all manner of qualities the matter which existed beside him, but was hitherto devoid of qualities. And he enveloped the whole body with a wrapping of immortality, that the matter might not seek to break away from the composite structure of the universe, and so dissolve into its primal disorder. For when matter was not yet formed into body, my son, it was in disorder; and even in our world, it retains something of disorder, which besets the small living creatures; for the process of growth and decay is a remnant of disorder. But it is only the living creatures upon earth that are involved in this disorder. The bodies of the celestial gods keep without change that order which has been assigned to them by the Father in the beginning; and that order is preserved unbroken by the reinstatement of each of them in its former place. But the reinstatement of the terrestrial bodies is brought about by the dissolution of their composition; and through this dissolution, they are reinstated by absorption into the bodies which are indissoluble, that is, immortal. When this takes place, consciousness ceases, but life is not destroyed.

And the third being is man, who has been made in the image of the Kosmos. Man differs from all other living creatures upon earth, in that he possesses mind, for so the Father has willed; and not only does man find himself to be in union with the second God, but he also apprehends by thought the first God. He perceives the second God as a body; he apprehends the first God as bodiless. *Tat.* Do you say then that this living creature does not perish? *Hermes.* Speak not of man as perishing, my son. Think what God is, and what the Kosmos is, and what is meant by a living creature that is immortal, and a living creature that is dissoluble. The Kosmos is made by God, and is contained in God; man is made by the Kosmos, and is contained in the Kosmos; and it is God that is the author of all, and encompasses all, and knits all things together.

LIBELLUS IX

A discourse of Hermes Trismegistus.
concerning thought and sense.

Yesterday, Asclepius, I delivered my crowning discourse; and today I think it necessary, by way of sequel to that discourse, to expound the doctrine of sense.

Men think that there is a difference between sense and thought, in that sense is connected with matter, and thought with incorporeal and eternal substance. But I hold that sense and thought are united, and cannot be separated, that is to say, in the case of men. In the lower animals, sense is united with instinct; in men, sense is united with thought. Mind differs from thought to the same extent that God differs from divine influence. Divine influence is put forth by God; and thought is put forth by mind, and is sister to speech. Thought and speech are instruments of one another; speech cannot be understood without thought, and thought cannot be uttered without speech. Sense and thought are infused into a man together, being intertwined with one another, so to speak; for a man can neither think without perceiving, nor perceive without thinking. It is sometimes said that men may think without sense-perception, as when one sees imaginary things in dreams; but I hold rather that both thought and sense-perception have taken place in the dream-vision; for when we are awake, thought is always combined with sense-perception. Sense belongs in part to the body, and in part to the soul; and when the body-sense and the soul-sense are in accord, then it results that thought manifests itself, being brought forth as offspring by the mind.

For all man's thoughts are brought forth by his mind, good thoughts, when the mind is impregnated by God, and bad thoughts, when it is impregnated by some daemon, who enters into the man that has not been illuminated by God, and deposits in his mind the seed of such thoughts as it is the special work of that daemon to beget; and the mind brings forth those things which spring from this seed, adulteries, murders, acts of parricide and sacrilege, and all manner of impious deeds. But the seeds which God deposits in the mind are few in number, but potent, and fair, and good; they are virtue, and self-control, and piety. Now piety is the knowledge of God; and he who has come to know God is filled with all things good; his thoughts are divine and are not like those of the many.

Hence it is that those who have attained to the knowledge of God are not pleasing to the many, nor the many to them. They are thought mad, and are laughed at; they are hated and despised, and perhaps they may even be put to death. For evil, as I have told you before, must needs dwell here on earth, where it is at home; for the home of evil is the earth, and not the whole universe as some will blasphemously say in days to come. But the pious man will endure all things, cleaving to his knowledge of God. For to such a man all things are good, even though they be evil to others. When men devise mischief against him, he sees all this in the light of his knowledge of God; and he, and none but he, changes things evil into good.

But let us return to the doctrine of sense. It is a property of man that sense in him is joined with thought; but as I have already told you, it is not every man that profits by his power of thought; for one man's thoughts are combined with evil, as I said, because he has got from the daemons the seed from which his thinking springs, and other men's thoughts are combined with good, because they are kept safe by God. God is the Maker of all things, and makes all things like to himself; but though good when first made, they (can be corrupted) when the cosmic force works on them; for the movement of the Kosmos varies the births of things, and gives them this or that quality; it fouls with evil the births of some things, and purifies with good the births of others.

The Kosmos also, Asclepius, has sense and thought; but its sense and thought are of a kind peculiar to itself, not like the sense and thought of man, nor varying like his, but mightier and less diversified. The sense and thought of the Kosmos are occupied solely in making all things, and dissolving them again into itself. The Kosmos is an instrument of God's will; and it was made by him to this end, that, having received from God the seeds of all things that belong to it, and keeping these seeds within itself, it might bring all things into actual existence. The Kosmos produces life in all things by its movement; and decomposing them, it renews the things that have been decomposed; for, like a good husbandman, it gives them renewal by sowing seed. There is nothing in which the Kosmos does not generate life; and it is both the place in which life is contained, and the maker of life. The bodies of all living beings are made of matter. They are diversely made, but all are composite, in greater or less degree; the heavier bodies are more composite, and the lighter less. It is the swiftness of the movement of the Kosmos that causes the diversity of the births. For the cosmic life-breath, working without intermission, conveys into the bodies a succession of qualities, and therewith makes the universe one mass of life. And rightly is the Kosmos so named; for all things in it are wrought into an ordered whole by the diversity of births and the incessant continuance of life, and by its unwearied activity, and the swiftness of its movement, and the immutable necessity that rules in it, and by the combining of the elements, and the fit disposal of all things that come into being. Thus the name 'Kosmos' may be applied to it in a secondary sense as well as literally.

Now the sense and thought of all living creatures enter into them from without, being breathed into them from the atmosphere; but the Kosmos received sense and thought once for all when it first came into being, and has got them from God. God is not devoid of sense and thought, as in time to come some men will think he is; those who speak thus of God blaspheme through excess of reverence. And the sense and thought of God consist in this, that he is ever moving all things. For all things that exist, Asclepius, are in God, and are made by God, and are dependent on him, whether they be things that put forth activity by means of their bodies, or things that effect movement by means of soul-stuff, or things that generate life by means of vital breath, or things that receive into themselves the bodies that life has quitted. And there will never come a time when anything that exists will cease to be; for God contains all things, and there is nothing which is not in God, and nothing in which God is not. Nay, I would rather say, not that God contains all things, but that, to speak the full truth, God is all things.

What I have told you, Asclepius, you will deem true if you apply your thought to it; but if not, you will not believe it; for belief follows on thinking, and disbelief follows on want of thinking. Speech does not attain to truth; but mind has mighty power, and when it has been led some distance on its way by speech, it attains to truth; and having thought over all things, and found all to be in accord with that which has been expounded to it by speech, the mind believes, and finds rest in that goodly belief. And so, if men grasp with their thought what I have said, they will believe it; but if they do not grasp it with their thought, they will not believe it.

Concerning thought and sense, let this suffice.

LIBELLUS X

A discourse of Hermes Trismegistus.
The Key

Hermes. The teaching which I gave yesterday, Asclepius, I dedicated to you; and it is only right that I should dedicate to Tat that which I am about to give today; for it is an abridgement of the General Discourses which I have addressed to him.

Know then, Tat, that God the Father is of one nature with the Good; or rather, the working of God the Father is one with the working of the Good. 'Nature' is a term applied to birth and growth, and birth and growth have to do with things subject to change and movement; but God's working has to do with things free from change and movement, that is, with things divine; and it is God's will that what is human should be divine. Of forces at work, divine and human, I have spoken elsewhere; and in dealing with our present topic, as well as in other matters, you must bear in mind what I have taught you concerning them.

The force with which God works is his will; and his very being consists in willing the existence of all things. What else is God the Father but the being of all things when as yet they are not? It is this that constitutes the existence of all things that are. Such then is God, such is the Father. And to him appertains the Good; for the Good is a thing that can appertain to none save God alone. It is true that the Kosmos also is father of things which are good in so far as they partake of the Good; but the Kosmos is not, in like measure with God, the author of what is good in living creatures; for the Kosmos is not the author of their life; or if it acts as an author of life, it does so only under the compulsion imposed on it by God's will, without which nothing can be or come into being. The Kosmos is to the things within it as a father to his children, in that it is the author of their generation and nutrition; but it has received from God its supply of good. It is the Good that is the creative principle; and it is impossible that the creative principle should come to be in any save God alone, God, who receives nothing, but wills the existence of all things. I will not say 'makes all things'; for he who 'makes' things falls short of the fulfilment of his function during long intervals of time, in that he is sometimes making, and at other times not making. And moreover, he who 'makes' things makes only qualities and magnitudes; for he makes things have certain magnitudes and qualities at one time, and contrary magnitudes and qualities at another time. But God makes by his will the very existence of all things; and it is in this sense that he is the Father of all things. For God wills things to be, and, in that way, these things also have existence. But the Good itself, my son, exists in the highest degree; for it is by reason of the Good that all other things exist.

For it is a property of the Good that it becomes known to him who is able to see it.—*Tat.* Father, you have given me my fill of this good and most beautiful sight; and my mind's eye is almost blinded by the splendour of the vision. *Hermes.* Nay, the vision of the Good is not a thing of fire, as are the sun's rays; it does not blaze down upon us and force us to close our eyes; it shines forth much or little, according as he who gazes on it is able to receive the inflow of the incorporeal radiance. It is more penetrating than visible light in its descent upon us; but it cannot harm us; it is full of all immortal life. Even those who are able to imbibe somewhat more than others of that vision are again and again sunk in blind sleep by the body; but when they have been released from the body, then they attain to full fruition of that most lovely sight, as Uranos and Kronos, our forefathers, have attained to it. *Tat.* Would that we too, my father, might attain to it. *Hermes.* Would that we might, my son. But in this life we are still too weak to see that sight; we have not strength to open our mental eyes, and to behold the beauty of the Good, that incorruptible beauty which no tongue can tell. Then only will you see it, when you cannot speak of it; for the knowledge of it is deep silence, and suppression of all the senses. He who has apprehended the beauty of the Good can apprehend nothing else; he who has seen it can see nothing else; he cannot hear speech about aught else; he cannot move his body at all; he forgets all bodily sensations and all bodily movements, and is still. But the beauty of the Good bathes his mind in light, and takes all his soul up to itself, and draws it forth from the body, and changes the whole man into eternal substance. For it cannot be, my son, that a soul should become a god while it abides in a human body; it must be changed, and then behold the beauty of the Good, and therewith become a god.

Tat. What do you mean, father, by saying that the soul 'must be changed'? *Hermes.* Every separated soul, my son, passes through many changes. *Tat.* And what is a 'separated' soul? —*Hermes.* Have you not heard me say in my General Discourses, that all these souls which shift about from place to place throughout the Kosmos are, so to speak, parted off and portioned out from one soul, even the soul of the universe? Now these souls undergo many changes, by which some of them pass to a happier lot, and others to a worse lot. Souls of the nature of creeping things change into things which dwell in the waters; souls which dwell in the waters change into beasts which dwell on land; souls which dwell on land change into birds of the air; souls which fly in air change into men. And human souls, when they have attained to a beginning of immortal life, change into daemons, and thereafter pass on into the choral dance of the gods; that is the crowning glory of the soul. But if a soul, when it has entered a human body, persists in evil, it does not taste the sweets of immortal life, but is dragged back again; it reverses its course, and takes its way back to the creeping things; and that ill-fated soul, having failed to know itself, lives in servitude to uncouth and noxious bodies. To this doom are vicious souls condemned. And the vice of the soul is lack of knowledge. A soul that has gained no knowledge of the things that are, and has not come to know their nature, nor to know the Good, but is blind, such a soul is tossed about among the passions which the body breeds; it carries the body as a burden, and is ruled by it, instead of ruling it. That is the vice of the soul. On the other hand, the virtue of the soul is knowledge. He who has got knowledge is good and pious; he is already divine. *Tat.* And who is such a one, my father? *Hermes.* One who does not speak many words, nor listen to much talk. He who spends his time in disputations and in listening to men's words is beating the air, my son; for knowledge of God the Father cannot be taught by speech, nor learnt by hearing. Knowledge differs greatly from sense-perception. Sense-perception takes place when that which is material has the mastery; and it uses the body as its organ, for it cannot exist apart from the body. But knowledge is the perfection of science, and science is the gift of God; for all science is incorporeal; the organ which it uses is the mind itself; and the mind is contrary to the body. A soul then, when it has entered into a body, admits into itself both things of the mind and things material. It cannot be other wise; for all things must needs be composed of opposites and contraries. And seeing that this is so in all things that exist, *Tat.* What then are we to think of this material God, the Kosmos? *Hermes.* The Kosmos is not indeed evil, but it is not good, as God is; for it is material, and subject to perturbation. It is first among all things that are subject to perturbation, but second among things that are. The Kosmos also is ever-existent; but it exists in process of becoming; it is ever becoming, in that the qualities and magnitudes of things are ever coming into being. It is therefore in motion; for all becoming is material movement. That which is incorporeal and motionless works the material movement; and it does so in the following way. The Kosmos is a sphere, that is to say, a head; and so, all things that are united to the cerebral membrane of this head, the membrane in which the soul is chiefly seated, are immortal, for they have in them more soul than body; but the things which are at a distance from the cerebral membrane are mortal, for they have in them more body than soul. Thus the universe is composed of a part that is material and a part that is incorporeal; and inasmuch as its body is made with soul in it, the universe is a living creature.

The Kosmos is first among all living creatures; man, as a living creature, ranks next after the Kosmos, and first among those which are mortal. Man is not merely not-good; he is evil, inasmuch as he is mortal. The Kosmos is not-good, as being subject to movement; but it is not-evil, as being immortal. Man, on the other hand, is both not-good, as being subject to movement, and evil, as being mortal. And the soul of man is vehicled thus. The mind has for its vehicle the soul; the soul has for its vehicle the vital spirit; and the vital spirit, traversing the arteries together with the blood, moves the body, and carries it like a burden. Hence some have thought that the soul is the blood. But those who think this are mistaken as to its nature; they do not know that at death the soul must quit the body first, and then, when the vital spirit has withdrawn into the atmosphere, the blood must coagulate along the course of the veins, and leave the arteries emptied. This is the death of the body. All things are dependent on one first cause; and that first cause is dependent on the One and Only. The first cause is moved, that it may come to be first cause of all things; the One alone stands fast, and is not moved.

There are these three then, God, Kosmos, Man. The Kosmos is contained by God, and man is contained by the Kosmos. The Kosmos is son of God; man is son of the Kosmos, and grandson, so to speak, of God. God then does not ignore man, but acknowledges him to the full, and wills to be acknowledged by him. And this alone, even the knowledge of God, is man's salvation; this is the ascent to Olympus; and by this alone can a soul become good and it never remains good, but becomes evil by necessity.

Tat. What do you mean, thrice-greatest one? *Hermes.* Look at the soul of a child, my son, a soul that has not yet come to accept its separation from its source; for its body is still small, and has not yet grown to its full bulk. How beautiful throughout is such a soul as that! It is not yet fouled by the bodily passions; it is still hardly detached from the soul of the Kosmos. But when the body has increased in bulk, and has drawn the soul down into its material mass, it generates oblivion; and so the soul separates itself from the Beautiful and Good, and no longer partakes of that; and through this oblivion the soul becomes evil.

But when men quit the body, the process is reversed. The soul ascends to its own place, and is separated from the vital spirit; and the mind is separated from the soul. Thus the mind, which is divine by nature, is freed from its integuments; and taking to itself a body of fire, it ranges through all space, leaving the soul to be judged and punished according to its deserts.

Tat. What do you mean, father, by saying that the mind is separated from the soul? *Hermes.* My son, the learner ought to share in his teacher's thought; he should be quicker in his listening than the teacher is in his speaking. It is in an earthy body only that the mind and the soul are joined together. The mind cannot, naked and alone, take up its abode in an earthy body; a body of earth could not endure the presence of that mighty and immortal being, nor could so great a power submit to contact with a body defiled by passion. And so the mind takes to itself the soul for a wrap; the soul, for the soul also is in some measure divine, uses as its wrap the vital spirit; and the vital spirit controls the body. For the vital spirit is enveloped in the blood, and the soul in the vital spirit. The mind then, when it departs from the earthy body, clothes itself forthwith in its own proper vesture, that is, a vesture of fire, which it could not retain when it took up its abode in the earthy body. For earth cannot sustain fire; even a little spark is enough to set it all in a blaze; and it is for this very reason that the earth is encompassed by water, which serves as a barrier and defence to protect it from the flaming heat of the fire. But mind, which is the keenest of all things incorporeal, has for its body fire, the keenest of all the material elements. Mind is the maker of things, and in making things it uses fire as its instrument. The mind of the universe is the maker of all things; but the human mind is a maker of earthly things alone; for the mind which is in man is stripped of its vesture of fire, and therefore cannot make divine things, being merely human, by reason of its place of abode. Now the human soul, not indeed every human soul, but the pious soul, is daemonic and divine. And such a soul, when it has run the race of piety, and this means, when it has Come to know God, and has wronged no man, becomes mind throughout; and it is ordained that after its departure from the body, when it becomes a daemon, it shall receive a body of fire, so that it may work in God's service. But the impious soul retains its own substance unchanged; it suffers self-inflicted punishment, and seeks an earthy body into which it may enter.

But it can enter a human body only; for no other kind of body can contain a human soul. It is not permitted that a human soul should fail so low at to enter the body of an irrational animal; it is a law of God that human souls must be kept safe from such outrage as that. *Tat.* Tell me then, father, how are human souls punished. *Hermes.* Why, what greater punishment can there be, my son, than impiety? What fire burns with so fierce a flame as impiety? What ravenous beast has such power to mangle the body, as impiety has to mangle the very soul? See you not what tortures the impious soul endures? It cries and shrieks 'I am burning, I am all on fire; I know not what to say or what to do; wretch that I am, I am devoured by the miseries that have hold on me.' Are not such cries as these the outcries of a soul that is suffering punishment? Or do you too, my son, suppose, as most men do, that a soul, when it quits the body, is turned into a beast? That is a very great error. Souls are punished thus: the mind, when it has entered an impious soul, torments it with the scourges of its sins, and by these scourgings it is punished; it is impelled to blasphemies against God, and murders and outrages and manifold deeds of violence by which men are wronged. But when the mind has entered a pious soul, it leads that soul to the light of knowledge; and such a soul is never weary of praising and blessing God, and doing all manner of good to all men by word and deed, in imitation of its Father. Therefore, my son, when you are giving thanks to God, you must pray that the mind assigned to you may be a good mind.

A soul then may rise to a higher grade of being, but cannot sink to a lower grade.

There is communion between soul and soul. The souls of the gods are in communion with those of men, and the souls of men with those of the creatures without reason. The higher have the lower in their charge; gods take care of men, and men take care of creatures without reason. And God takes care of all; for He is higher than all. The Kosmos then is subject to God; man is subject to the Kosmos; the creatures without reason are subject to man; and God is above all, and watches over all. The divine forces are, so to speak, radiations emitted by God; the forces that work birth and growth are radiations emitted by the Kosmos; the arts and crafts are radiations emitted by man. The divine forces operate by means of the Kosmos, and their operation reaches man by means of the cosmic radiations to which birth and growth are due; and the forces that work birth and growth operate by means of the material elements. Thus is the universe administered. All things are dependent on the being of God alone, and are administered by means of mind alone. There is nothing more divine than mind, nothing more potent in its operation, nothing more apt to unite men to gods, and gods to men. Mind is 'the good daemon'; blessed is the soul that is filled with mind, and ill-fated is the soul that is devoid of it. *Tat* Again I ask you, father, what do you mean by that? *Hermes.* Do you think then, my son, that every soul has mind? That is the good mind; for it is of the good mind I am now speaking, and not of that mind of which I spoke before, namely the mind which is employed in service, and is sent down in penal justice. Oftentimes the mind quits the soul; and at such times, the soul can neither see nor hear, but is like a beast devoid of reason. For a soul without mind 'can neither say aught nor do aught'; so great is the power of mind. Nor does mind endure a torpid soul; it abandons the soul which is fastened to the body, and held down in the grip of the body. Such a soul, my son, has no mind in it; and therefore such a one ought not to be deemed a man.

For man is a being of divine nature; he is comparable, not to the other living creatures upon earth, but to the gods in heaven. Nay, if we are to speak the truth without fear, he who is indeed a man is even above the gods of heaven, or at any rate he equals them in power. None of the gods of heaven will ever quit heaven, and pass its boundary, and come down to earth; but man ascends even to heaven, and measures it; and what is more than all beside, he mounts to heaven without quitting the earth; to so vast a distance can he put forth his power. We must not shrink then from saying that a man on earth is a mortal god, and that a god in heaven is an immortal man.

All things then are administered through these two, the Kosmos and Man; but all things are governed by God alone.

LIBELLUS XI. (i)

A discourse of Mind to Hermes

God, Aeon, Kosmos, Time, Coming-to-be.
God makes the Aeon,
the Aeon makes the Kosmos,
the Kosmos makes Time,
and Time makes Coming-to-be.

The essence of God is the Good,
the essence of the Aeon is sameness,
the essence of the Kosmos is order,
the essence of Time is change,
and the essence of Coming-to-be is life.

The workings of God are mind and soul,
the workings of the Aeon are immortality and duration,
the workings of the Kosmos are reinstatement in identity
and reinstatement by substitution,
the workings of Time are increase and decrease,
and the workings of Coming-to-be are quality and quantity.

The Aeon then is in God,
the Kosmos is in the Aeon,
Time is in the Kosmos,
and Coming-to-be is in Time.

The Aeon stands fast in connection with God,
the Kosmos moves in the Aeon,
Time passes in the Kosmos,
and Coming-to-be takes place in Time.

God then is the source of all things; the Aeon is the power of
God; and the work of the Aeon is the Kosmos, which never
came into being, but is ever coming into being by the action of
the Aeon. And so the Kosmos will never be destroyed; for the
Aeon is indestructible. Nor will anything in the Kosmos perish;
for the Kosmos is encompassed by the Aeon. And the Aeon
imposes order on matter, putting immortality and duration
into matter. For things come into being in two different ways;
the things that come into being in heaven are immutable and
imperishable, but those that come into being on earth are mutable and perishable. The Kosmos then is dependent on the
Aeon, as the Aeon is dependent on God; the Aeon's source of
being is God, and that of the Kosmos is the Aeon.

And this whole body, in which all bodies are contained, is
filled with soul; soul is filled with mind; and mind is filled with
God. Soul fills the whole body within, and encompasses it
without, giving life to the universe; without, it gives life to this
great and perfect living creature, and within, to all the living
creatures. In heaven above, soul persists in sameness; on earth
below, it changes as things come into being.

That which holds this universe together is the Aeon; (some perhaps think, or will think in time to come, that it is Necessity, or Providence, or Nature, or something else;) that is to say, it is God at work. And God's working is unsurpassable in power; nothing human or divine can be compared to it. Deem not then, Hermes, that anything on earth below or in heaven above is like to God; else you will err from the truth; for nothing can be like to the One and Only. And deem not that God resigns aught of his power to another; for who is as God is? Who else is the author of life, and the maker both of immortality and of the changing life of mortals? And what is God's work, if not to make things? God is not idle; if he were, then all things would be idle; for all things are full of God. Nay, in the Kosmos also there is no idleness anywhere; idleness, whether of the Maker or of that which he makes, is a word devoid of meaning. It needs must be that all things come into being, and that things are ; coming into being always and everywhere. For the Maker is in all things; his abode is not in some one place, nor does he make some one thing; no, he makes all things, and everywhere he is at work. The things that come into being have no independent power; to God is subject all that comes into being.

Grasp this my teaching then, thrice-greatest Hermes, and keep in memory what I tell you.

LIBELLUS XI.(ii)

A discourse of Mind to Hermes

Hermes. But I will not shrink from speaking as the thought has come to me. Many men have told me many and diverse things concerning the universe and God, and yet I have not learnt the truth. I ask you therefore, Master, to make this matter clear to me. You, and you alone, I shall believe, if you will show me the truth about it.

Mind. Hearken then, my son, and I will tell you how things are, as to God and the universe. Look upon things through me, and contemplate the Kosmos as it lies before your eyes, that body which no harm can touch, the most ancient of all things, yet ever in its prime, and ever new. See too the seven subject worlds, marshalled in everlasting order, and filling up the measure of everlasting time as they run their diverse courses. And all things are filled with light; but nowhere is there fire for by the friendship of contraries, and the blending of things unlike, the fire of heaven has been changed into light, which is shed on all below by the working of the Sun; and the Sun is the begetter of all good, the ruler of all ordered movement, and governor of the seven worlds. Look at the Moon, who outstrips all the other planets in her course, the instrument by which birth and growth are wrought, the worker of change in matter here below. Look at the Earth, firm-seated at the centre, the foundation of this goodly universe, the feeder and nurse of all terrestrial creatures. See too how great is the multitude of living beings, both those which are immortal and those which are mortal; and note how the Moon, as she goes her round, divides the immortals from the mortals. And all are filled with soul, and all are in movement, immortals in heaven, and mortals upon earth.

Now all these have been made. There is no need for me to tell you that, dear Hermes. It must be so, because they are bodies with soul in them; it is the soul that moves them, and body and soul cannot meet in one, unless there is some one who brings them together. There must then be such a one; and he must needs be one. The movements are diverse and many, and the bodies differ one from another, but there is one ordered system which extends through all; therefore, there cannot be two or more makers. Where there are many makers, one order cannot be maintained; there will be rivalry among the many; the weaker will hate the stronger, and they will be at strife. And if the maker of mutable and mortal creatures had been another than the maker of immortals, he would have wanted to make immortals also; and the maker of immortals would have wanted to make mortals. Yes, and if there are two makers, then, seeing that matter is one and soul is one, to which of the two does the supply of matter and soul belong? Or if it belongs to both, to which of the two does it belong in larger measure? You must understand that every living body, be it immortal or mortal, rational or irrational, is composed of matter and soul. All living bodies have soul in them; things which are not alive are matter

apart by itself; and there is likewise soul by itself, laid up in the
Maker's keeping; for soul is the substance of which life is made.
How then can the life which is in the immortals be other than
the life which is in mortal creatures? And how can it be maintained that the maker of those living beings which are immortal
is not the maker of those which are mortal also? He therefore is
the author of all life, who is the author of the life of the immortals.

It is clear that there is some one who makes these things. And
it is manifest that the maker is one; for soul is one, and life is one,
and matter is one. And who is that maker? Who else can he be
but God alone? To whom save God alone should it belong to
put soul into things? You have agreed that the Cosmos is one,
and that the Sun is one, and the Moon is one, and the Earth is
one; and would you have it that God himself is but one among
many? It would be absurd to suppose that there are many Gods.
God also then is one. Moreover, if all things, both those in
heaven and those on earth, are alive, and there is one life in
them all, and life is made by God, it follows that all things are
made by God.

And why should it be thought strange for God to make both
what is immortal and what is mutable, when you yourself do so
many different things? You see; you speak and hear; you smell,
and feel by touch; you walk; you think; you breathe. It is not one
that sees, another that hears, and another that speaks; it is not
one that feels by touch, another that smells, another that walks,
another that thinks, and another that breathes; but he who does
all these things is one.

Nay it is not possible for God to exist without doing what I
said he does. You, if you cease to do the things I spoke of, are
no longer a living being; and even so, God, if he ceases to do his
work, is no longer God, a thing which none may dare to say. I
have shown that a man cannot exist and yet be doing nothing;
and still more does this hold good of God. If there is anything
which God does not make, then God himself is incomplete, a
thing which none may dare to say; but if he is idle in nothing,
then he is perfect. God then makes all things.

And if you give yourself up to me, Hermes, for a little while,
you will find it easy to understand that God's work is this, and
this alone, to bring all things into being; and this is the good.

For as a man cannot live without breathing, even so God cannot exist without making that which is good; and that, dear Hermes, is life. For it is, so to speak, God's very being to generate movement and life in all things. If you wish to understand this by your own experience, note what takes place in you when you desire to beget off-spring. Yet what God does is not like what you do; for God does not find carnal pleasure in it; he has no consort to work with him. He works alone then; and he is ever at his work, and is himself that which he makes. If what he makes were separated from him, all things would of necessity collapse and die; for there would be no life in them. But seeing that all things are alive, but life is the union of body and soul, death then is not the destruction of the things which have been brought together but the dissolution of their union.

The Aeon then is an image of God;

The Kosmos is an image of the Aeon.

The Sun is an image of the Kosmos;

And Man is an image of the Sun.

But men call the change 'death', because, when it takes place, the body is decomposed, and the life departs and is no longer seen.

And speaking in this way, dear Hermes, I say that the Kosmos also is changing through all time, inasmuch as day by day a part of its life passes away out of our sight, but that it is never decomposed. And the things that befall the Kosmos are . And the Kosmos assumes all forms; it does not contain the forms as things placed in it, but the Kosmos itself changes.

Now if the Kosmos is so made that it assumes all forms, what is to be said of its Maker? Shall we say that he is formless? Surely not that! Yet if he too assumes all forms, he will be like the Kosmos; and if he has but one form, he will in that respect be inferior to the Kosmos. What then are we to say of him? We must not let the discussion end in unsolved doubt; for in our thoughts of God, no question is insoluble. We will say then that God has one form, and one alone, but it is a form that no eye can see; for it is incorporeal. And marvel not that there is an incorporeal form. Such things there are; for instance, in pictures we see mountaintops standing out high, though the picture itself is quite smooth and flat.

And if you boldly grasp this conception, you will get a truer notion of Him who contains all things. There are terms which must be taken in a sense peculiar to the thing spoken of; and of this, what I am now saying is an instance. All things are in God; but things are not situated in God as in a place. A place is a body,' and all bodies are subject to movement; but that which is incorporeal is motionless, and the things situated in it have no movement; for it is in a different sense that things 'are situated in' what is incorporeal. And the incorporeal cannot be enclosed by anything; but it can itself enclose all things; it is the quickest of all things, and the mightiest. Think of yourself, and you will see that it is so. Bid your soul travel to any land you choose, and sooner than you can bid it go, it will be there. Bid it pass on from land to ocean, and it will be there too no less quickly; it has not moved as one moves from place to place, but it is there. Bid it fly up to heaven, and it will have no need of wings; nothing can bar its way, neither the fiery heat of the sun, nor the swirl of the planet-spheres; cleaving its way through all, it will fly up till it reaches the outermost of all corporeal things.' And should you wish to break forth from the universe itself, and gaze on the things outside the Kosmos (if indeed there is anything outside the Kosmos), even that is permitted to you. See what power, what quickness is yours. And when you yourself can all this, cannot God do it? You must understand then that it is in this way that God contains within himself the Kosmos, and himself, and all that is; it is as thoughts which God thinks, that all things are contained in him.

If then you do not make yourself equal to God, you cannot apprehend God; for like is known by like. Leap clear of all that is corporeal, and make yourself grow to a like expanse with that greatness which is beyond all measure; rise above all time, and become eternal; then you will apprehend God. Think that for you too nothing is impossible; deem that you too are immortal, and that you are able to grasp all things in your thought, to know every craft and every science; find your home in the haunts of every living creature; make yourself higher than all heights, and lower than all depths; bring together in yourself all opposites of quality, heat and cold, dryness and fluidity; think that you are everywhere at once, on land, at sea, in heaven; think that you are not yet begotten, that you are in the womb, that you are young, that you are old, that you have died, that you are in the world beyond the grave; grasp in your thought all this at once, all times and places, all substances and qualities and magnitudes together; then you can apprehend God. But if you shut up your soul in your body, and abase yourself, and say 'I know nothing, I can do nothing; I am afraid of earth and sea, I cannot mount to heaven; I know not what I was, nor what I shall be'; then, what have you to do with God? Your thought can grasp nothing beautiful and good, if you cleave to the body, and are evil.

For it is the height of evil not to know God; but to be capable of knowing God, and to wish and hope to know him, is the road which leads straight to the Good; and it is an easy road to travel. Everywhere God will come to meet you, everywhere he will appear to you, at places and times at which you look not for it, in your waking hours and in your sleep, when you are journeying water and by land, in the night-time and in the daytime, when you are speaking and when you are silent; for there is nothing which is not God. And do you say 'God is invisible'? Speak not so. Who is more manifest than God? For this very purpose has he made all things, that through all things you may see him. This is God's goodness, that he manifests himself through all things. Nothing is invisible, not even an incorporeal thing; mind is seen in its thinking, and God in his working.

So far, thrice-greatest one, I have shown you the truth. Think out all else in like manner for yourself, and you will not be misled.

LIBELLUS XII.(i)

A discourse of Hermes Trismegistus to Tat, concerning mind in men.

Hermes. Mind, my son Tat, is of the very substance of God, if indeed there is a substance of God; and of what nature that substance is, God alone knows precisely. Mind then is not severed from the substantiality of God, but is, so to speak, spread abroad from that source, as the light of the sun is spread abroad. In men, this mind is productive of divinity. Hence some men are divine, and the humanity of such men is near to deity; for the Agathos Daimon said 'gods are immortal men, and men are mortal gods'. But in the irrational animals, there is instinct in place of mind. Wherever there is life, there is soul; but in the irrational animals, the soul is devoid of mind. Mind is a benefactor to the souls of men; it produces good for them. In the case of the irrational animals, mind cooperates with the special form of instinct which belongs to each several kind of beast; but in men, mind works against the natural instincts. Every soul, as soon as it has been embodied, is depraved by pain and pleasure; for pain and pleasure belong to a composite body, and seethe like juices in it, and the soul steps into them and is plunged in them. Those souls then of which mind takes command are illuminated by its light, and it counteracts their prepossessions; for as a good physician inflicts pain on the body, burning or cutting it, when disease has taken possession of it, even so mind inflicts pain on the soul, ridding it of pleasure, from which spring all the soul's diseases. And godlessness is a great disease of the soul; for the beliefs of the godless bring in their train all kinds of evils, and nothing that is good. Clearly then, mind, inasmuch as it counteracts this disease, confers good on the soul, just as the physician confers health on the body. But those human souls which have not got mind to guide them are in the same case as the souls of the irrational animals. For mind cooperates with them, and gives free course to their desires; and such souls are swept along by the rush of appetite to the gratification of their desires, and strive towards irrational ends; and like the irrational animals, they cease not from irrational anger and irrational desire, and are insatiable in their craving for evils; for irrational angers and desires are passions that exceed all else in evil. And to punish and convict such souls as these, God has established penal law.

Tat. But if that is so, father, it would almost seem that the doctrine of destiny which you have explained to me before is overthrown. If a man is inevitably destined to commit adultery, or sacrilege, or some other crime, why is punishment inflicted on one who has been compelled by destiny to do the deed? It is destiny that has committed all these crimes. *Hermes.* It is true, my son, that, and that nothing, whether good or bad, which has to do with the body, can come to pass apart from destiny. But it is destined also that he who has done evil shall suffer evil; and to this end he does it, that he may suffer the penalty for having done it. But for the present, we are not discussing evil-doing and destiny. Of those matters I have spoken elsewhere; but we are now concerned with mind, and the questions we have to consider are these, what mind can do, and how it admits of differences, being of one sort in men, and of another sort in irrational animals. And further, we have to consider that in the irrational animals mind does not work good, whereas in men it works good, but not alike in all men; for not in all men does it quench the passions of anger and desire. The one sort of men we must hold to be rational, and the other sort irrational. Now all men are subject to destiny, inasmuch as all are subject to birth and death ; for a man's destiny begins at his birth, and ends at his death. And all men undergo what destiny has appointed for them; but rational men (that is, those who, as I said, are governed by mind) do not undergo it in the same way as the irrational. They are freed from wickedness; they undergo what is destined, but they are not wicked. *Tat.* Once more, father, what do you mean? The adulterer, and the murderer, and all the rest, are they not wicked? *Hermes.* Nay, my son, the rational man has not committed adultery or murder, yet he must undergo what is destined, as the adulterer and the murderer undergo it. It is impossible for a man to escape from his destined death, just as it is impossible for him to escape from his destined birth; but from wickedness a man can escape, if he has mind in him. I will tell you, my son, what I heard the Agathos Daimon say. If he had put forth in writing what he said, he would have conferred a great benefit on the human race; for being the first-born god, he alone, my son, had seen all things, and spoke words that are in very truth divine. I once heard him say . Think on these words, and apply this teaching to the question which you asked me just now, that is, the question about destiny. For if you are careful to put aside contentious arguments, my son, you will find that in very truth mind is master of all things, master of destiny, and of penal law, and of all else; and for mind nothing is impossible, neither to exalt a human soul above destiny, nor, if the soul, as sometimes happens, gives no heed, to make it subject to destiny. As to destiny then, let this suffice.

Tat. This teaching, father, is divine; it is both true and helpful. But there is yet another thing which I must ask you to explain. You said that in the irrational animals mind works in the way of instinct, cooperating with their impulses. Now the impulses of the irrational animals are passive affections, I suppose; and if mind cooperates with the impulses, and the impulses are passive affections, then mind also must be passively affected, being polluted by contact with the passive affections. *Hermes.* Well said, my son! Your question shows the right spirit, and it is only fair that I should answer it. All things that are in a body, my son, are subject to passive affection. It is the bodies themselves that are subject to passive affection in the primary sense of the term; but the incorporeals also are passively affected under certain circumstances. For everything that moves something is incorporeal, and everything that is moved is body; both the mover then and that which is moved are passively affected, the one being the ruler, and the other that which is ruled. And so, mind, as long as it is in a body, is subject to passive affection; but when it is freed from the body, it is freed from the passive affection also. You must not let yourself be confused by the use of these terms; 'but there is no harm in using the better-sounding word.' *Tat.* You have explained the matter most clearly, father.

Hermes. There is another thing to be considered, my son. There are two gifts which God has bestowed on man alone, and on no other mortal creature. These two are mind and speech; and the gift of mind and speech is equivalent to that of immortality. If a man uses these two gifts rightly, he will differ in nothing from the immortals; or rather, he will differ from them only in this, that he is embodied upon earth; and when he quits the body, mind and speech will be his guides, and by them he will be brought into the troop of the gods and the souls that have attained to bliss. *Tat.* But do not the other living creatures use speech, father? *Hermes.* No, my son; they have voice, but not speech; and speech is very different from voice. All men have speech in common; but each kind of living creatures has its special sort of voice. *Tat.* But among men also, father, each nation has a different speech. *Hermes.* Languages differ, my son, but mankind is one; and speech likewise is one. It is translated from tongue to tongue, and we find it to be the same in Egypt, Persia, and Greece. Speech then is an image of mind; and mind is an image of God.

That blessed god, the Agathos Daimon, said 'soul is in body, mind is in soul, and God is in mind'. The rarest part of matter then is air; the rarest part of air is soul; the rarest part of soul is mind; and the rarest part of mind is God. And God deals with all things, and permeates all things; mind deals with soul; soul deals with air; and air deals with gross matter.

LIBELLUS XII.(ii)

A discourse of Hermes to Tat.

Hermes. And necessity and providence and nature are instruments by means of which the Kosmos is governed, and by means of which matter is set in order.

Each of the intelligibles is one, and sameness is their essence; but each of the bodies contained in the universe is many. And matter is one; for the incomposite bodies cleave to sameness, and though they change into one another, they maintain their sameness unimpaired for ever. But in every composite body there is number; for there cannot be combination or composition unless there is number. And the units generate number and increase it, and receive it back into themselves when it is broken up.

Now this whole Kosmos, which is a great god, and an image of Him who is greater, and is united with Him, and maintains its order in accordance with the Father's will, is one mass of life; and there is not anything in the Kosmos, nor has been through all time from the first foundation of the universe, neither in the whole nor among the several things contained in it, that is not alive. There is not, and has never been, and never will be in the Kosmos anything that is dead. For it was the Father's will that the Kosmos, as long as it exists, should be a living being; and therefore it must needs be a god also. How then, my son, could there be dead things in that which is a god, in that which is an image of the Father, in that which is one mass of life? Deadness is corruption, and corruption is destruction. How then can any part of that which is incorruptible be corrupted, or any part of that which is a god be destroyed? *Tat.* Is it not true then, father, that the living creatures in the Kosmos die? And are they not parts of the Kosmos? *Hermes.* Say not so, my son. You are misled by the terms that men apply to that which takes place. The living creatures do not die, my son; but they are composite bodies, and as such, they undergo dissolution. Dissolution is not death; it is only the separation of things which were combined; and they undergo dissolution, not to perish, but to be made new. Why, wherein does life manifest its force? Surely, in movement. And what is there in the Kosmos that is motionless? Nothing, my son. *Tat.* Do you think then, father, that not even the earth is motionless? *Hermes.* No, my son, not even the earth; but the earth, alone of all things, is both in notion in manifold ways, and at the same time stationary. Would it not be absurd to say that the nurse of all things is motionless, she who brings forth and generates all things? Without motion, it is impossible to bring forth anything. And it is utterly absurd to ask, as you did, whether the fourth part of the universe is idle; for if you say that a body is motionless, that means nothing else than that it is idle. Know then, my son, that everything which exists in the Kosmos, everything without exception is in motion; and that which is in motion must be alive. But it is not necessary that in every case it should be one and the same thing that is alive at all times. Considered as one whole, my son, the Kosmos is exempt from change; but all its parts are subject to change. But there is nothing in it that suffers corruption or destruction; if men think otherwise, their thoughts are confused by the terms in use. Birth is not a beginning of life, but only a beginning of consciousness; and the change to another state is not death, but oblivion. And this being so, all the things of which every living creature is composed, gross matter, and vital spirit, and soul, are immortal; and so, reason of their immortality, every living creature is immortal.

But more than all the rest, man is immortal; for he can receive God, and hold intercourse with God. With man alone of living creatures God associates. God speaks to man by dreams at night, and by signs in the daytime; God foretells the future to him in manifold ways, by the flight of birds, by the inward parts of beasts, by inspiration, or by the whispering of an oaktree. And so man can boast that he knows things past, things present, and things future. Mark this too, my son; each of the other kinds of living creatures haunts but one part of the Kosmos; fishes live in the water, beasts on the earth, and birds in the air; but man makes use of all these elements, earth, water, air; yes, and heaven too he beholds, and grasps that also with his sense of sight.

And it is not difficult, my son, to contemplate God in thought, or even, if you will, to see him. Look at the order of the Kosmos; look at the necessity which governs all that is presented to our sight, and the providence shown in things that have been, and in things that come to be; look at matter filled to the full with life, and see this great god in movement, with all things that are contained in him. *Tat.* But these, father, are nothing but forces at work. *Hermes.* If they are forces at work, my son, who is it that works them? Is it not God? Do you not know that, just as heaven and earth and water and air are parts of the Kosmos, even so destiny and necessity and providence and nature are parts of God? And there is nothing that comes to be or has come to be, in which God is not. *Tat.* Is God in matter then, father? *Hermes.* Why, what is matter apart from God, my son, that you should assign a place to it? What else but an inert mass do you suppose matter would be, if it were not worked upon? And if it is worked upon, who is it that works upon it? I have told you that the forces at work are parts of God; who is it then that puts life into all living creatures? Who is it that gives immortal beings their immortality? Who is it that works change in things subject to change?   And whether you speak of matter, or body, or substance, know that these also are manifestations of God's working; for it is God that by his .working makes matter material, and bodies corporeal, and substance substantial. God is the

All; and there is nothing that is not included in the All. Hence there is neither magnitude nor place nor quality nor shape nor time beside God; for God and the All permeates all things, and has to do with all things.

This God, my son, I bid you worship and adore. And there is but one way to worship God; it is to be devoid of evil.

LIBELLUS XIII

A secret discourse of Hermes Trismegistus to his son Tat, concerning Rebirth.

Tat. In your general discourses, father, you spoke in riddles, and did not make your meaning clear, when you were discussing the divinity of man. You said that no one can be saved until he has been born again; but you did not make known to me what you meant by this. After your talk with me , I besought you to let me learn the doctrine of Rebirth, as this was the one part of your teaching that I did not know; but you did not think fit to transmit it to me at that time; you said, 'When you are ready to alienate yourself from the world, then I will teach it to you '. I am now prepared to receive it; I have alienated the thoughts of my heart from the world's deceptions; and I entreat you to supply what is yet lacking to me, as you said you would, when you promised to transmit the Rebirth to me. I know not, thrice- greatest one, from what womb a man can be born again, nor from what seed. *Hermes.* My son, the womb is Wisdom, conceiving in silence; and the seed is the true Good. *Tat.* And who is it, father, that begets? I am wholly at a loss. *Hermes.* The Will of God, my son, is the begetter. *Tat.* Tell me this too; who is the ministrant by whom the consummation of the Rebirth is brought to pass? *Hermes.* Some man who is a son of God, working in subordination to God's will. *Tat.* And what manner of man is he that is brought into being by the Rebirth? *Hermes.* He that is born by that birth is another; he is a god, and son of God. He is the All, and is in all; for he has no part in corporeal substance; he partakes of the substance of things intelligible, being wholly composed of Powers of God. *Tat.* Your words are riddles, father; you do not speak to me as a father to his son. *Hermes.* This sort of thing cannot be taught, my son; but God, when he so wills, recalls it to our memory. *Tat.* But what you say is impossible, father; it does violence to common sense. When you treat me thus, I have good reason to ask, 'Am I an alien to my father's race? Do not grudge me this boon, father; I am your true-born son; explain to me what manner of thing the Rebirth is. *Hermes.* What can I say, my son? This thing cannot be taught; and it is not possible for you to see it with your organs of sight, which are fashioned out of material elements. I can tell you nothing but this; I see that by God's mercy there has come to be in me a form which is not fashioned out of matter, and I have passed forth out of myself, and entered into an immortal body. I am not now the man I was; I have been born again in Mind, and the bodily shape which was mine before has been put away from me. I am no longer an object coloured and tangible, a thing of spatial dimensions; I am now alien to all this, and to all that you perceive when you gaze with bodily eyesight. To such eyes as yours, my son, I am not now visible. *Tat.* Father, you have driven me to raving madness. Will you tell me that I do not at this moment see my own self? *Hermes.* Would that you too, my son, had passed forth out of yourself, so that you might have seen, not as men see dream-figures in their sleep, but as one who is awake. *Tat.* Now indeed, father, you have reduced me to speechless amazement. Why, I see you, father, with your stature unchanged, and your features the same as ever. *Hermes.* Even in this you are mistaken. The mortal form changes day by day; it is altered by lapse of time, and becomes larger and smaller; for it is an illusion. *Tat.* What then is real, thrice-greatest one? *Hermes.* That which is not sullied by matter, my son, nor limited by boundaries, that which has no colour and no shape, that which is without integument, and is luminous, that which is apprehended by itself alone, that which is changeless and unalterable, that which is good. *Tat.* I must indeed have gone mad, father; I have lost the wits I had. I thought your teaching had made me wise; but when you put this thought before me, my senses are stopped up. *Hermes.* It is even so, my son. The fire which rises, and the earth which sinks, the liquid water, and the air we breathe, are perceived by the senses; but how can you perceive by mere sense a thing of other nature, a thing that is neither rigid nor fluid that is incomposite and indissoluble, a thing which can be apprehended only by divine power, and demands one who has power to apprehend the incorporeal. *Tat.* Is it then beyond my power, father? *Hermes.* Heaven forbid, my son. Draw it into you, and it will come; will it, and it comes to be. Stop the working of your bodily senses, and then will deity be born in you.

But if you would be born again, you must cleanse yourself from the irrational torments of matter. *Tat.* What, father, have I torturers within me? *Hermes.* Yes, my son, and not a few; they are terrible, and they are many. *Tat.* I do not know them, father. *Hermes.* This very ignorance, my son, is one of the torments.

The second is Grief;
the third is Incontinence;
the fourth is Desire;
the fifth is Injustice;
the sixth is Covetousness;
the seventh is Deceitfulness;
the eighth is Envy;
the ninth is Fraud;
the tenth is Anger;
the eleventh is Rashness;
the twelfth is Vice.

These are twelve in number; and under them there are many others also, my son; and by means of the senses they force the man who is bound in the prison of the body to suffer what they inflict. But when God has had mercy on a man, they depart from him together, one and all; and then is reason built up in him. Such is the manner of the Rebirth.

And now, my son, speak not, but keep solemn silence; so will the mercy come down on us from God.

Rejoice now, my son; you are being cleansed by the Powers of God; for they have come to build up in you the body of reason. The knowledge of God has come to us; and at its coming, my son, ignorance has been driven out. Joy has come to us; and at her coming, my son, Grief will flee away, to enter into those in whom there is room for her. And after Joy, I summon a third Power, even Continence. O sweetest Power! Let us receive her, my son, most gladly. See how, at the instant of her coming, she has pushed Incontinence away.

And now I summon the fourth Power, Endurance, the opponent of Desire.

And this, my son, is the tribunal on which Justice sits enthroned. See how she has driven out Injustice. We have been justified, my son, without being brought to judgement; for Injustice is no longer here.

As the sixth Power, I call to us Unselfishness, the opponent of Covetousness. And when Covetousness has departed, .

As the seventh, I invoke Truth. Flee away, Deceit; for Truth has come.

See, my son, how, on the coming of Truth, the Good is completed; for Envy has departed from us, and the other torments also.

Truth 'has come to us, and on it has followed the Good, with Life and Light. No longer has there come upon us any of the torments of darkness; they have flown away with rushing wings. Thus, my son, has the intellectual being: been made up in us; and by its coming to be, we have been made gods. Whoever then has by God's mercy attained to this divine birth, abandons bodily sense; he knows himself to be composed of Powers of God, and knowing this, is glad.

Tat Father, God has made me a new being, and I perceive things now, not with bodily eyesight, but by the working of mind. *Hermes.* Even so it is, my son, when a man is born again; it is no longer body of three dimensions that he perceives, but the incorporeal. *Tat.* Father, now that I see in mind, I see myself to be the All. I am in heaven and in earth, in water and in air; I am in beasts and plants; I am a babe in the womb, and one that is not yet conceived, and one that has been born; I am present everywhere. *Hermes.* Now, my son, you know what the Rebirth is. *Tat.* But tell me further; how is it that the torments of darkness, which are twelve in number are driven off by ten Powers? How does this come about, thrice-greatest one? *Hermes.* This earthly tabernacle, my son, out of which we have passed forth, has been put together by the working of the Zodiac, which produces manifold forms of one and the same thing to lead men astray. and as the Signs of which the Zodiac consists are twelve in number, the forms produced by it, my son, fall into twelve divisions. But at the same time they are inseparable, being united in their action; for the reckless vehemence of irrational impulse is indivisible. It is with good reason then that they all depart together, as I said before. And it is also in accordance with reason that they are driven out by ten Powers, that is, by the Decad; for the Decad, my son, is the number by which soul is generated. Life and Light united are a Unit; and the number One is the source of the Decad. It is reasonable then that the Unit contains in itself the Decad.

Tat. Tell me, father, will this body which is composed of divine Powers ever suffer dissolution? *Hermes.* Hush! Speak not of a thing that cannot be; it would be impious to say that. Has the eye of your mind been blinded? The physical body, which is an object of sense, differs widely from that other body, which is of the nature of true Being. The one is dissoluble, the other is indissoluble. The one is mortal, the other is immortal.

Do you not know that you have become a god, and son of the One, even as I have?

Tat. Father, I would fain be taught that hymn of praise which, as you have told us, Poimandres predicted that you would hear the Powers sing when you had ascended to the eighth sphere of heaven. *Hermes.* My son, you do well to seek that; for you are purified, now that you have put away from you the earthly tabernacle. Poimandres, the Mind of the Sovereignty, told me no more than stands written in the book; for he knew that I should be able of myself to apprehend all things, and to hear what I would, and to see all; and he left it to me [to think out what he did not tell me.]

And so the Powers which are in all things sing within me also.

Tat. Father, I would fain hear that song; I wish to make it mine in thought. *Hermes.* Be still then, my son, and listen to the hymn of praise which is appropriate to the Rebirth. I had not meant to make it known to you so readily. [This hymn therefore is not taught, except at the end of all, but is kept hidden in silence. You must take your place then in a place open to the sky, and worship thus, facing to the South, at the hour of sunset; and you must worship in like manner at sunrise, facing to the East.] Let every bar of the universe be flung open to me; and let all nature receive the sound of my hymn.

Be thou opened, O Earth, and ye trees, wave not your boughs;
I am about to sing the praise of Him who is both the All and
the One.
Be ye opened, ye heavens, and ye winds, be still;
Let the immortal sphere of heaven receive my utterance.
For I am about to sing the praise of Him who created all
things,
who fixed the earth, and hung heaven above;
who made the sweet water flow from Ocean into the lands
wherein
men dwell,
that it might serve for the sustenance of all mankind,
and gave command that fire should come forth,
to be used by gods and men in all their works.
Let us all with one accord give praise to Him,
who is seated high upon the heavens, creator of all that is.
It is He that is the eye of my mind;
may He accept the praise sung by my Powers.
Ye Powers that are within me, praise ye the One and All
sing ye in concord with my will, all ye Powers that are within
me.
O holy Knowledge, by thee am I illumined,
and through thee do I sing praise to the incorporeal Light.
I rejoice in joy of mind;
rejoice with me, all ye Powers.

And do thou, O Continence, sing praise;
and thou, Endurance;
and thou, my Justice, praise the Just through me;
thou, my Unselfishness, praise the All through me;
O Truth, sing praise to Truth.
O Good that is in me, praise the Good;
O Life and Light, from you comes the song of praise, and to
you does it go forth.
I give thanks to thee, O Father, who workest in my Powers;
I give thanks to thee, O God, .
Thus crying, the Powers that are in me accomplish thy will;
praising the All, they fulfil thy purpose.

It is thy Word that through me sings thy praise;
for by thee, O Mind, is my speech shepherded.
Through me accept from all an offering of speech;
for the All is from thee, and to thee returns the All.
O Light, illumine thou the mind that is in us;
O Life, keep my soul alive.
Thy man cries thus to thee by means of the things thou hast made;
but he has got from thine eternity the praises which he utters.
I have seen that which I seek;
I have found rest according to thy purpose;
by thy will I am born again.

Tat. Father, by your song of praise to God you have put into my world also. *Hermes.* Nay, my son, say rather my incorporeal-world. *Tat.* By your hymn you have put fresh power into my incorporeal world, and through your song of praise my mind has been further illumined. But now I too wish to present to God an offering of praise of my own devising.

Hermes My son, venture not heedlessly. *Tat.* Nay, father, it is that which I behold in Mind that I would utter in speech.

O thou first author of the work by which the Rebirth has been wrought in me, to thee, O God, do I, Tat bring offerings of speech. O God, thou art the Father; O Lord, thou art Mind. From me accept praises such as thou willest; for by thy will it is that all is accomplished for me.

Hermes. Good, my son; you have presented an offering acceptable to God the Father of all. But add, my son, 'by thy Word'. *Tat.* I thank you, father. *Hermes.* I rejoice, my son, that you are like to bring forth fruit. Out of the Truth will spring up in you the immortal brood of virtue; for by the working of mind you have come to know yourself and our Father.

Now that you have learnt this from me, my son, you must promise to keep silence, and not to reveal to any one how the Rebirth is transmitted, that we may not be deemed maligners of the universe.

And now, no more; for we have both of us done enough to satisfy our wants, I as teacher, and you as learner.

This discourse about the Rebirth I have set down in writing privately, to be read by those to whom God himself wills it to be made known, and not by the many, that we may not be deemed maligners of the universe.

LIBELLUS XIV

Hermes Trismegistus writes to Asclepius, wishing him health of mind.

In your absence, my son Tat desired to be taught the nature of things, and would not let me postpone his instruction; and as he was young, and had only just begun to learn the gnosis~ I was obliged to discourse to him on each several matter at some length, in order to make it easy for him to understand the doctrine. But since you are older, and have knowledge of the nature of things, I have thought fit to select and send to you in writing, in the form of a short summary, the most important of the truths I taught him.

The things presented to our sight are many, and all different, and not like to one another; and seeing that all these things have come into being, and are ever coming into being, and that things which come into being are brought into being by another, there must be one who makes these things. And he who makes them cannot have been generated; for he must be prior to the things that are generated. These things, as I said, are brought into being by another; and it is impossible that anything should be prior to them all, save only that which has not been generated. And the Maker is one; he is mightier than all, and he alone is truly wise in all things, for there is nothing that is prior to him. He rules over the multitude of things made, in virtue of his greatness; and he rules over all their differences, because he makes things without intermission. And inasmuch as the things generated are seen, the Maker also can be seen; for to this end he makes them, that he may be seen. Since then he is at all times making things, he can be seen at all times.

Thus is it meet for us to think, and thus thinking, to marvel, and marvelling, to deem ourselves blest, in that we have come to recognise our Father; for what is dearer to a son than his true father? Who is he then, and how are we to recognise him? Are we to say that it is right that the name of God alone should be assigned to him, or that of Maker, or that of Father? Nay, all three names are his; he is rightly named God by reason of his power, and Maker by reason of the work he does, and Father by reason of his goodness. In power he surpasses the things that come into being; he is at work in bringing all things into being; (and his goodness is shown in).

We ought therefore to get rid of superfluous and idle talk and keep our thoughts fixed upon these two, the thing made and the Maker. Between them there is nothing; there is no third. In all your thoughts then, and in all that you are told, keep in mind these two, and hold them to be all that is, making no difficulty or mystery about anything in heaven above or here below, divine or mutable. All things are but two, that which is made and that which makes. And the one cannot be separated from the other; the Maker cannot exist apart from the thing made, nor the thing made, apart from the Maker. Each of them is just that and nothing else; and so the one can no more be parted from the other than it can be parted from itself. For if the Maker is nothing else but that which makes, and that alone, simple and incomposite, he must of necessity make. And again, what is made cannot be made by itself; if it is made, it must of necessity be made by another; without the Maker, the thing made can neither come into being nor exist. If the one is wanting, the other ceases to be itself. If then it is admitted that there are two things, that which is made and that which makes, these two are one in virtue of their union, the one of them going before, and the other following after. It is the Maker, that is, God, that goes before: and it is the thing made, whatsoever it be, that follows after.

And if the things made vary in quality, do not for that reason hesitate through fear of degrading God, or impairing his glory. For God's glory is this, and this alone, that he makes all things; and the making of things is, so to speak, God's very being. In relation to the Maker himself, nothing is to be deemed evil or foul. Evil and foulness are accidents which follow on the making of things, just as rust forms on metal, or dirt collects on a man's body; but the metal-worker did not make the rust, nor did the father who begot the body make the dirt. And even so, God is not the author of evil; but it is the lasting on of the things made that causes evil to break out on them. And that is why God has subjected things to change; for by transmutation the things made are purged of evil.

The same painter can make heaven and earth and sea, gods and men, and beasts of every kind, and things without life; and is it impossible for God to make all things? What fools men are! How little they know of God ! It is a strange mistake; such men profess to honour God by refusing to ascribe to him the making of all things; but they know not God, and not only that, but they are guilty of the worst impiety against him; for they attribute a bad quality to God; they make him out to be either disdainful or incapable. If God does not make all things, it must be either because he disdains to make things, or because he is not able; and it is impious to say that. God has one quality, and one alone, the quality of goodness; and he who is good is neither disdainful nor incapable. All that has come into being then has been brought into being by God, that is, by him who is good, and is able to make all; for God is the Good, and the Good has all power to make all.

And if you wish to know how God makes things, and how the things made come into being, you may see an image of it, a goodly sight, and very like. Look at a husbandman sowing seed, here wheat, there barley, and elsewhere some other kind of seed. Look at him planting now a vine, and now an apple-tree, and trees of other kinds; the same man plants them all. And even so, God sows immortality in heaven, and change on earth, and in all the universe, life and movement. For in these two, God, and the world of things made, is comprised all that exists.

LIBELLUS XVI

An epistle of Asclepius to King Ammon.

Of weighty import is this discourse which I send to you, my King; it is, so to speak, a summing up of all the other discourses, and a reminder of their teaching. It is not composed in accordance with the opinion of the many; it contains much that contradicts their beliefs . For my teacher Hermes often used to say in talk with me when we were alone, and sometimes when Tat

was with us, that those who read my writings will think them
to be quite simply and clearly written, but those who hold
opposite principles to start with will say that the style is obscure, and conceals the meaning. And it will be thought still
more obscure in time to come, when the Greeks think fit to
translate
    these writings from our tongue (Egyptian) into theirs. Transla-
tion will greatly distort the sense of the writings, and cause
much obscurity. Expressed in our native language, a the teaching conveys its meaning clearly; for the very quality of the
sounds ; and when the Egyptian words are spoken, the force of
the things signified works in them. Therefore, my King, as far
as it is in your power, (and you are all-powerful,) keep the
teaching untranslated, in order that secrets so holy may not be
revealed to Greeks, and that the Greek mode of speech, with its
arrogance, and feebleness, and showy tricks of style, may not
reduce to impotence the impressive strength of the language,
and the cogent force of the words. For the speech of the Greeks,
my King, is devoid of power to convince; and the Greek philosophy is nothing but a noise of talk. But our speech is not mere
talk; it is an utterance replete with workings.
    I will begin by invoking God, the Master and Maker and
Father and Encompasser of all, who is both One and all things;
not that the One is two, but that these two are one; for the whole
which is made up of all things is one. And I beg you to keep this
in mind, my King, throughout your study of my teaching. For
if any one attempts to separate all things from the One, taking
the term 'all things' to signify a mere plurality of things, and not
a whole made up of things, he will sever the All from the One,
and will thereby bring to naught the All; but that is impossible
It needs must be that all things are one, if they exist, (and they
do exist, and never cease to exist,) in order that the whole which
is made up of them may not be dissolved.
    You can see that in the earth there gush forth many springs
of water and of air in its midmost parts, and that these three
things, air, water, and earth, are found in the same place, being
attached to one single root. Hence we believe that the earth is
the store house of all matter; it gives forth the supply of matter,
and in return receives that thing which comes from above.' For
in this way the Demiurgus (that is, the Sun) brings together

heaven and earth, sending down true being from above, and raising up matter from below. And he orders all things in connection with himself, both drawing life to himself, and giving forth life from himself; for he lavishes light on all things without stint. For the Sun is he whose beneficent workings operate not only in heaven, but also upon earth, and penetrate even to the lowest depths. The material body of the Sun is the source of visible light; and if there is such a thing as a substance not perceptible by sense, the light of the Sun must be the receptacle of that substance. But of what that substance consists, or whence it flows in, God only knows. The Sun, being near to us in position, and like to us in nature, presents himself to our sight. God does not manifest himself to us; we cannot see him, and it is only by conjecture, and with hard effort, that we can apprehend him in thought. But it is not by conjecture that we contemplate the Sun; we see him with our very eyes. He shines most brightly on all the universe, illuminating both the world above and the world below; for he is stationed in the midst, and wears the Kosmos as a wreath around him. And so he lets the Kosmos go on its course, not leaving it far separated from himself, but, to speak truly, keeping it joined to himself; for like a skilled driver, he has made fast and bound to himself the chariot of the Kosmos, lest it should rush away in disorder. And the reins with which he controls it are his light rays.

In this wise he makes all things. He assigns to the immortals their everlasting permanence, and with that part of his light which tends upwards (that is, the light which he sends forth from that side of him which faces heaven), he maintains the immortal parts of the Kosmos; but with the light which is shed downward, and illuminates all the sphere of water, earth, and air, he puts life into the things in this region of the Kosmos, and stirs them up to birth, and by successive changes remakes the living creatures and transforms them. For the permanence of every kind of body is maintained by change. Immortal bodies undergo change without dissolution, but the changes of mortal bodies are accompanied by dissolution; that is the difference between immortals and mortals. And as the light of the Sun is poured forth continuously, so his production of life also is continuous and without intermission

The Sun then is the preserver and maintainer of every kind of living beings; and as the intelligible Kosmos, encompassing the sensible Kosmos, fills its material mass with manifold forms of every shape, so the Sun also fills all things in the Kosmos with his light, and makes them live. And the Earth, supplying matter for the birth of things, gives mass and strength to all things, and when they fail and sink away, receives the matter back into itself.

And to the Sun is subject the troop of daemons, or rather, troops; for there are many and diverse troops of them, placed under the command of the planets, an equal number of daemons being assigned to each planet. Thus marshalled in separate corps, the daemons serve under the several planets. They are both good and bad in their natures, that is, in their workings; for the being of a daemon consists in his working. To these daemons is given dominion over all things upon earth, They are also the authors of the disturbances upon earth, and work manifold trouble both for cities and nations collectively and for individual men. For they mould our souls into another shape, and pull them away to themselves, being seated in our nerves and marrow and veins and arteries, and penetrating even to our inmost organs. For at the time when each one of us is born and made alive, the daemons who are at that moment on duty as ministers of birth take charge of us, that is, the daemons who are subject to some one planet. For the planets replace one another from moment to moment ; they do not go on working without change, but succeed one another in rotation. These daemons then make their way in through the body, and enter into the two irrational parts of the soul (viz. the part that feels desire and the part that feels repugnance); and each daemon perverts the soul in a different way, according to his special mode of action. But the rational part of the soul remains free from the dominion of the daemons, and fit to receive God into itself. If then the rational part of a man's soul is illumined by a ray of light from God, for that man the working of the daemons is brought to naught; for no daemon and no god (i.e. no planetary god) has power against a single ray of the light of God. But such men are few indeed; and all others are led and driven, soul and body, by the daemons, setting their hearts and affections on the workings of the daemons. This is that love which is devoid of reason, that love which goes astray and leads men astray. The daemons then govern all our earthly life, using our bodies as their instruments; and this government Hermes called 'destiny'.

The intelligible Kosmos then is dependent on God; and the Sun receives from God, through the intelligible Kosmos, the influx of good (that is, of life-giving energy), with which he is supplied. And round about the Sun, and dependent on the Sun, are the eight spheres, namely, the sphere of the fixed stars, and the six planet-spheres, and the sphere which surrounds the earth; and the daemons are dependent on these spheres; and men are dependent on the daemons. Thus all things and all persons are dependent on God. God then is the Father of all; the Sun is the Demiurgus and the Kosmos is the instrument by means of which the Demiurgus works . The Kosmos governs the gods; and the daemons are subject to the gods, and govern men. Thus is marshalled the army of gods and daemons. Working through gods and daemons, God makes all things for himself; and all things are parts of God. And inasmuch as all things are parts of him, God is all things. Therefore, in making all things, God makes himself. And it is impossible that he should ever cease from making; for God himself can never cease to be.

LIBELLUS XVII

'And if you think of it, my King, there are incorporeal images of bodies also.' 'What sort of things do you mean?' asked the King. 'Do you not think that the images seen in mirrors are incorporeal?' 'Yes, Tat, it is so,' said the King. 'And there are other things also that are incorporeal; for instance, do you not think that the forms which are seen not only in the bodies of living beings, but also in those of lifeless things, are incorporeal?' 'Yes, Tat, you are right.' 'Well then, as bodies are reflected in mirrors, so incorporeal things are reflected in bodies, and the intelligible Kosmos is reflected in the sensible Kosmos. Therefore, my King, worship the statues of the gods, seeing that these statues too have in them forms which come from the intelligible Kosmos.'

Thereupon the King rose from his seat, and said, 'Prophet, it is time for me to see to the entertainment of my guests;' but tomorrow we will continue our discussion about the gods, and deal with the next part of the subject.'

LIBELLUS XVIII

When musicians undertake to make harmonious melody, then, if in the performance their good intent is thwarted by the discordance of their instruments, one does not impute the blame to the musician's inspiration, but one ascribes the fault to the unsoundness of the instrument; it is this, we say, that has made the music fall short of perfect beauty, obstructing the musician in his rendering of the melody, and depriving the audience of the joy of hearing the clear sweet strain. And even so, let no man who is present at this festival find fault with my art by reason of my personal defects; but be it known that the spirit which God breathes into men of my sort is unfailing. For God, who is by nature a musician, and not only works harmony in the universe at large, but also transmits to individuals the rhythm of his own music, God, I say, can never fail; there is no variation in his skill, and his bounties are the same for ever. And even if the matter which the craftsman has to use does not yield such obedience to his hand as would bring the work of art to perfection, [it is not he that is at fault. If then the music goes amiss but] the musician has done his part as far as it is in his power, we must not lay the blame on him, but we must charge the fault to the shortcoming of the lyre-string, for that it has lowered the pitch of the note, and so has marred the beauty of true music.

But I see that it sometimes comes to pass that, when an artist has made ready to deal with a noble theme, he gets his lyre put in tune by mysterious means, in such wise as to bring its deficiency to a glorious issue, to the amazement of his hearers. It is told of a certain lute-player, one that enjoyed the favour of the god who presides over music, that when he was playing the lute for a prize, and was hindered in his competition by the breaking of a string,. For by God's providence, a cicala settled on his lute, and made good the defect in the music; and so the lute-player's grief was stayed, and he won the honour of the victory. And even so I feel it is with me, most honoured Sirs. Just now I confessed my weakness; but by God's power methinks the defect in the melody has been made good, and I am like to make right pleasant music.

The aim of my endeavour is the glory of kings; and it is the trophies which our kings have won that make me eager to speak. Onward then! for so God wills; and the melody that the musician makes will sound the sweeter by reason of the greatness of his theme.

Since then his lyre is tuned to treat of kings, and is set to the right pitch for songs of praise, he first uplifts his voice to laud the supreme King of the universe, and comes down thereafter to those who hold their sovereignty after His likeness. For this our kings themselves would wish, that the song should come down step by step from heaven above, and that our praise of them should be derived in due succession from the Power that has conferred on them their victories. Let the musician then address his song to that most mighty King, who is immortal, and reigns from all eternity; that primal Victor, from whom all victories come to those who follow after.

Thus let us praise God; but from Him we will pass down to those who have received the sceptre from his hand. For we must practise ourselves by praising earthly kings, and so habituate and train ourselves for adoration of the Deity. My discourse comes down then to the praise of those who rule on earth, and hastens on to these our kings, whose rule provides safety and peace for all; these to whom God has given the topmost height of sovereignty, and on whom victory has been conferred by God's right hand; for whom the prizes have been made ready even before they win them by their prowess in the wars; whose trophies are set up even before the armies meet in battle; who strike terror into the barbarians even before the troops march forth to fight. For we must make requital to our kings, for that they have spread abroad among us the prosperity which comes of this great peace. The virtue of a king is shown in making peace; nay, the very name of king confers peace; for the king is so called for this cause, that with smooth tread' he plants his feet upon the topmost heights, and prevails by means of reason; so that this name is in itself a token of peace. Moreover, even the statues of the king serve as havens to men tossed by the fiercest storms; and it has come to pass ere now that the sight of a mere image of the king has given protection from all fears.

Among those then who dwell in that world above there is no disagreement; all have one purpose; there is one mind, one feeling in them all; for the spell which binds them one to another is Love, the same in all, and by it all are wrought together into one harmonious whole.

But now the speaker hastens on to end as he began, and to conclude his speech with praise of God. For as the Sun, who nurtures all vegetation, also gathers the first fruits of the produce with his rays, as it were with mighty hands, plucking the sweetest odours of the plants; even so we too, having received into our souls (which are plants of heavenly origin) the efflux of God's wisdom, must, in return, use in his service all that springs up in us.

To God then, the Father of our souls, it is fitting that praise should rise from countless tongues and voices, even though our words cannot be worthy of him, seeing that it is a task beyond our power to tell of him. Even so, little children are not able worthily to sing their father's praise; but they do what is fitting when they render to him such honour as they can. Nay, this very thing redounds to God's glory, that his greatness transcends the praises of his offspring; and the beginning and middle and end of our praise is to confess that our Father is infinite in power, and ... But we must beseech him to pardon us; though his children do indeed get pardon from their Father even before they ask it; and just as it is to be looked for that a father, so far from turning his face away from his babes because they can do so little, should be glad when they acknowledge him, even so [does God take pleasure in our praises]. For God, inasmuch as he is good, and has in himself the only limit of his own preeminence, and inasmuch as he is immortal, and from his everlasting energy supplies to this world also its appointed lot of endless duration, ...

ASCLEPIUS

A holy book of Hermes Trismegistus, addressed to Asclepius.

Prologue

Trismegistus. 'It is God that has brought you to me, Asclepius, to hear a teaching' which comes from God. My discourse will be of such a nature, that by reason of its pious fervour it will be rightly deemed that there is in it more of God's working than in all that I have spoken before, —or rather, that God's power has inspired me to speak. And if you understand my words, and thereby come to see God, your mind will be wholly filled with all things good, —if indeed there are many goods, and not rather one Good, in which all goods are comprised. For we find that these two things agree with one another; they are so linked together that it is impossible to part them. But this you will learn from my discourse today, if you listen with earnest attention.

But go forth for a moment, Asclepius, and summon Tat to join us.' When Tat had entered, Asclepius proposed that Ammon also should be present. Trismegistus replied, 'I do not grudge permission to Ammon to be with us; for I bear in mind that many of my writings have been addressed to him, as again many of my treatises on nature, and a very large number of my explanatory writings, have been addressed to Tat, my dear and loving son. As for our discussion today, I will inscribe on it your name, Asclepius. You may call Ammon; but summon no one else, lest a discourse which treats of the loftiest of themes, and breathes the deepest reverence, should be profaned by the entrance and presence of a throng of listeners. For it would be impiety to make public through the presence of many witnesses a discussion which is replete with God in all his majesty.' Then Ammon also entered the sanctuary; and the place was made holy by the pious awe of the four men, and was filled with God's presence. And the hearers listened in fitting silence, and with heart and soul each of them hung on the words in reverence, as through the lips of Hermes the divine Eros thus began to speak.

Asclepius I

Trism. All human souls, Asclepius, are immortal. But souls are not all of one kind; different souls have been created in different fashions; for souls differ in quality. *Ascl.* But tell me, Trismegistus, are not souls uncreated ? —*Trism.* How quickly, Asclepius, you have lost your hold on the true doctrine! Have I not told you this before, that all things are one, and the One is all things, seeing that all things were in the Creator before he created them all? And rightly has it been said of him that he is all things; for all things are parts of him. Throughout our discussion then, be careful to remember him, the One who is all things, —him who is the creator of all things.

From heaven are derived all .... (Air) enters into earth and water; and fire enters into air. That only which tends upward is life-giving; and that which tends downward is subservient to it. Moreover, all that descends from on high is generative; and that which issues upward from below is nutritive. Earth, which alone stands fast in its own place, receives all that is generative into itself, and renders back all that it has received. This whole then, which is made up of all things, or is all things, consists, as you have heard me say before, of soul and corporeal substance. Soul and corporeal substance together are embraced by nature, and are by nature's working kept in movement; and by this movement, the manifold qualities of all things that take shape are made to differ among themselves, in such sort that there come into existence individual things of infinitely numerous forms, by reason of the differences of their qualities, and yet all individuals are united to the whole; so that we see that the whole is one, and of the one are all things. The elements through which all matter has been imbued with form are four in number, fire, water, earth, and air; but matter is one, soul is one, and God is one.

And now give me your whole attention, exerting to the utmost your power of thought and keenness of intelligence. For the doctrine which teaches of God's being needs for its apprehension such effort of thought as man cannot make save by God's help. It is like a torrent plunging downward with headlong rush, so that in its swiftness it outstrips the man who strives to follow it, and leaves behind not only the hearers, but even the teacher himself.

To Heaven, a god perceptible by sense, is committed the administration of all bodies; and the growth and decay of bodies fall under the charge of Sun and Moon. But Heaven itself, and all things in it, are governed by God; and he, working through nature, is the maker of all general and individual forms of living things. For by all the heavenly bodies, which all alike are governed by God, there is poured into all matter an uninterrupted stream of soul. Matter has been made ready by God beforehand to be the recipient of individual forms of every shape; and nature, fashioning matter in individual forms by means of the four elements, brings into being, up to the height of heaven, all things that will be pleasing in God's sight. All portions of soul are dependent on the powers above, and are distributed among individuals in the way that I will now describe. The individuals of each kind are fashioned in accordance with the form of their kind. The kind is the whole made up of the individuals; the individual is a part of the kind. Thus the god-kind produces individual gods, and the daemon-kind produces individual daemons. And so too the kind or race of men, and that of birds, and those of all beings which the universe contains, generate individuals of like form to their kind. And there is yet another kind of living beings, which are devoid of soul indeed, yet not without sensation, so that they are gladdened by all that does them good, and suffer pain from all that impairs and harms them. This kind consists of all things which are implanted in the soil, and spring into life with firm-fixed roots; and the individuals of this kind are spread abroad over all the earth. Heaven itself is filled with gods; and the gods are individually immortal. The other kinds of which I have spoken dwell in the space which extends from earth to the abode of the gods; and in all these kinds, the individuals are mortal. For the individual is a part of the kind, —as a man, for instance, is a part of mankind, —and must necessarily agree in quality with the kind of which it is a part. Hence, though all kinds are immortal, not all individuals are immortal. In the case of the gods, both the kind and the individuals are immortal. All other kinds, though they perish in their individuals, are kept in being by their reproductive fertility. Thus the individuals are mortal, but the kind is everlasting ; So that men are mortal, but mankind is immortal.

But though all individuals exactly resemble the type of their kind, yet individuals of each kind intermingle with all other kinds. All daemons who have dissociated themselves from their own kind, and have come to be united to the god-kind through close connection and fellowship with some individual of the god-kind, are held to be 'god-like daemons'; individuals of the daemon-kind who maintain unchanged the character of their own kind are called ...; and those who associate with men are called 'daemons friendly to man'. And the like is to be said of men; indeed, the range of men is yet wider than that of the daemons. The individuals of the human kind are diverse, and of many characters. They, like the daemons, come from above; and entering into fellowship with other individuals, they make for themselves many and intimate connections with almost all other kinds. Accordingly, the man who, in virtue of the mind in him, through which he is akin to the gods, has attached himself to them by pious devotion, becomes like to the gods; he who has attached himself to daemons becomes like to the daemons; those who are content with the intermediate station of their kind remain mere men and nothing more; and all other individuals of the human kind, according as they have attached themselves to individuals of this kind or that, will resemble the beings to which they have attached themselves.

Man is a marvel then, Asclepius; honour and reverence to such a being! Man takes on him the attributes of a god, as though he were himself a god; he is familiar with the daemon kind, for he comes to know that he is sprung from the same source as they; and strong in the assurance of that in him which is divine, he scorns the merely human part of his own nature. How far more happily blended are the properties of man than those of other beings! He is linked to the gods, inasmuch as there is in him a divinity akin to theirs; he scorns that part of his own being which makes him a thing of earth; and all else with which he finds himself connected by heaven's ordering, he binds to himself by the tie of his affection. He raises reverent eyes to heaven above; he tends the earth below. Blest in his intermediate station, he is so placed that he loves all below him, and is loved by all above him. He has access to all; he descends to the depths of the sea by the keenness of his thought; and heaven is not found too high for him, for he measures it by his sagacity, as though it were within his reach. With his quick wit he penetrates the elements; air cannot blind his mental vision with its thickest darkness; dense earth cannot impede his work; the deepest water cannot blur his downward gaze. Man is all things; man is everywhere.

Now of all the different kinds or races, those which possess soul have roots extending downward to them from above; and those which are soulless sprout from roots which reach upward from below. The one sort are nourished with two kinds of food; the other sort, with food of one kind only. Animals are composed of soul and body; and their food is of two kinds —The soul is nourished by the ceaseless movement of fire and air, the higher elements; the growth of bodies is supplied from water and earth, the lower elements. Mind, a fifth component part, which comes from the aether, has been bestowed on man alone; and of all beings that have soul, man is the only one whose faculty of cognition is, by this gift of mind, so strengthened, elevated, and exalted, that he can attain to knowledge of the truth concerning God.

As I have been led to speak of mind, I will later on expound to you the true doctrine concerning mind also; for it is a high and holy doctrine, and one no less sublime than that which treats of God himself. But for the present, I will continue the explanation I have begun. I was speaking of that attachment to the gods which men, and men alone, are by the grace of the gods permitted to enjoy, —that is to say, such men as have attained to the great happiness of acquiring that divine faculty of apprehending truth, that diviner sort of mind, which exists only in

God and in the intellect of man. —*Ascl.* But tell me then, Trismegistus, is not the mind of all men of one quality? —*Trism.* Not all men, Asclepius, have attained to true knowledge. Many men, yielding to reckless impulse, and seeing nothing of the truth, are misled by illusions and these illusions breed evil in their hearts, and transform man, the best of living beings, into a wild and savage beast. But concerning mind and the like I will fully set forth the truth to you later on, when I come to treat of spirit also.

Man, and man alone of all beings that have soul, is of twofold nature. Of the two parts of which he is composed, the one is single and undivided; this part is incorporeal and eternal, and we call it 'that which is formed in the likeness of God'. The other part of man is fourfold, and material; and within it is enclosed that part of him which I just now called divine, to the end that, sheltered therein, the divine mind, together with the thoughts of pure mind, which are cognate to it, secluded from all else, may dwell at rest, fenced in by the body, as it were by a wall. —

Ascl. But what need was there, Trismegistus, that man should be placed in this material world? Why might he not have dwelt in the region where God is, and there enjoyed perfect happiness? —*Trism.* You are right, Asclepius, in asking that question; and I pray God to give me power to answer it. For on his will depend all things, and above all else, the investigation of that which is highest and most comprehensive; and such is that with which our present inquiry is concerned. Listen then, Asclepius. When the Master, the Maker of all things, whom by usage we name God, had made him who is second, a god visible and sensible; —and I call him 'sensible', not because he perceives things by sense, (for the question whether he perceives things by sense or not, we will discuss later on,) but because he can be perceived by sense and sight; —when, I say, God had made this being, his first and one and only creation, and when he saw that the being he had made was beautiful, and wholly filled with all things good, he rejoiced in him, and loved him dearly, as being his own offspring. Therefore, being wise and good himself, he willed that there should be another who might look upon the being whom he had begotten; and in that act of willing, he made man, to be an imitator of his wisdom and his fostering care. For with God, to will is to accomplish, inasmuch as, when he wills, the doing is completed in the self-same moment as the willing. And so, having made man as an incorporeal and eternal being, and perceiving that the man whom he had made could not tend all things on earth unless he enclosed him in a material envelope, God gave him the shelter of a body to dwell in, and ordained that all men should be formed in like manner. Thus he fashioned man of the substance of mind and the substance of body, —of that which is eternal and that which is mortal, —blending and mingling together portions of either substance in adequate measure, to the end that the creature so fashioned might be able to fulfil the demands of both sources of his being, that is to say, to venerate and worship the things of heaven, and at the same time to tend and administer the things of earth. And when I say 'the things of earth', I do not mean merely the two elements, water and earth, which nature has placed in subjection to men; I mean all things that men do on land and water, or make out of earth and water, as for instance tillage and pasture, building, harbour-works and navigation, and intercourse and mutual service, that strong bond by which the members of the human race are linked together. For to man is given the charge of that part of the universe which consists of earth and water; and this earthly part of the universe is kept in order by means of man's knowledge and application of the arts and sciences. For God willed that the universe should not be complete until man had done his part.

But I see, Asclepius, that you are eager and impatient to be told how man can tend heaven or the things in heaven. Listen then, Asclepius. Tendance of heaven and of all things that are therein is nothing else than constant worship; and there is no other being, divine or mortal, that worships, but man alone. For in the reverence and adoration, the praise and worship of men, heaven and the gods of heaven find pleasure. And not without good reason has the supreme Deity sent down the choir of the Muses to dwell among mankind. The earthly part of the universe would have seemed but rude and savage, if it had been wanting in sweet melody; and lest this should be, God sent the Muses down, to the intent that men might adore with hymns of praise Him who is all things in one, the Father of all, and that thus sweet music might not be lacking upon earth, to sound in concord with the singing of his praise in heaven. To some men then, but to very few, men who are endowed with mind uncontaminate, has fallen the high task of raising reverent eyes to heaven. But to all who, through the intermingling of the diverse parts of their twofold being, are weighed down by the burden of the body, and have sunk to a lower grade of intelligence, —to all such men is assigned the charge of tending the elements, and the things of this lower world. Thus man is a being partly divine, and partly mortal; not that he is to be thought the lower because he is mortal in part; we ought rather to regard him as exalted by his mortality, in that he is by such a lot more fitly and effectively constituted for a purpose pre-ordained. For since he could not have met the demands of both his functions if he had not been made of both kinds of substance, he was fashioned out of both, to the end that he might be able both to tend the earth and to do service to the Deity.

And now, Asclepius, I desire you to listen with a strong effort of thought, as well as with keen penetration, to that which I am about to expound to you. It is a doctrine which the many do not believe, but which should be accepted as sound and true by men of saintlier mind. Thus I begin. God, the Master of eternity, is first; the Kosmos is second; man is third. God, the maker of the Kosmos and of all things that are therein, governs all things, but has made man as a composite being to govern in conjunction with him. And if man takes upon him in all its fullness the function assigned to him, that is, the tendance which is his special task, he becomes the means of right order to the Kosmos, and the Kosmos to him; so that it seems the Kosmos (that is, the ordered universe) has been rightly so named, because man's composite structure has been thus ordered by God. Man knows himself, and knows the Kosmos also, provided that he bears in mind what action is suited to the part he has to play, and recognises what things he is to use for his own ends, and to what things he in turn is to do service, rendering praise and thanks in full measure to God, and revering God's image (the Kosmos), not unaware that he himself is a second image of God. For there are two images of God; the Kosmos is one, and man is another, inasmuch as he, like the Kosmos, is a single whole built up of diverse parts. For you must note that man, in order that he may be fully equipped on both sides, has been so fashioned that each of his two parts is made up of four elements;

and so, in respect of the divine part of him, which is composed of other and higher 'elements', so to speak, namely, mind, intellect, spirit, and reason, he is found capable of rising to heaven; but in respect of his material part, which consists of fire, water, earth, and air, he is mortal, and remains on earth, that he may not leave forsaken and abandoned all things that are entrusted to his keeping. Thus it is that man, though in part divine, has been made mortal also in part, being placed in a body. Now the right regulation of the two parts, that is, of the whole man, consists first and chiefly in piety; and piety is accompanied by goodness. But goodness is to be seen in its perfection only when man's virtue is fortified against desire, and he scorns all things that are alien to him. Now all earthly things which man holds in his possession to gratify his bodily desires are alien to all that part of his nature which is akin to God; and these things are rightly called 'possessions' for this reason, that they were not born with us, but we began to get possession of them at a later time. All such things then are alien to man; yes, and the body too we must regard as alien, that so we may scorn not only the objects of our greed, but also that which is the source of the vicious greed within us. For according to the view to which my thinking leads me, it is man's duty not to acquiesce in his merely human state, but rather, in the strength of his contemplation of things divine, to scorn and despise that mortal part which has been attached to him because it was needful that he should keep and tend this lower world.

Seeing then that man has been thus made and fashioned, and has been appointed by the supreme God to such tasks of service and of worship, what, think you, should be his reward, if by a well-ordered life of labour in the world committed to his charge, and by honouring God with pious observance, in both respects alike he worthily and fittingly obeys God's will? For since the world is God's handiwork, he who maintains and heightens its beauty by his tendance is cooperating with the will of God, when he contributes the aid of his bodily strength, and by his care and labour day by day makes things assume that shape and aspect which God's purpose has designed. What shall be his reward? Shall it not be that which our fathers have received, and which we pray with heartfelt piety that we too may receive, if God in his mercy is pleased to grant it? And that is, that when

our term of service is ended, when we are divested of our
guardianship of the material world, and freed from the bonds
of mortality, he will restore us, cleansed and sanctified, to the
primal condition of that higher part of us which is divine.
—*Ascl.* Right and true Trismegistus. —*Trism.* Yes, such is the
reward of those who spend their lives in piety to God above,
and in tendance of the world around them. But those who have
lived evil and impious lives are not permitted to return to
heaven. For such men is ordained a shameful transmigration
into bodies of another kind, bodies unworthy to be the abode of
holy mind. —*Ascl.* According to your teaching then,
Trismegistus, souls have at stake in this earthly life their hope
of eternity in the life to come. —*Trism.* Yes. But some cannot
believe this; and some regard it as an empty tale; and to some,
perhaps, it seems a thing to mock at. For in our bodily life on
earth, the enjoyment derived from possessions is a pleasant
thing; and the pleasure which they yield grips the soul by the
throat, so to speak, and holds it down to earth, compelling it to
cleave to man's mortal part.

Moreover, there are some whose ungenerous temper grudges
men the boon of immortality, and will not suffer them to get
knowledge of that in them which is divine. For speaking as a
prophet speaks, I tell you that in after times none will pursue
philosophy in singleness of heart. Philosophy is nothing else
than striving through constant contemplation and saintly piety
to attain to knowledge of God ; but there will be many who will
make philosophy hard to understand, and corrupt it with manifold speculations —*Ascl.* How so? —*Trism.* In this way,
Asclepius; by a cunning sort of study, in which philosophy will
be mixed with diverse and unintelligible sciences, such as arith-
metic, music, and geometry. Whereas the student of philosophy
undefiled, which is dependent on devotion to God, and on that
alone, ought to direct his attention to the other sciences only so
far as he may thereby learn to see and marvel how the returns
of the heavenly bodies to their former places, their halts in
preordained positions, and the variations of their movements,
are true to the reckonings of number; only so far as, learning the
measurements of the earth, the depth of the sea, <the —of air,>
the force of fire, and the properties, magnitudes, workings, and
natures of all material things, he may be led to revere, adore,

and praise God's skill and wisdom. And to know the science of music is nothing else than this, —to know how all things are ordered, and how God's design has assigned to each its place; for the ordered system in which each and all by the supreme Artist's skill are wrought together into a single whole yields a divinely musical harmony, sweet and true beyond all melodious sounds. I tell you then that the men of after times will be misled by cunning sophists, and will be turned away from the pure and holy teachings of true philosophy. For to worship God in thought and spirit with singleness of heart, to revere God in all his works, and to give thanks to God, whose will, and his alone, is wholly filled with goodness, —this is philosophy unsullied by intrusive cravings for unprofitable knowledge.

Asclepius II

[Here let the discussion of these things end; and let us now begin to speak of spirit and the like.]

Trism. In the beginning were God and Matter. The elements of which the universe is composed were not then in existence, because they had not yet come into being; but they were already in that from which they were to be generated.

Now all things which possess the faculty of generating are generative; and it is possible for something else to be generated from them, even if they are self-generated. For there is no doubt that from things self-generated can easily be generated ⁞ from which all things come into being.

God is everlasting, God is eternal. That he should come into being, or should ever have come into being, is impossible. He is, he was, he will be for ever. Such is God's being; he is wholly self-generated.

Matter, though it is manifestly ungenerated, yet has in itself from the first the power of generating; for an original fecundity is inherent in the properties of matter, which possesses in itself the power of conceiving things and giving birth to them. Matter then is generative by itself, without the help of anything else. It undoubtedly contains in itself the power of generating all things.

On the other hand, we must class apart from matter those things which are enabled to conceive only when something else is intermingled with them; though <such things also may be ungenerated>. Thus the space in which is contained the universe with all things that are therein is manifestly ungenerated. (By 'space' I here mean that in which all things are contained.) For the existence of all things that are would have been impossible, if space had not existed as an antecedent condition of their being. For if anything is to exist, space for it must be provided beforehand; if things were nowhere, their properties, magnitudes, positions, and operations could not be discerned.

Matter then, though it is likewise ungenerated, yet contains in itself the births of all things, inasmuch as it presents a womb most fertile for the conception of all things that come into being.

This sum of things therefore is of diverse quality, in accordance with the varying action of the generative power of matter, which, though uncreated, is creative. For as the generative power of matter is productive of good, so it is equally productive of evil also.

You must not then, my pupils, speak as many do, who say that God ought by all means to have freed the world from evil. To those who speak thus, not a word ought to be said in answer; but for your sake I will pursue my argument, and therewith explain this. It was beyond God's power to put a stop to evil, and expel it from the universe; for evil is present in the world in such sort that it is manifestly an inseparable part thereof. But the supreme God provided and guarded against evil as far as he reasonably could, by deigning to endow the minds of men with intellect, knowledge, and intuition. It is in virtue of these gifts that we stand higher than the beasts; and by these, and these alone, are we enabled to shun the traps and deceptions and corruptions of evil. If a man shuns them when he sees them from afar, before he is entangled in them, it is by God's wisdom and forethought that he is protected from them; for man's knowledge is based on the supreme goodness of God.

[On this topic then, let this explanation suffice.]

Asclepius III

Trism. He whom we name God supreme, a God apprehensible by thought alone, is the ruler and director of that god perceptible by sense, who embraces within himself all substances and all matter, and all things without exception that have to do with birth and production. Spirit, which is subject to the will of the supreme God, and serves him as his instrument, is that by means of which are moved or directed all kinds of beings in the universe, each in accordance with the special character assigned to it by God. Matter is the recipient of all forms; and the changes and unbroken successions of the forms <are wrought by means of spirit>. The process is directed by God, who distributes <life> to all things in the universe, giving to each one of them as much as it needs. Into all things he infuses spirit, assigning it to each in larger measure, in proportion as the thing stands higher in the scale of being.

These then are the primary things, the prior things, the heads or first principles of all things in the universe; for all cosmic things are contained in them, or wrought by means of them, or made of them.

But as to Void, which most people think to be a thing of great importance, I hold that no such thing as void exists, or can have existed in the past, or ever will exist. For all the several parts of the Kosmos are wholly filled with bodies of various qualities and forms, each having its own shape and magnitude; and thus the Kosmos as a whole is full and complete. Of these bodies, some are larger, some are smaller; and they differ in the greater or lesser firmness of their substance. Those of them which are of firmer substance are more easily seen, as are also those which are larger; whereas smaller bodies, and those which are of less firm substance, are almost or quite invisible, and it is only by the sense of touch that we are made aware of their existence. Hence many people have come to think that these bodies do not exist, and that there are void spaces; but that is impossible. And the like holds good of what is called 'the extra-mundane', if indeed any such thing exists; for I hold that not even the region outside the Kosmos is void, seeing that it is filled with things apprehensible by thought alone, that is, with things of like nature with its own divine being. And so our Kosmos also,

—the sensible universe, as it is called, —is wholly filled with bodies, and living bodies, suited to its character. The shapes presented by these bodies to our sight differ in magnitude; some of these shapes are very large; others are very small, when the distance of the objects makes them appear small to us; and some things, on account of their extreme minuteness or tenuity, are wholly invisible to us, and are consequently supposed by many people to be non-existent.

And so, Asclepius, you must not call anything void, without saying what the thing in question is void of, as when you say that a thing is void of fire or water or the like. For it is possible for a thing to be void of such things as these, and it may consequently come to *seem* void; but the thing that seems void, however small it be, cannot possibly be empty of spirit and of air.

And the like must be said of Space. The word 'space ' is unmeaning when it stands alone; for it is only by regarding something which is in space, that we come to see what space is; and apart from the thing to which it belongs, the meaning of the term 'space' is incomplete. Thus we may rightly speak of the space occupied by water, and fire, and so on, <but not of space alone.> For as there cannot be a void, so it is impossible to determine what space is, if you regard it by itself. For if you assume a space apart from something which is in it, it will follow that there is a void space; and I hold that there is no such thing as that in the universe. If void has no existence, then it is impossible to find any real thing answering to the word 'space' taken by itself.

...Gross matter then is the nutriment of bodies, and spirit is the nutriment of souls. But besides these, there is mind, which is a gift from heaven, and one with which mankind alone are blessed, —not indeed all men, but those few whose souls are of such quality as to be capable of receiving so great a boon. By the light of mind the human soul is illumined, as the world is illumined by the sun, —nay, in yet fuller measure. For all things on which the sun shines are deprived of his light from time to time by the interposition of the earth, when night comes on; but when mind has once been interfused with the soul of man, there results from the intimate blending of mind with soul a thing that is one and indivisible, so that such men's thought is never obstructed by the darkness of error.

Hence it has been rightly said that the souls of gods consist wholly of mind. But for my part, I hold that, even as regards the gods, this cannot be said of all, but of certain great and chief gods only. —*Ascl.* And which are they, Trismegistus . —*Trism.* It is a weighty secret that I am about to disclose, a holy mystery that I am about to reveal to you ; and I pray for the grace of Heaven to aid me as I speak. There are many kinds of gods; some of them are apprehensible by thought alone, and others are perceptible by sense. The gods apprehensible by thought are so called, not because it is held that they are not subject to our perception; for we perceive them more truly than we perceive those gods whom we call visible as my discourse will show, and as you will be able to see for yourself, —but only if you exert to the utter most your powers of thought. For so lofty is the doctrine of things divine, that it is beyond the reach of any effort of merely human thought; and if you do not hearken to my words with keen attention, my teaching will wing its way beyond you, and flow past you, or rather, will flow back thither whence it came, and mingle with its source. —*Ascl.* And what then, Trismegistus, is this doctrine of things divine, of which you speak? —*Trism.* Be it known to you that the intelligible Kosmos, that is to say, that Kosmos which is discerned by thought alone, is incorporeal, and that nothing corporeal can be mingled with its being, —nothing, that is, which admits of determination by quality, magnitude, or number; for nothing of this kind exists in it. You cannot measure it as you would measure a body, affixing marks of length and breadth and height.

...There are then certain gods apprehensible by thought alone, who preside over all departments of the world, and are called 'Rulers over material things' and subordinate to them are the gods perceptible by sense. These sensible gods bear the likeness of both the sources of their being; and these are they who make all things throughout the sensible world, working one through another, each pouring light into the things he makes.

The Ruler of Heaven, or of whatsoever is included under the name 'Heaven', is Zeus <Hypatos>; for life is given to all beings by Zeus through the medium of Heaven.

The Ruler of the Decani, —that is, the thirty-six fixed stars which are called Horoscopi, —is the god named Pantomorphos; he it is that gives to the individuals of each kind their diverse forms.

The seven spheres, as they are called, have as their Ruler the deity called Fortune or Destiny, who changes all things according to the law of natural growth, working with a fixity which is immutable, and which yet is varied by everlasting movement. The air is the instrument with which all these gods work and by means of which all is done. The Ruler of the air is the subordinate distributor of life; to him belongs the region between heaven and earth; and we call him Zeus <Neatos>.

Earth and sea are ruled by Zeus Chthonios; he it is that supplies nutriment to all mortal beings that have soul, and to all trees that bear fruit; and it is by his power that the fruits of the earth are produced.

And there are other gods beside, whose powers and operations are distributed through all things that exist.

But God, who dwells above the summit of the highest heaven, is present everywhere, and from all around he watches all things; his abode is beyond heaven, in a starless region, far removed from all things corporeal.

Thus mortal things are joined to things immortal, and things perceptible by sense are linked to things beyond the reach of sense; but the supreme control is subject to the will of the Master who is high above all. And this being so, all things are linked together, and connected one with another in a chain extending from the lowest to the highest; so that we see that they are not many, or rather, that all are one. For inasmuch as all things hang on the One and flow from the One, we think indeed that they are many when we look at them apart, but when we regard them as united, we hold them to be one.

This sensible Kosmos then is the recipient of all the sensible forms or qualities of bodies; and all bodies can receive life only from God. For God is all things; from him are all things; and all things are dependent on his will, and on his inimitable wisdom. And this whole sum of things is good and beautiful, and is apprehensible by sense and thought to God alone. Without God nothing has been or is or will be; from God and in God and through God are all things, —all the various and multiform qualities, the vast and measureless magnitudes, and the forms of every aspect. If you learn to understand this, Asclepius, you will render thanks to God.

And if you consider the whole, you will learn that in truth the sensible Kosmos itself, with all things that are therein, is woven like a garment by that higher Kosmos. For matter, having no quality or form of its own to make it visible, is in itself wholly invisible; and for that reason many people think that it is like space, and has the properties of space. It is only by reason of the shapes derived from those ideal forms in the likeness of which we see it carved, so to speak, that men suppose it to be visible; but in reality, matter in itself is ever invisible; for the substance of each thing, in so far as the thing is actually existent, consists wholly of the visible shapes which are present in all things.

For the ideal form, which is divine, is incorporeal, as are all things apprehensible by thought alone.

Since therefore the two constituents of which bodies consist (namely, form and matter) are incorporeal, ...

For every living being, Asclepius, whatever be its kind, and whether that kind be mortal or immortal, rational or irrational, endowed with soul or devoid of soul, bears the likeness of its kind, according as the character of that kind may be. But though each living being has in all respects the form which is proper to its kind, the individuals, while one and all have the same form, yet differ among themselves. For instance, though the human race has a common form, so that we can know from a man's appearance that he is a man, at the same time individual men, for all their sameness of form; yet differ one from another. For it is impossible that any single form should come into being which is exactly like a second, if they originate at different points of time, and at places differently situated; but the forms change at every moment in each hour of the revolution of that celestial circle in which resides the god whom we have named Pantomorphos. Thus the type persists unchanged, but generates at successive instants copies of itself as numerous and different as are the moments in the revolution of the sphere of heaven; for the sphere of heaven changes as it revolves, but the type neither changes nor revolves. Thus the generic forms persist unchanged, but the individuals, for all their sameness of generic form, yet differ one from another.

Ascl. And does the Kosmos also, Trismegistus, change its forms? —*Trism.* Why, you must have been asleep, Asclepius; you cannot have heard what I have been telling you all this while. What is the Kosmos, and of what is it composed, if not of things which have all come into being? When you speak of the Kosmos then, you are speaking of sky, and earth, and the elements. And do not these change their forms as often as anything that exists? The sky is moist and dry, cold and hot, bright and obscured by turns; these are the rapidly alternating <sensible> forms included under the one <ideal or universal> form of the sky. The earth is ever passing through many changes of form; it generates produce, it nourishes the produce it has generated, it yields all manner of crops, with manifold differences of quality and quantity; and above all, it puts forth many sorts of trees, differing in the scent of their flowers and the taste of their fruits. Water takes different forms, now standing and now running. Fire undergoes many changes, and assumes god-like forms; thus the aspects of the sun and moon pass through all manner of forms; they are like our mirrors, and reproduce <the ideal or universal form> in visible copies with rival brilliance.

*   *   *   *   *

Ascl. And what is this other doctrine, Trismegistus? —*Trism,* It is this, Asclepius. Whether he of whom I speak be called God, or Father, or Master of all, whatever be the name by which we name him to convey our meaning in our talk one with another, it is for men to hallow the name with a higher sanctity by contemplation of his supreme divinity; for his being cannot be accurately described by any of the names we call him. For if a word is but a sound made by the impact of our breath upon the air, whereby a man makes known any thought which has entered his mind through his senses, whenever he wills to do so; and if a name is nothing more than a few syllables, and is restricted in length, so as to render possible the indispensable intercourse of man with man by speech and hearing, —if this is so, the full name of God must include the names of sense, and breath, and air, and all names that are contained in sense and breath and air or are uttered by means of them, or are composed of them. For I deem it impossible that he who is the maker of the universe in all its greatness, the Father or Master of all things, can be named by a single name, though it be made up of ever so many others; I hold that he is nameless, or rather, that all names are names of him. For he in his unity is all things; so that we must either call all things by his name, or call him by the names of all things.

He, filled with all the fecundity of both sexes in one, and ever teeming with his own goodness, unceasingly brings into being all that he has willed to generate; and all that he wills is good. From his divine being has sprung the goodness of all things in this world below; and hence it is that all things are productive, and that their procreative power is adequate to ensure that all shall hereafter be as it is now, and as it has been in the past. Take this, Asclepius, as my answer to the question why and how it comes to pass that all kinds of beings are male and female.

—*Ascl.* You say then, Trismegistus, that God is bisexual?
—*Trism.* Yes, Asclepius; and not God alone, but all kinds of beings, whether endowed with soul or soulless. Nothing that exists can be barren; for if all things that now exist are deprived of fertility, it will be impossible for the now existing races to endure for ever. I tell you <that God eternally generates the Kosmos,> and that the Kosmos possesses generative power, and thereby maintains all races that have come into being. For either sex is filled with procreative force; and in that conjunction of the two sexes, or, to speak more truly, that fusion of them into one, which may be rightly named Eros, or Aphrodite, or both at once, there is a deeper meaning than man can comprehend. It is a truth to be accepted as sure and evident above all other truths, that by God, the Master of all generative power, has been devised and bestowed upon all creatures this sacrament of eternal reproduction, with all the affection, all the joy and gladness, all the yearning and the heavenly love that are inherent in its being. And there were need that I should tell of the compelling force with which this sacrament binds man and woman together, were it not that each one of us, if he directs his thought upon himself, can learn it from his inmost feeling. For if you note that supreme moment when, through interaction I without pause, we come at last to this, that either sex infuses itself into the other, the one giving forth its issue, and the other eagerly taking hold on it and laying it up within, you will find

that at that moment, through the inter mingling of the two natures, the female acquires masculine vigour, and the male is relaxed in feminine languor. And so this sacramental act, sweet as it is, and a thing that must needs be done, is done in secret, lest, if it were done openly, the ignorant should mock, and thereby the deity manifested in either sex through the mingling of male and female should be put to the blush, —and the more so, if the act is exposed to the eyes of impious men.

Now there are not many pious men in the world, —nay, there are so few that they could easily be numbered; for men lack wisdom and knowledge of all truth, and hence it is that in the many vice persists. For if a man understands the design of God by which all things are ordained, he will despise all material things, and his vices will be healed; but when folly and ignorance continue, all the vices grow in strength, and lacerate the soul with incurable sores; and infected and corrupted by the poison, the soul breaks out in tumours, so to speak, save in the case of those whose souls are cured by the sovereign remedy of knowledge and intelligence.

If then my words are likely to be profitable only to such men as these, few though they be, it is worth while to pursue this discussion, and explain why God has deigned to impart his intelligence and knowledge to men alone. Listen then. Since God, the Father and Master, after he had made the gods, made man of ingredients weighed out in equal measure from the more corrupt part of matter and from that part which is divine, it came to pass that evils inherent in matter were intermingled with the human body, and so persisted, while other evils enter in by reason of the eating of food, in which we must needs take part together with all living creatures; whence it necessarily results that lustful appetites and all other evil passions find place in the human soul. But the gods are made of the purest part of matter, and have no need of reason and knowledge to aid them; and accordingly, though their immortality and the vigour of their everlasting youth are mightier than any wisdom or knowledge, yet in place of knowledge and intelligence God appointed for them an ordered movement determined by necessity and prescribed by eternal law. On the other hand, God saw that of all living creatures men alone had need of reason and knowledge, whereby they might repel and put away from them the evil passions inherent in their bodies; and for this cause he imparted to them the gift of reason; and at the same time, to the end that they might not be severed from the gods, he held out to them the hope of immortality, and gave them power to strive towards it. Willing then that man should be at once ...and capable of immortality, God compacted him of these two substances, the one divine, the other mortal; and in that he is thus compacted, it is ordained by God's will that man is not only better than all mortal beings, but also better than the gods, who are made wholly of immortal substance. Hence man, being joined to the gods by kinship, worships them with piety and holy thoughts; while the gods on their side regard and watch over all the concerns of men with loving mercy. But you must take this as said only of the few who are endowed with piety. Of the vicious it is better to say nothing, lest by turning our thoughts on them we should profane the high sanctity of our discourse.

And now that the topic of men's kinship and association with the gods has been introduced, let me tell you, Asclepius, how great is the power and might of man. Even as the Master and Father, or, to call him by his highest name, even as God is the maker of the gods of heaven, so man is the fashioner of the gods who dwell in temples and are content to have men for their neighbours. Thus man not only receives the light of divine life, but gives it also; he not only makes his way upward to God, but he even fashions gods. Do you wonder at this, Asclepius? Or do you too doubt it, as many do? —*Ascl.* I am amazed, Trismegistus; but I gladly give assent to what you say, and deem man most highly blest, in that he has attained to such felicity. —*Trism.* Yes, you may well hold man to be a marvel; he surpasses all other creatures. As to the celestial gods, it is admitted by all men that they are manifestly generated from the purest part of matter, and that their astral forms are heads, as it were, and heads alone, in place of bodily frames. But the gods whose shapes are fashioned by mankind are made of both substances, that is, of the divine substance, which is purer and far nobler, and the substance which is lower than man, namely, the material of which they are wrought; and they are fashioned not in the shape of a head alone, but in the shape of a body with all its members. Mankind is ever mindful of its own parentage and the source whence it has sprung, and steadfastly persists in following God's example; and consequently, just as the Father and Master made the gods of heaven eternal, that they might resemble him who made them, even so do men also fashion their gods in the likeness of their own aspect. —*Ascl.* Do you mean statues, Trismegistus? —*Trism.* Yes, Asclepius. See how even you give way to doubt! I mean statues, but statues living and conscious, filled with the breath of life, and doing many mighty works; statues which have fore-knowledge, and predict future events by the drawing of lots, and by prophetic inspiration, and by dreams, and in many other ways; statues which inflict diseases and heal them, dispensing sorrow and joy according to men's deserts.

Do you not know, Asclepius, that Egypt is an image of heaven, or, to speak more exactly, in Egypt all the operations of the powers which rule and work in heaven have been transferred to earth below? Nay, it should rather be said that the whole Kosmos dwells in this our land as in its sanctuary. And yet, since it is fitting that wise men should have knowledge of all events before they come to pass, you must not be left in ignorance of this: there will come a time when it will be seen that in vain have the Egyptians honoured the deity with heart felt piety and assiduous service; and all our holy worship will be found bootless and ineffectual. For the gods will return from earth to heaven; Egypt will be forsaken, and the land which was once the home of religion will be left desolate, bereft of the presence of its deities. This land and region will be filled with foreigners; not only will men neglect the service of the gods, but ...; and Egypt will be occupied by Scythians or Indians, or by some such race from the barbarian countries thereabout. In that day will our most holy land, this land of shrines and temples, be filled with funerals and corpses. To thee, most holy Nile, I cry, to thee I foretell that which shall be; swollen with torrents of blood, thou wilt rise to the level of thy banks, and thy sacred waves will be not only stained, but utterly fouled with gore. Do you weep at this, Asclepius? There is worse to come; Egypt herself will have yet more to suffer; she will fall into a far more piteous plight, and will be infected with yet more grievous plagues; and this land, which once was holy, a land which loved the gods, and wherein alone, in reward for her devotion, the gods deigned to sojourn upon earth, a land which was the teacher of mankind in holiness and piety, —this land will go beyond all in cruel deeds. The dead will far out number the living; and the survivors will be known for Egyptians by their tongue alone, but in their actions they will seem to be men of another race. O Egypt, Egypt, of thy religion nothing will remain but an empty tale, which thine own children in time to come will not believe; nothing will be left but graven words, and only the stones will tell of thy piety. And in that day men will be weary of life, and they will cease to think the universe worthy of reverent wonder and of worship. And so religion, the greatest of all blessings, —for there is nothing, nor has been, nor ever shall be, that can be deemed a greater boon, —will be threatened with destruction; men will think it a burden, and will come to scorn it. They will no longer love this world around us, this incomparable work of God, this glorious structure which he has built, this sum of good made up of things of many diverse forms, this instrument whereby the will of God operates in that which he has made, ungrudgingly devouring man's welfare, this combination and accumulation of all the manifold things that can call forth the veneration, praise, and love of the beholder. Darkness will be preferred to light, and death will be thought more profitable than life; no one will raise his eyes to heaven; the pious will be deemed insane, and the impious wise; the madman will be thought a brave man, and the wicked will be esteemed as good. As to the soul, and the belief that it is immortal by nature, or may hope to attain to immortality, as I have taught you, —all this they will mock at, and will even persuade themselves that it is false. No word of reverence or piety, no utterance worthy of heaven and of the gods of heaven, will be heard or believed.

And so the gods will depart from mankind, —a grievous thing! —and only evil angels will remain, who will mingle with men, and drive the poor wretches by main force into all manner of reckless crime, into wars, and robberies, and frauds, and all things hostile to the nature of the soul. Then will the earth no longer stand unshaken, and the sea will bear no ships; heaven will not support the stars in their orbits, nor will the stars pursue their constant course in heaven; all voices of the gods will of necessity be silenced and dumb; the fruits of the earth will rot; the soil will turn barren, and the very air will sicken in sullen stagnation. After this manner will old age come upon the world. Religion will be no more; all things will be disordered and awry; all good will disappear.

But when all this has befallen, Asclepius, then the Master and Father, God, the first before all, the maker of that god who first came into being, will look on that which has come to pass, and will stay the disorder by the counter-working of his will, which is the good. He will call back to the right path those who have gone astray; he will cleanse the world from evil, now washing it away with water-floods, now burning it out with fiercest fire, or again expelling it by war and pestilence. And thus he will bring back his world to its former aspect, so that the Kosmos will once more be deemed worthy of worship and wondering reverence, and God, the maker and restorer of the mighty fabric, will be adored by the men of that day with unceasing hymns of praise and blessing. Such is the new birth of the Kosmos; it is a making again of all things good, a holy and awe-striking restoration of all nature; and it is wrought in the process of time by the eternal will of God.

For God's will has no beginning; it is ever the same, and as it now is, even so it has ever been, without beginning. For it is the very being of God to purpose good. —*Ascl.* Is 'will' then, Trismegistus, summed up in 'purpose' —*Trism.* Will, Asclepius, issues from purpose; and from will issues each several act of will. Not without effect does God will a thing, for he is fully supplied with all things; and all things that he wills are good. He has all things which he wills, and wills the things which he has; and all that he purposes and wills is good.

Such is God. The Kosmos is God's image; and since God is good, the Kosmos also is good. —*Ascl.* Do you say, Trismegistus, that the Kosmos is good? —*Trism.* Yes, Asclepius; and I will show you that it is so. God dispenses and distributes goods, namely, sense, soul, and life, to all kinds of beings in the Kosmos; and in like manner, the Kosmos gives and supplies all things which seem good to mortals, namely, the succession of births in time, the formation, growth, and ripening of the fruits of the earth, and the like. For you must deem the Kosmos a second god, Asclepius, a god who governs all living things, both those which have souls and those which are soulless. For if the Kosmos has been and is and will be a living and ever-living being, nothing in the Kosmos is mortal. It is the everlasting life of each of its several parts that makes the Kosmos what it is; and seeing that the Kosmos is ever one, and is a living and ever-living being, mortality can have no place in it. It must therefore be filled with life, and with eternal life, if it needs must live for ever.

It is God then that everlastingly governs all the sources of life in the Kosmos; he is the eternal dispenser of life itself. But when life has once been dispensed to all the (intra-cosmic) sources of life, the supply of it is maintained in accordance with eternal law; and the manner of its maintenance I will proceed to explain. The Kosmos moves within the very life of eternity, and is contained in that very eternity whence all life issues; and for this reason it is impossible that it should at any time come to a stand, or be destroyed, since it is walled in and bound together, so to speak, by eternal life. And the Kosmos is itself the dispenser of life to all things in it here below, and the place in which are contained all things which are subject to control beneath the sun. The movement of the Kosmos itself consists of a twofold working; life is infused into the Kosmos from without by eternity; and the Kosmos infuses life into all things that are within it, distributing all things according to fixed and determined relations of number and time, by the operation of the sun and the movements of the stars. The process of time is wholly determined by God's law; but the lapse of terrestrial time is marked by the changing states of the atmosphere, and the variations of heat and cold; while that of celestial time is marked by the return of the heavenly bodies to their former positions as they move in their periodic revolutions. The Kosmos is that in which time is contained; and it is by the progress and movement of time that life is maintained in the Kosmos. The process of time is regulated by a fixed order; and time in its ordered course renews all things in the Kosmos by alternation. All things being subject to this process, there is nothing that stands fast, nothing fixed, nothing free from change, among the things which come into being, neither among those in heaven nor among those on earth. God alone stands unmoved, and with good reason; for he is self-contained, and self-derived, and wholly self-centred, and in him is no deficiency or imperfection.

He stands fast in virtue of his own immobility, nor can he be moved by any force impinging on him from without seeing that in him are all things, and that it is he alone that is in all things; unless indeed one should presume to say that he moves (not in time, but) in eternity. But it should rather be said that eternity also is motionless; into eternity all movements of time go back, and from eternity all movements of time take their beginning. God then stands unmoved; and eternity likewise is ever changeless, containing in itself a Kosmos which is without beginning, even that Kosmos which we rightly call 'imperceptible to sense'. This (sensible) Kosmos has been made in the image of that other Kosmos, and reproduces eternity in a copy. Now time, though it is ever in movement, possesses a faculty of stability peculiar to itself, in that its return into itself is determined by necessity. And accordingly, though eternity is stable, fixed, and motionless, yet since time is mobile, and its movement ever goes back into eternity, it results from this that eternity also, though motionless in itself, appears to be in motion, on account of its relation to time; for eternity enters into time, and it is in time that all movement takes place. Hence it follows that on the one hand eternity, stable though it be, is also mobile, and on the other hand, time, mobile though it be, is rendered stable by the immutability of the law by which its movement is determined. And in this way it is possible to hold that God also moves within himself, though God, like eternity, is motionless; for the movement of God, being made stable by his greatness, is no movement, inasmuch as his greatness is necessarily motionless. The being, then, of which I speak, —whether it is to be called God, or eternity, or both, and whether God is in eternity, or eternity in God, or each in the other, —this being, I say, is imperceptible by sense; it is infinite, incomprehensible, immeasurable; it exceeds our powers, and is beyond our scrutiny. The place of it, the whither and the whence, the manner and quality of its being, are unknown to us. It moves in absolute stability, and its stability moves within it. Eternity then is not limited by the conditions of time; and time, which admits of numerical limitations, is eternal in virtue of its cyclic recurrence. Thus time as well as eternity is infinite, and is thought to be eternal. But eternity is rightly held to rank above time, in virtue of its fixity; for it is firmly fixed, so as to be able, by its rigid immobility, to sustain those things which are in motion. God and eternity then are the first principles of all things which exist. The Kosmos does not hold the first and highest place, because it is mobile; for its mobility takes precedence of the immutability with which it obeys the law of its everlasting movement, which is a secondary sort of eternity. It is this sort of eternity that enters into all the parts of which the Kosmos is composed. For the Kosmos, changeless in virtue of the unalterable law by which its motion is determined, revolves with an everlasting movement. That movement has had no beginning, and will have no end; it manifests itself and disappears by turns in the several parts of the Kosmos, and that in such fashion that again and again in the chequered course of time it manifests itself anew in those same parts in which it disappeared before. Such is the nature of circular movement; all points in the circle are so linked together, that you can find no place at which the movement can begin; for it is evident that all points in the line of movement both precede and follow one another for ever. And it is in this manner that time revolves.

The divine mind is wholly of like nature with eternity. It is motionless in itself, but though stable, is yet self-moving; it is holy, and incorruptible, and everlasting, and has all attributes yet higher, if higher there be, that can be assigned to the eternal life of the supreme God, that life which stands fast in absolute reality. It is wholly filled with all things imperceptible to sense, and with all-embracing knowledge; it is, so to speak, consubstantial with God.

The cosmic mind is the recipient of all sensible forms and of all kinds of knowledge of sensible things.

The (merely) human mind is ..., and is dependent on the retentiveness of man's memory, that is, on his remembrance of all his past experiences.

The divine mind descends in the scale of being as far as man, but no farther; for the supreme God willed not that the divine mind should be interfused with all things, lest it should be put to shame by mingling with the lower animals.

The knowledge which corresponds to the character and extent of the human mind is based wholly on man's memory of the past; it is the retentiveness of his memory that has given him dominion over the earth. The knowledge which corresponds to the nature and character of the cosmic mind is such as can be procured from all the sensible things in the Kosmos. But the knowledge which corresponds to the character of the supreme God's mind —this knowledge, and this alone, is truth; and of this truth not the faintest outline or shadow is discernible in the Kosmos. For where things are discerned at intervals of time, there is falsehood; and where things have an origin in time, there errors arise.

Thought, however, differs from mind in this respect, that our thought attains by mental effort to the kind of knowledge which corresponds to the character of the cosmic mind; and having come to know cosmic things, it furthermore attains to a knowledge of eternity and the supra-cosmic gods. And thus it comes to pass that we men see, as through dark mist, the things of heaven, so far as this is compatible with the conditions of the human mind. Our powers, when we aspire to the sight of things so high, are limited by narrow bounds; but great is man's happiness when he has seen that vision. You see, Asclepius, how lowly is our station, and how lofty are the things of which we treat; but to thee, O God supreme, I give my thanks, that thou hast shed on me the light whereby I see that which is divine. [And you, Tat and Asclepius and Ammon, I bid you keep these divine mysteries hidden in your hearts, and cover them with the veil of silence.]

But as to these matters, let this suffice; and let us now return to the topic of man, and that divine gift of reason, in virtue of which man is called a rational animal. Marvellous is all that I have told you of man; but one thing there is, more marvellous than all the rest; for all marvels are surpassed by this, that man has been able to find out how gods can be brought into being, and to make them. Our ancestors were at first far astray from the truth about the gods; they had no belief in them, and gave no heed to worship and religion. But afterwards, they invented the art of making gods out of some material substance suited for the purpose. And to this invention they added a supernatural force whereby the images might have power to work good or hurt, and combined it with the material substance; that is to say, being unable to make souls, they invoked the souls of daemons, and implanted them in the statues by means of certain holy and sacred rites. We have an instance in your grandfather, Asclepius,

who was the first inventor of the art of healing, and to whom a
temple has been dedicated in the Libyan mountain, near the
shore of crocodiles. There lies the material man, that is, the
body; but the rest of him,—or rather, the whole of him, if it is
conscious life that constitutes a man's whole being,—has returned to heaven. And to this day he renders to the sick by his
divine power all the aid which he used to render to them by his
medicinal art. Again, there is my grandfather Hermes, whose
name I bear. Has he not taken up his abode in his native city,
which is named after him, and does he not help and safeguard
all mortal men who come to him from every quarter? And Isis
too, the wife of Osiris, —do we not know how many boons she
confers when she is gracious, and how many men she harms
when she is angry? For terrestrial and material gods are easily
provoked to anger, inasmuch as they are made and put together by men out of both kinds of substance. And hence it has
come about that the sacred animals are recognised as such by
the Egyptians, and that in the several cities of Egypt people
worship the souls of the men to whom these animals have been
consecrated as living statues; so that the cities are governed by
the laws which those men made, and bear their names. Thus the
same animals which some cities think it right to worship and
revere are in other cities held in small esteem; and this, Asclepius,
is the reason why the cities of Egypt are wont to make war on
one another. Moreover, in time to come the rulers of the land
will be made gods, and their worship will be established in a
city at the very border of Egypt, a city which will be founded
towards the setting sun, and to which men of every race will
speed by land and sea. —*Ascl.* But tell me, Trismegistus, where
are such deified rulers to be found in our own day? —*Trism.*
Their worship is established in the great city in the Libyan
mountain.

Ascl. And these gods who are called 'terrestrial', Trismegistus,
by what means are they induced to take up their abode among
us? *Trism.* They are induced, Asclepius, by means of herbs and
stones and scents which have in them something divine.' And
would you know why frequent sacrifices are offered to do them
pleasure, with hymns and praises and concord of sweet sounds
that imitate heaven's harmony. These things are done to the end
that, gladdened by oft-repeated worship, the heavenly beings

who have been enticed into the images may continue through long ages to acquiesce in the companionship of men. Thus it is that man makes gods.

And you must not suppose, Asclepius, that the operations of the terrestrial gods are to no purpose. The celestial gods dwell in the heights of heaven, and there each one of them unswervingly accomplishes the part assigned to him in the ordering of the Kosmos; but these our gods on earth below see to things one by one, predict events by means of sacred lots and divination, foresee what is coming and render aid accordingly; they assist, like loving kinsmen, in the affairs of men. Thus the celestial gods rule over things universal; the terrestrial gods administer particulars.

Ascl. But tell me, Trismegistus, what part of the government of the universe is administered by Destiny ? —*Trism.* That which we name Destiny, Asclepius, is the force by which all events are brought to pass; for all events are bound together in a never-broken chain by the bonds of necessity. Destiny then is either God himself, or else it is the force which ranks next after God; it is the power which, in conjunction with Necessity, orders all things in heaven and earth according to God's law. Thus Destiny and Necessity are inseparably linked together and cemented to each other. Destiny generates the beginnings of things; Necessity compels the results to follow. And in the train of Destiny and Necessity goes Order, that is, the interweaving of events, and their arrangement in temporal succession. There is nothing that is not arranged in order; it is by order above all else that the Kosmos itself is borne upon its course; nay, the Kosmos consists wholly of order.

Of these three, the first is Destiny, which sows the seed, as it were, and thereby gives rise to all that is to issue from the seed thereafter; the second is Necessity, by which all results are inevitably compelled to follow; and the third is Order, which maintains the inter-connection of the events which Destiny and Necessity determine. But Destiny, Necessity, and Order, all three together, are wrought by the decree of God, who governs the Kosmos by his law and by his holy ordinance. Hence all will to do or not to do is by God's ruling wholly alien from them. They are neither disturbed by anger nor swayed by favour; they obey the compulsion of God's eternal ordinance, which is inflexible, immutable, indissoluble.

Yet chance or contingency also exists in the Kosmos, being intermingled with all material things. ...

*   *   *   *   *

But enough of this. I must now speak of the mortal and immortal parts of man. The many are afraid of death, thinking it the greatest of evils, through ignorance of the truth. Death comes to pass through the dissolution of a worn-out body, and takes place at the completion of the number of years for which the bodily parts are co-adjusted to form a single instrument for the discharge of the vital functions; for the body dies when it is no longer able to sustain the stress of human life. Death then is the dissolution of the body, and the cessation of bodily sense; and about this we have no cause to be troubled. But there is something else, which demands our anxious thought, though men in general disregard it through ignorance or unbelief. —*Ascl.* What is it, Trismegistus, that men do not know of, or do not believe to be possible? —*Trism.* I will tell you, Asclepius. When the soul has quitted the body, there will be held a trial and investigation of its deserts. The soul will come under the power of the chief of the daemons. When he finds a soul to be devout and righteous, he allows it to abide in the region which is suited to its character; but if he sees it to be marked with stains of sin, and defiled with <incurable> vices, he flings it downward, and delivers it to the storms and whirlwinds of that portion of the air which is in frequent conflict with fire and water, that the wicked soul may pay everlasting penalty, being ever swept and tossed hither and thither between sky and earth by the billows of cosmic matter. And so the everlasting existence of the soul is to its detriment in this respect, that its imperishable faculty of feeling makes it subject to everlasting punishment. Know then that we have good cause for fear and dread, and need to be on our guard, lest we should be involved in such a doom as this. Those who disbelieve will, after they have sinned, be forced to believe; they will be convinced, not by words, but by hard facts, not by mere threats, but by suffering the punishment in very deed. All things are known to God, and the punishments inflicted will vary in accordance with the character of men's offences. —*Ascl.* It is not true then, Trismegistus, that men's offences are punished only by human law —*Trism.* Some parts of man, Asclepius, are mortal; that is to say, firstly, all those parts of him which are of earthy substance, and secondly, those parts of him also which live their life after the manner of the body, and likewise cease from life after the manner of the body. All these parts are liable to punishment in this life, so far as the man has deserved punishment by his offences. But man's immortal part is subject to punishment after death; and that punishment is all the more severe, if his offences chance to have escaped detection during his life on earth. —*Ascl.* But why, Trismegistus, do such men deserve severer punishment? —*Trism.* Because those who are condemned by human laws are forcibly deprived of life, and so it is held that they have not yielded up their life as a debt due to nature, but have paid by its loss the penalty which they deserved. But to the righteous man, on the other hand, ...

*   *   *   *   *

I say that there are daemons who dwell with us here on earth, and others who dwell above us in the lower air, and others against whose abode is in the purest part of the air, where no mist or cloud can be, and where no disturbance is caused by the motion of any of the heavenly bodies.

*   *   *   *   *

(Lydus *De mens. 4. 148 :*) And the souls which have transgressed the rule of piety, when they depart from the body, are handed over to these daemons, and are swept and hurled to and fro in those strata of the air which teem with fire and hail.

*   *   *   *   *

The one safeguard is piety. Over the pious man neither evil daemon nor destiny has dominion; for God saves the pious from every ill. Piety is the one and only good among men. The Father and Master of all, he who alone is all things, willingly reveals himself to all men. He does not indeed enable them to perceive him as situated in a certain place, or as having certain (sensible) qualities, or a certain magnitude; but he illuminates man with that knowledge alone which is the property of mind; whereby the darkness of error is dispelled from the soul, and truth is seen in all its brightness, and so man's consciousness is wholly absorbed in the knowledge of God; and being freed, by his ardent love of God, from that part of his being which makes him mortal, he is assured of his immortality in time to come. In this consists the difference between the good man and the bad. For in so far as a man is illumined by piety and devotion, by knowledge of God, and worship and adoration of him, ... he surpasses other men as much as the sun outshines the other lights of heaven.

Epilogue.

Trism. 'I have explained each of these matters to you, as far as my human powers availed, and as far as God willed and allowed. This only remains for us to do, that we should praise God and pray to him, and then turn our attention to the needs of the body; for our minds have been fed full with discourse concerning things divine.'

Having come forth from the sanctuary, they began their prayers to God, looking towards the South; for when a man wishes to pray to God at sunset, he ought to face southward, as at sunrise he ought to face eastward. But when they had begun to pray, Asclepius whispered, 'Tell me, Tat, shall we propose to your father that we should add to our prayer, as men are wont to do, an offering of incense and perfumes?' Trismegistus heard; and much disturbed, he said, 'Hush, hush, Asclepius; it is the height of impiety to think of such a thing with regard to Him who alone is good. Such gifts as these are unfit for him; for he is filled with all things that exist, and lacks nothing. Let us adore him rather with thanksgiving; for words of praise are the only offering that he accepts.

'We thank thee, O thou Most High, with heart and soul wholly uplifted to thee; for it is by thy grace alone that we have attained to the light, and come to know thee. We thank thee, O thou whose name no man can tell, but whom men honour by the appellation 'God', because thou alone art Master, and bless by the appellation 'Father', because thou hast shown in act toward all men and in all things loving-kindness and affection such as a father feels, nay, yet sweeter than a father's; for thou hast bestowed on us mind, and speech, and knowledge: mind, that we may apprehend thee; speech, that we may call upon thee; and knowledge, that having come to know thee, and found salvation in the light thou givest, we may be filled with gladness. We are glad because thou hast revealed thyself to us in all thy being; we are glad because, while we are yet in the body, thou hast deigned to make us gods by the gift of thine own eternal life.

Man can thank thee only by learning to know thy greatness. We have learnt to know thee, O thou most brightly shining light of the world of mind;
we have learnt to know thee, O thou true life of the life of man.
We have learnt to know thee, O thou all-prolific Womb, made pregnant by the Father's begetting;
we have learnt to know thee, O thou eternal constancy of that which stands unmoved, yet makes the universe revolve. With such words of praise do we adore thee, who alone art good; and let us crave from thy goodness no boon save this: be it thy will that we be kept still knowing and loving thee, and that we may never fall away from this blest way of life.

'Having prayed thus, let us betake ourselves to a meal unpolluted by flesh of living things.'

STOBAEUS

EXCERPT I

An extract from the Discourses of Hermes to Tat.

TO CONCEIVE GOD is difficult; and to describe Him is impossible, even if one is able to conceive Him. For it is not easy for that which is imperfect to apprehend that which is perfect, and it is hard for that which is of short duration to have dealings with that which is everlasting. The one ever is, the other passes; the one is real, the other is but shadowed forth by sense-picturing. So widely is that which is mortal separated from that which is divine. And the wide interval between them dims men's vision of the Beautiful. With our eyes we can see bodies; but that which is incorporeal and invisible and without shape, and is not composed of matter, cannot be apprehended by senses such as ours.

EXCERPT II A

From the Discourses of Hermes to Tat.

Hermes. Concerning reality, my son Tat, it is not possible for one who is but a man to speak adequately; for man is an imperfect creature, composed of parts which are imperfect, and his mortal frame is made up of many alien bodies. But what it is within my power to say, that I do say, namely, that reality exists only in things everlasting —. The everlasting bodies, as they are in themselves,—fire that is very fire, earth that is very earth, air that is very air, and water that is very water,—these

indeed are real. But our bodies are made up of all these elements together; they have in them something of fire, but also
something of earth and water and air; and there is in them
neither real fire nor real earth nor real water nor real air, nor
anything that is real. And if our composite fabric has not got
reality in it to begin with, how can it see reality, or tell of reality?

All things on earth then, my son, are unreal; but some of
them,—not all, but some few only,—are copies of reality. The
rest are illusion and deceit, my son; for they consist of mere
appearance. When the appearance flows in from above, it becomes an imitation of reality. But apart from the working of
power from above, it remains an illusion; just as a painted
portrait presents to us in appearance the body of the man we see
in it, but is not itself a human body. It is seen to have eyes, and
yet it sees nothing; it is seen to have ears, and yet it hears
nothing at all. The picture has all else too that a living man has,
but all this is false, and deceives the eyes of those who look at
it; they think that what they see is real, but it is really an illusion.

Those then <who see mere appearances> see illusion; but
those who <see things as they rally are> see reality. If then we
think or see each of these things as it is, we think and see truly;
if we think and see them otherwise than they are, we shall
neither think nor see truly. And so, when I think and say that
nothing on earth is real, I am thinking and speaking truly.—*Tat.*
Well then, when a man thinks and speaks truly, is it not right to
call that 'truth' (or 'reality')? —*Hermes.* What do you infer from
that?—*Tat.* If that is so, father, it follows that there is some
reality even on earth.—*Hermes.* You are mistaken, my son.
There is no reality on earth; it cannot come into being here
below; but none the less it is possible for some men to think
truly about reality; and I was not speaking inadvisably, when
I said that it is true that there is nothing real here below.

How is it possible, my son, that anything real should come
into being on earth? For reality is the absolute and unmixed
Good; it is that which is not fouled by matter, nor muffled in
body; it is bare of coverings, and shines with light undimmed;
it is immutable and unalterable. But the things on earth, my
son,—what *they* are, you can see. They are not capable of receiving the Good; they are subject to destruction and to perturbation; they are dissoluble and mutable, ever altering, and chang-

ing from one thing into another. And seeing that they are not even true to themselves, how could they possibly be real? Everything that changes is illusory, because it does not stay in the state in which it is, but presents appearances that vary. And all things on earth are overtaken by destruction; for without destruction things cannot come into being. The things which come into being must needs arise out of those which are destroyed; and the things which come into being must needs be destroyed, in order that coming-into-being may not stop. The things which come into being out of destruction must therefore be illusory, because they come to be different things at different times. For it is not possible that the same things should come into being again; and how can that be real, which is not the same that it was before? Inasmuch as things change, they are illusory. But at the same time you must understand, my son, that these illusory things are dependent on Reality itself, which is above; and that being so, I say that the illusion is a thing wrought by the working of Reality.'—

Tat. But what of man, father? Is not man real?—Hermes. In so far as he is man, my son, he is not real. For the real is that which consists of itself alone, and continues to be such as it is in itself; but man is composed of many different things, and does not continue to be such as he is in himself, but shifts and changes from one time of life to another, and from one form to another. Oftentimes men fail to recognise their own children after a short interval, and children likewise fail to recognise their parents. And when a thing so changes that it is not known, how can that thing be real, my son? Is it not an illusion, inasmuch as its changes manifest themselves in varying appearances? You must understand that which ever is, and that alone, is real. But man is not a thing that ever is; and therefore man is not real, but is only an appearance. We ought then to call men 'appearances', my son, if we name them rightly. We ought to call a child 'the appearance of a child', and a youth 'the appearance of a youth', and an adult man 'the appearance of an adult man', and an old man 'the appearance of an old man'; for the child does not remain a child, nor the youth a youth, nor the adult man an adult man, nor the old man an old man. And appearance must be illusion.

Tat. And what of these everlasting bodies, father? Are they too unreal? For they too suffer change.—*Hermes.* Everything that is subject to change is unreal; and the everlasting bodies also have in them something that is illusory, inasmuch as they suffer change; for nothing is real, which does not continue to be as it is. But seeing that they have been made indestructible by the Forefather, it may well be that the existence which they have received from him is real.—

(*Tat.* What then can we call real father?—*Hermes.* The Sun alone; because the Sun, unlike all other things, does not suffer change, but continues to be as he is. Wherefore the Sun alone has been entrusted with the task of making all things in the Universe he rules over all things, and makes all things. Him do I worship, and I adore his reality, acknowledging him, next after the one supreme God, as the Maker.—)

Tat. What then, father, can be called real in the supreme degree?—*Hermes.* He alone, my son, and none but He, who is not made of matter, nor embodied; who is colourless and formless; who is changeless and unalterable; who ever is.—

EXCERPT II B

An extract from the Discourses of Hermes to Tat.

(I esteem this treatise more highly than any other, on account of the benevolence towards men and piety towards God that is expressed in it; for there is nothing that could more rightly be called piety than to apprehend in thought the things that are, and to give thanks for them to Him who made them. And this I will continue to do without ceasing.)

Tat. If then there is nothing real here below, what must a man do, father, to live his life aright?—*Hermes.* He must be pious, my son. And he who seeks to be pious will pursue philosophy. Without philosophy, it is impossible to be pious; but he who has learnt what things are, and how they are ordered, and by whom, and to what end, will give thanks for all things to the Maker, deeming him a good father and kind fosterer and faithful guardian; and thus rendering thanks, he will be pious.

And he who pursues philosophy to its highest reach will learn where Reality is, and what it is; and having learnt this, he will be yet more pious. And thence-forward it will be impossible for him to fall away from the Good. For never, my son, can a soul that has so far uplifted itself as to grasp the truly good and real slip back to the evil and unreal; for the soul acquires a wondrous yearning for the Good, and oblivion of all evils, when it has learnt to know its own Forefather. This, my son, this is the consummation of piety; and when you have attained to it, you will live your life aright, and be blest in your death; for your soul will not fail to know whither it must wing its upward flight.

— For this, my son, is the only road that leads to Reality. It is the road our ancestors trod; and thereby they attained to the Good. It is a holy and divine road; but it is hard for the soul to travel on that road while it is in the body. For the soul must begin by warring against itself, and stirring up within itself a mighty feud; and the one part of the soul must win victory over the others, which are more in number. It is a feud of one against two, the one part struggling to mount upward, and the two dragging it down; and there is much strife and fighting between them. And it makes no small difference whether the one side or the other wins; for the one part strives towards the Good, the others make their home among evils; the one yearns for freedom, the others are content with slavery. And if the two parts are vanquished, they stay quiet in themselves, and submissive to the ruling part; but if the one part is defeated, it is carried off as a captive by the two, and the life it lives on earth is a life of penal torment. Such is the contest about the journey to the world above. You must begin, my son, by winning victory in this contest, and then, having won, mount upward.

EXCERPT III

(From the Discourses of Hermes to Tat.)

A holy discourse.

Hermes. A body, my son, cannot hold together without soul; but it is possible for it to have forces working in it, though it be without soul.—*Tat.* What do you mean by that, father? —*Hermes.* You must understand the matter thus, my son Tat. When the soul has been separated from the body, the body itself lasts on; and as long as the body lasts on, it is being acted on by forces. It is being broken up, and gradually disappearing; and the body could not undergo these processes if there were not a force at work in it. This force then stays on in the body after the soul has been parted from it.

This then is the difference between an immortal body and a mortal body. The immortal body consists of a single kind of matter; the mortal body does not, The immortal body acts on other things; the mortal body is acted on. <The immortal body has the mastery, and the mortal body is mastered ;> for everything which puts forces in action has the mastery, and that which is acted on by forces is mastered. And that which has the mastery is free, and takes the lead; but that which is mastered is in servitude, and is passively borne along.

Moreover, the forces work not only in bodies that have souls in them, but also in soulless bodies, such as logs and stones and the like, increasing their bulk and bringing them to maturity, corrupting, dissolving, rotting and crumbling them, and carrying on in them all processes of that sort that it is possible for soulless bodies to undergo. For this, my son, is the very meaning of the term 'a force-at-work'; it signifies <that by which is worked> every sort of process that goes on.

And there must be going on at all times many processes, or rather, every kind of process. For the Kosmos is never bereft of any of the things that are; ever in movement, it is ever breeding within itself the things that are.

*   *   *   *   *

You must understand then that every force is incorporeal, whatever force may be at work in any kind of body.

For forces, my son, though they are themselves incorporeal, are in bodies, and work by means of these bodies. And so, my son, inasmuch as they are incorporeal, I say that they are immortal; but inasmuch as they cannot work apart from bodies, I say that they are always in a body.

Hence it follows that there are always bodies in existence. And for this reason I say that the production of bodies must be everlasting. For if earthly bodies are dissoluble, and there must be bodies to serve as places and instruments for the working of the forces, and the forces are immortal, and that which is immortal exists for ever, then it follows that the production of bodies must go on for ever.

The forces, though they are themselves incorporeal, are dependent on the bodies; for they come from the divine bodies, and enter into mortal bodies. But each of them acts either on the body or on the soul; for they enter into connection with the soul also, but not apart from the body. The soul is not always in a body; it can exist apart from the body; but the forces cannot exist apart from the bodies.

The forces which accompany the soul do not all arrive at the same time. Some of them arrive at the moment of the man's birth, entering into his body together with the soul, and acting on the irrational parts of the soul; but the purer forces arrive when he reaches the age of adolescence, and cooperate with the rational part of the soul.

Of the forces at work, some act on the divine bodies, and others act on perishable bodies. <Of those which act on perishable bodies,> some are universal, <some are general,> and some are special. Those forces which act on the everlasting bodies are divine; and these are also perfect; for the bodies on which they act are perfect. <Those forces are universal, which act on all perishable bodies together;> those forces are general, the action of which extends throughout any one kind of living beings; and those forces are special, which act on an individual.

Hence it is to be inferred, my son, that all things are full of forces at work. If there are many bodies in the Kosmos, I say that the forces at work are more in number than the bodies. For in a single body there are often a first and a second and a third —

besides the universal forces which accompany the birth of bodies. I call those forces 'universal', which bring the bodies of
things into being; without them the body cannot be built up.
And besides these there are special forces....

... and made manifest by means of the sensations; for the
sensations accompany the forces, or rather, the sensations are
effects produced by the forces.

You must understand, my son, the difference between a
force at work and a sensation. The force is sent down from
above; but sense, which is in the body, and gets its being from
the body, receives the force and makes it manifest, giving it a
bodily existence, so to speak. I say then that the forces are
incorporeal and immortal, but the senses are corporeal and
mortal, continuing in existence only so long as the body does;
for the senses are generated together with the body, and perish
with it. And mortal bodies have sense; but the immortal bodies
have not sense, because they do not consist of that sort of
substance. For sense cannot apprehend anything whatever except that which is added to the body, or that which on the other
hand is taken from the body; but nothing is added to or taken
from the everlasting bodies, and therefore sensation does not
take place in them. For sensations have to do with changes that
befall the body, and take place only in connection with increase
and decrease of the body. The bodily change and the sensation
are attached to a single head, and joined in one; and both
together are effected by the forces at work.

Tat. Does sensation take place then in every body that is
subject to change ?—Hermes. Yes, my son; for there are forces at
work in all such bodies.—Tat. Even in soulless bodies, father?—
Hermes. Yes my son, even in soulless bodies. But there are
different kinds of sense. The sensations of rational beings are
accompanied by reason; those of irrational animals are merely...;
and those of soulless things ...

But beings that have souls in them have two other things,
which accompany the sensations and the bodily changes, namely,
pain and enjoyment. It is impossible for an irrational animal to
have a sensation without feeling pain or enjoyment; and so I say
that pain and enjoyment are proper to the irrational animals
rather than to men; for the irrational animals are more completely mastered by them. Pain and enjoyment, being corpo-

real, are stirred up by the sensations, and take hold of the irrational parts of the soul; and therefore I say that both of them work mischief. Enjoyment causes sensation to be accompanied by pleasure, and so forthwith becomes the cause of many evil to the man who feels it; and pain, producing intense distress and anguish, <spoils a man's life>. It may therefore be said with good reason that both of them work mischief.

Tat <Does sense belong both to the body and to the soul> father? —*Hermes*. What do you mean, my son, by 'sense belonging to the soul'? Is not the soul incorporeal, and is not sense a body?—*Tat...* , *Hermes*. If we say that sense is incorporeal, my son, we shall be making it a thing like the soul, or the forces at work; for these, we say, are incorporeal and are in bodies. But sense is neither force at work nor soul ...; it cannot therefore be incorporeal. And if it is not incorporeal, it must be a body.

EXCERPT IV A

From a Discourse of Hermes.

I said in my General Discourses, that of the movements of bodies some are worked by the forces of nature, and others by souls.

All bodies then of which the coming-into-being is followed destruction must necessarily be accompanied by two movements namely, the movement worked by the soul, by which bodies are moved in space, and the movement worked by nature, by which bodies are made to grow and to waste away, and are resolved into their elements when they have been destroyed. Thus I define the movement of perishable bodies.

... Soul is ever in motion; for it is ever moving within itself, and works movement for other things. And for this reason all soul is immortal, inasmuch as it is ever in motion, having its motive force within itself.

There are three different kinds of souls,—divine soul, human soul, and irrational soul.

The divine soul is that which moves the divine body , its motive force; it moves itself in the divine body, and it moves that body.

The human soul has in it something that is divine; but there are joined to it also the irrational parts, namely, desire and repugnance. These also are motive forces, but motive forces that have to do with mortal bodies. And so, as long as the divine part of the soul is in the divine body, desire and repugnance are far away from it; but when the divine part has entered into a mortal body, they come into being as accretions on it, and it is through their presence that the soul becomes bad. For when the soul has been released from the mortal body it is separated from its irrational parts; and it enters into the divine body, and, as it is ever in motion, it is moved in that body, being borne along in the circling movement of the universe.

But the soul of irrational animals consists of repugnance and desire; and that is why these animals are called 'irrational', because they are deprived of the rational part of the soul.

And you must understand that there is a fourth kind of motive force, which acts on soulless bodies. It is outside the bodies, and is operative in moving them. This must be the soul that is in motion in the divine body, and moves soulless bodies incidentally, so to speak.—

EXCERPT IV B

From the Discourses of Hermes to Tat.

Tat. You have explained these things rightly, father; but there is another thing about which I ask you to give me further instruction. You said before that knowledge and skill are forces put in action by the rational part of the soul. But now you tell me that it is because the irrational animals are deprived of the rational part of the soul, that they are irrational and are so called; and it is clear that it follows of necessity from this that the irrational animals have no portion of knowledge or skill, since they are deprived of the rational part.—*Hermes.* Yes, my son, it necessarily follows.—*Tat.* How is it then, father, that we see 2 some of the irrational animals using knowledge and skill,—the ants, for instance, storing up their food, and the birds of the air building nests for themselves, and the four-footed beasts knowing their own lairs ?—*Hermes.* It is not by knowledge or skill, my son, that they do these things, but by natural instinct. Knowledge and skill are things that are taught; but none of the irrational animals are taught to do the things you speak of. And the things that are done by instinct are done by a force that is universal in its working; but the things that are done by know ledge and skill are acquired by some, and not by all. For instance, all men look upward; for this is done by nature's working; but not all men are musicians, nor are all men archers or hunters; and all other such things also are done, not by all men, but by some of them, that is, by those who have learnt to do this or that; for it is knowledge and skill that are at work. In the same way, if some ants only did this, and others did not, you would have been right in saying that it is by knowledge and skill that they collect their food; but if all of them alike are led to do this, and do it involuntarily, it is clear that it is not by knowledge or skill that they do it, but by nature's leading.

EXCERPT V

From the Discourses of Hermes to Tat.

And the Maker of the everlasting bodies, my son, having once made them, did not thereafter make them, nor does he make them now; he gave them over into their own keeping, and having united them to one another, left them to go their way, as things that are in need of nothing. If they need anything, they need one another; but they have no need of the addition of anything from without. <Those bodies then are> immortal; for the bodies which were made by Him could not but be of such nature.

But the Maker (i.e. the Kosmos or Sun) by whom we men were made, being himself embodied, made us, and ever is and will be making us, as beings whose bodies are dissoluble and mortal. For it was not permitted to him to imitate his own Maker, especially as <—. Moreover, was> impossible; for the Maker of the everlasting bodies made them of the first substance, which is incorporeal, but our Maker made us of the corporeal things that had been made.

It is with good reason then that the everlasting bodies are immortal, inasmuch as they have been made of incorporeal substance; but our bodies are dissoluble and mortal, inasmuch as our fabric is composed of bodies. And for this reason our bodies are weak, and need much help. How could the bond that holds our bodies together have endured even for a little time, were it not that they receive into them nutriment which comes from the elements, and that this nutriment renews our bodies day by day? For we receive an influx of earth and water, fire and air, which renovates our bodies, and holds our mortal frame together, so that we are too weak to endure the strain of our movements, and cannot bear them for one day. Be assured, my son, that, were it not that our bodies rest at night, we could not hold out for a single day. And so the Maker,—being good, and fore-knowing all things,—to the end that the living being might last on, made sleep, a potent remedy for the weariness produced by movement; and he assigned time in equal portions to movement and to sleep. Know then, my son, that the work wrought by sleep is a great work. It is contrary to that wrought by the soul, but of no less import; for as the soul works movement, even so <sleep works repose. And for this reason> our bodies cannot live without sleep; for sleep is a relaxing of —. Moreover, sleep works within us, building into the body the matter that has entered in, and distributing to each part of the body that kind of matter which is appropriate to it, water to the blood, earth to the bones and marrow, air to the nerves, and fire to the organs of sight. And so the body feels intense pleasure when sleep is doing this work.

EXCERPT VI

From the Discourses of Hermes to Tat.

Tat. In your former General Discourses you promised to explain about the thirty-six Decans; I therefore ask you to tell me about them now, and to explain their working.—*Hermes.* I am quite willing, Tat; and of all my teachings, this will be of supreme importance, and will stand highest among them. I bid you mark it well.

I have told you before about the zodiacal circle, which is also called the animal-bearing circle, and about the five planet-stars and the sun and the moon, and the several circles of these seven bodies.—*Tat.* You have, thrice-greatest one.—*Hermes.* I desire you then, in your thoughts about the thirty-six Decans also, to bear in mind what I have told you, that so my teaching about the Decans also may be intelligible to you.—*Tat.* I bear in mind what you have told me, father.—

Hermes. I told you, my son, that there is a body which encloses all things. You must conceive the shape of that body as circular; for such is the shape of the universe.—*Tat.* I conceive its shape as circular, even as you bid me, father.—*Hermes.* And you must understand that below the circle of this body are placed the thirty-six Decans, between the circle of the universe and that of the zodiac, separating the one circle from the other; they bear up, as it were, the circle of the universe, and look down on the circle of the zodiac.

They retard the all-enclosing body,—for that body would move with extreme velocity if it were left to itself,—but they urge on the seven other circles, because these circles move with a slower movement than the circle of the universe.

And subject to the Decans is the constellation called the Bear, which is centrally situated with regard to the zodiac. The Bear is composed of seven stars, and has overhead another Bear to match it. The function of the Bear resembles that of the axle of a wheel; it never sets nor rises, but abides in one place, revolving about a fixed point, and making the zodiacal circle revolve, transmitting the world from night to day, and from day to night.

Let us understand then that both the ...of the seven planets and all ...;'or rather, that the Decans stand round about all things in the Kosmos as guardians, holding all things together, and watching over the good order of all things. —*Tat.* Even so I conceive them, father, according to your words.

— *Hermes.* And further, my son, you must understand that the Decans are exempt from the things that befall the other stars. They are not checked in their course and brought to a standstill, nor hindered and made to move backwards, as the planets are; nor yet are they as are the other stars. They are free, and exalted above all things; and as careful guardians and overseers of the universe, they go round it in the space of a night and a day.—

Tat. Tell me then, father, do the Decans act on us men also?'—*Hermes.* Yes, my son, they act on us most potently. If they act on the heavenly bodies, how could it be that they should not act on us also, both on individual men and on communities The force which works in all events that befall men collectively comes from the Decans; for instance, overthrows of kingdoms, revolts of cities, famines, pestilences, overflowings of the sea, earthquakes,—none of these things, my son, take place without the working of the Decans—. For if the Decans rule over the seven planets, and we are subject to the planets, do you not see that the force set in action by the Decans reaches us also, whether it is worked by the Decans themselves or by means of the planets?

And besides this, my son, you must know that there is yet another sort of work which the Decans do; they sow upon the earth the seed of certain forces, some salutary and others most pernicious, which the many call daemons.—*Tat.* And what is the bodily form of these beings, father?—*Hermes.* They do not possess bodies made of some special kind of matter, nor are they moved by soul, as we are; for there is no such thing as a race of daemons distinct from other beings; but they are forces put in action by these six and thirty gods.

Moreover, there are other stars also which travel in heaven and obey the Decans, namely, the so-called Liturgi, whom the Decans have under their command as servants and private soldiers. The Liturgi, commanded by the Decans, are borne along floating in the aether, filling all the region of that element, that there may be no place in heaven that is empty of stars; and they help to maintain the order of the universe, putting forth a force that is their own, but is subject to the force put forth by the six and thirty Decans. From the Liturgi come the destructions of other living beings that take place in this or that region, and the swarming of creatures that spoil the crops.

And after the Liturgi comes another company of stars, to which we have not cared to give names; but the men that shall live after us will assign names to these also.

And below the moon are stars of another sort, perishable and inert, which are so composed as to last but for a little time, rising as exhalations from the earth itself into the air above the earth; and we can see their dissolution with our own eyes. These are of like nature to the animals on earth that are good for nothing and are produced only to be destroyed, as for instance the races of flies and fleas and worms and the like. For as those creatures, my son, are in no way serviceable either to us or to the Kosmos, but on the contrary, vex and annoy us, being by-products of nature, and things the production of which is superfluous, even so the stars which rise as exhalations from the earth do not attain to the region of heaven,—for they are not able to do that, because they rise from below,—and, as they have in them much heavy stuff, they are dragged down by their own matter, and are quickly dissipated, and being broken up, they fall down again to earth, having effected nothing except a troubling of the air above the earth.

And there are stars of another kind, my son, which are called comets. They appear at their appointed times, and disappear again after a little while. They neither rise nor set, nor do they suffer dissolution. They come as visible messengers and heralds to announce destined events that are about to befall mankind in general. The comets have their abode below the circle of the sun. When something is about to befall the world, they appear; and having appeared for a few days, they go back to their place below the circle of the sun, and abide invisible. Some of them appear in the East, some in the North, some in the West, and some in the South. We have named them 'prophet-stars'.

*   *   *   *   *

He who has not failed to get knowledge of these things is able to form an exact conception of God; nay, if I am to speak boldly, he is able to see God with his own eyes, and having seen God, to be blest.—*Tat.* Blest indeed, father, is he who has seen God.—*Hermes.* But it is impossible, my son, for one who is yet in the body to attain to this happiness. A man must train his soul in this life, in order that, when it has entered the other world, where it is permitted to see God, it may not miss the way <which leads to Him>. But men who love the body will never see the vision of the Beautiful and Good. How glorious, my son, is the beauty of that which has neither shape nor colour! —*Tat.*

But can there be anything, father, that is beautiful apart from shape and colour?—*Hermes.* God alone, my son, or rather, that which is too great to be called God.

EXCERPT VII

Hermes.

Hermes. For there is a mighty deity, my son, who is posted in the midst of the universe, and watches over all things done on earth by men. For as Necessity has been set over the divine order, even so has Penal Justice been set over men. For Necessity holds in her grasp the order of those above, inasmuch as they are divine, and do not wish to err, and cannot err;—for it is impossible that that which is divine should go astray;—but Penal Justice has been appointed to punish those who err on earth. For the human race is apt to err, because it is mortal, and is composed of evil matter; [and the men most liable to slip are those who do not possess the power of seeking God; and on those men above all does Penal Justice lay her hold'] and men are subject to Destiny by reason of the forces at work in their birth, but are subject to Penal Justice by reason of their errors in the conduct of life.

EXCERPT VIII

A discourse of Hermes to his son.

Tat. In all this, father, you have spoken rightly. But go on, and tell me again what are the incorporeal things in us that are according to Providence, and likewise what are those that are according to Necessity, and those that are according to Destiny.—

Hermes. I told you, my son Tat, that there are in us three kinds of incorporeals. The first of these is apprehensible by thought alone This is a thing without colour and without shape; it issues from nothing else than the primary intelligible substance.

But there is also in us a second kind of incorporeal thing, <which is in itself irrational, but is capable of being moved rationally>. For when the irrational part is moved by the intelligible substance, it is moved rationally in some degree, and being so moved, is at once transformed into an image of the Maker's thought.

And there is in us a third kind of incorporeals also, namely, the attributes of our bodies. Of these there are two different classes. Those of the one class are qualities characteristic of the individual; those of the other class are <separable accidents> of the body. The qualities characteristic of the individual are —; the —of the body are —

Now the intelligible substance, if it has drawn near to God, has power over itself, [i.e. has free will] and in saving itself, it also saves the other part. As long as it is by itself, [i.e. as long as it is not influenced or interfered with by the body and bodily things] it is not subject to Necessity, and its choice is in accordance with Providence. But if it falls away from God, it chooses the corporeal world, and in that way it becomes subject to Necessity, which rules over the Kosmos.

The irrational part of the soul [i.e. that part of the soul in which the passions reside] is moved rationally in some degree, [and is thereby brought into accord with Providence; but if it is not obedient to the intelligible substance, it is subject to Necessity.]

...And reason is according to Providence; that which is irrational is according to Necessity; and the attributes of the body are according to Destiny. This is my teaching concerning the things that are according to Providence, Necessity, and Destiny.

EXCERPT IX

An extract from the Discourses of Hermes to Tat.

Matter, my son, has come into being; but it also was always in being. For matter is a receptacle in which the process of coming into being takes place; and that process is a mode of the working of God, who is without beginning, and was in being before the world began. Matter then has received from God the germ from which has sprung its coming-into-being, and has thereby come into being. And it came into being as a thing that is mutable; and it takes many forms, being fashioned into various shapes; for in passing through its changes it is governed by God's working, which fabricates the forms taken by it in the course of its mutation. In respect of its formlessness then, matter was without beginning; but in respect of God's working on it, it has come into being.

EXCERPT X

An extract from the Discourses of Hermes to Tat.
— concerning the three times [i.e. Past, present and future time] For they are neither independent of one another nor united with one another; and again, they are both united and independent.

If you suppose the present time to be separate from the past time <and the future from the present, you will find yourself in a difficulty. For> it is impossible for the present to come into being unless the past also has come into being, <and for the future to come into being unless the present has ;> for the present issues from the past, and the future from the present. And inasmuch as the past joins on to the present, and the present to the future, they are made one by their continuity. They are therefore not separate from one another.

<On the other hand, if you suppose them to be united with one another, you will again find yourself in a difficulty—. Thus it appears that, though time is one and the same throughout, its parts are separate.

If we are to investigate the matter yet further, let us reason as follows. The past time has departed, so that it no longer is; and the future is not in existence, in that it has not yet arrived. And even the present is not in that it does not abide. For seeing that the present does not stand fast, and does not abide even for an instant, how can it be said to be 'present', when it cannot stand fast for one moment?

EXCERPT XI

Hermes. <*Hitherto*, I have given you instruction by means of numerous discourses;> but now, my son, I will sum up in brief sentences all that I have taught you. You will understand what I say, if you bear in mind what you have been told before.

(1) All bodies are moved; only that which is incorporeal is motionless.

(2) All bodies are subject to change; but not all bodies are dissoluble.

(3) [Every living being has come into being; but not every living being is mortal].

(4) That which is dissoluble is destructible; only that which is indissoluble is everlasting.

(5) That which is ever coming into being is ever being destroyed, but that which has come into being once for all is never destroyed.

(6) God is first; the Kosmos is second; Man is third.

(7) [The Kosmos has been made by God, and man has been made by means of the Kosmos].

(8) The sensitive part of the soul is mortal; but the rational part of the soul is immortal.

(9) Everything that exists is subject to change; (but not everything that exists is destructible.)

(10) Everything that is, is movable; nothing that is stands fast.

(11) Not all things are moved; but everything that is moved is moved by soul.

(12) Everything that has sensation is passively affected; mind alone is free from passive affections.

(13) Everything that feels pain feels pleasure also; but not everything that feels pleasure feels pain.

(14) Not all bodies are diseased; but all bodies that are diseased are dissoluble.

(15) Mind is in God; and reason is in mind.

(16) Nothing that is corporeal is real; only that which is incorporeal is devoid of illusion.

(17) Everything that has come into being is subject to change; but not everything that has come into being is destructible. (18) There is nothing good on earth; there is nothing bad in heaven. (19) God is good; man is bad. (20) The good is voluntary; the bad is involuntary. (21) The gods choose the things that are good; men choose the things that are bad, thinking them to be good.

(22) [Obedience to law is unanimity with God; lawlessness is strife against God.] (23) [God's law is virtue; man's law is vice.] (24) [For the Kosmos, time is revolving movement; for man, time is destruction. (25) Everything in heaven is unalterable; everything on earth is alterable. (26) Nothing in heaven is in bondage; nothing on earth is free. (27) Nothing is unknown (or unknowable) in heaven; nothing is known (knowable) on earth. (28) The things in heaven have no communion with the things on earth; but the things on earth have communion with the things in heaven. (29) All things in heaven are without blemish; all things on earth are marred by blemishes. (30) [That which is immortal is not subject to passive affections (or disturbing passions); only that which is mortal is passively affected (or is disturbed by passion]. (31) That which has been generated is not in all cases mortal; but that which is mortal is in all cases a thing that has been generated. (32) A dissoluble body has two times, namely, and ; an everlasting body has only one time, namely, (33) Dissoluble bodies increase and diminish; everlasting bodies [neither increase nor diminish]. (34) [Dissoluble things are changed into their opposites; everlasting things are changed into things like themselves.] (35) Coming into being is the beginning of destruction, and destruction is the beginning of coming into being.

(36) That which goes out of being also comes into being; and that which comes into being also goes out of being.

(37) Of the things that are, some are bodies, some are forms, and some are forces. Forms and forces are incorporeal things, but are in bodies.

(38) That which is immortal has no part in that which is mortal; but that which is mortal has part in that which is immortal.

(39) That which is mortal does not go into an immortal body; but that which is immortal enters into a mortal body.

(40) The <cosmic> forces do not work upward from below, but downward from above.

(41) The things in heaven receive no benefit from the things on earth; but the things on earth receive all benefits from the things in heaven.

(42) Heaven is receptive of everlasting bodies; earth is receptive of destructible bodies.

(43) Earth is irrational; heaven is rational.

(44) The things in heaven are subject to providence; the things on earth are subject to Necessity.

(45) Heaven is the first of the elements; earth is the last of the elements.

(46) Providence is God's ordering; Necessity is subservient to Providence.

(47) Chance is a movement without order; [skill is a force which works in good order]

(48) What is God? A thing immutable and good. What is man? A thing mutable and bad.

If you keep in mind these aphorisms, you will easily recall the fuller explanations I have given you in numerous discourses; for my previous teaching is summed up in these brief sentences.

But avoid converse with the many. Not that I wish you to grudge a benefit to others; my reason for this warning is rather that the many will think you one to be laughed at (if you speak to them as I have spoken to you). Like welcomes like; but men that are unlike are never friends. And these discourses will find few indeed that are worthy to hear them; nay, perhaps not even the few will be worthy. Moreover, my teaching has a certain property which is peculiar to it; it urges on bad men to worse wickedness.—*Tat.* What do you mean, father?—*Hermes.* This is what I mean, my son. The living being called man is inclined to evil; he is brought up amidst evil, and therefore he takes pleasure in it. If then this being is told that the Kosmos has had a beginning, and that all things take place by necessity, inasmuch as Destiny governs all,—if he is told that, he will be far worse than he was before; for he will despise the Kosmos, as a thing that has had a beginning, and he will put off on Destiny the responsibility for evil, and so he will never refrain from any evil deed. You must therefore beware of talking to them, in order that, being in ignorance, they may be less wicked.

EXCERPT XII

From the teachings of Hermes to Ammon.

But all things come to pass, and there is no place destitute of Providence. Now Providence is the sovereign design of the God who rules over the heavens; and that sovereign design has under it two subordinate powers, namely, Necessity and Destiny. <Necessity is a firm and unalterable decision of Providence> and Destiny is subservient to Providence <in accordance with Necessity>. And the stars are subservient to Destiny. [For no man can either escape from Destiny, or guard himself from the terribleness of the stars]. For the stars are the instrument of Destiny; it is in accordance with Destiny that they bring all things to pass for the world of nature and for men.

EXCERPT XIII

From the teachings of Hermes to Ammon.

Necessity is a firm and unalterable decision of Providence.

EXCERPT XIV

From the teachings of Hermes to Ammon?

And the power which holds the whole Kosmos in its grasp is Providence; but that which [puts constraint on <particular things within the Kosmos> is Necessity. And Destiny makes all things move with a cyclic movement, working in accordance with Necessity; for it is the nature of Destiny to compel.

—<The working of> Providence is spread out in heaven; —the star-gods circle in heaven with a movement which continues without failing and without cease. But Destiny And Providence takes thought for; but Destiny [operating in subservience to Providence, works the unvarying movement of the stars, and] is the cause of [the birth and destruction of things on earth by means of] the arrangement of the stars.

<Providence is the> inevitable law according to which all things have been ordered.

EXCERPT XV

From the teachings of Hermes to Ammon.

And that which is moved is moved in accordance with the force exerted by Nature, which moves the universe, and permeates all things. For Nature gives movements to the universe; <but the Mental Substance>. And Nature pervades the whole Kosmos, and holds it together within; but the <Mental Substance> transcends the Kosmos, and encompasses it without.

And Nature, producing all things that come into being, gives form to the things that are produced. She sows in matter her own seeds; and the matter which she has at her disposal is capable of being moved. And matter, being moved by her, is made hot and cold; and so there come into being fire and water. The fire is strong and powerful, the water is feeble; the fire is active, the water is passive. And the fire, being opposed to the water, dried some of the water, and thereby the earth came into being. And when the water and the earth were being dried round about by the fire, there arose from them a vapour; and so the air came into being, borne up on earth and water. And these four elements entered into combination according to the plan of the cosmic structure, hot combining with cold, and dry with fluid; and from their co operation came into being—.

*   *   *   *   *

[There is the semen genitale of men and beasts] a vital spirit, analogous to the atmospheric vital spirit of the Kosmos. This vital spirit, when it has been injected into the womb, is not inactive; and inasmuch as it is not inactive, it works change in the [matter supplied by secretion in the womb]. And this, through the change worked in it, grows, and acquires bulk; and thereupon, it assumes a definite shape, and is shaped; and thereafter, it takes to itself the species-form, whereby the thing that is coming into being is fashioned according to its species. And after a measured interval of time, <Nature> brings the foetus to its birth, and acts as midwife, and draws it forth into the external air.

Now the vital spirit, as long as it was in the womb, had not the movement of animal life, but only that of vegetable growth; and so <Nature, at the time of the birth,> joined on <a soul> also to the bodily structure, as a receptacle for the force which works in animal life; for <the soul> insinuates itself into the vital spirit, and makes it move with the movement of animal life. And it is the soul which is nearest at hand that is assigned to the organism; and this soul comes to it, not because of any congenital likeness, but according to destiny; for the soul is not impelled by a desire to be combined with a body. For this reason, it is according to destiny that [Nature] gives the man that has been born the movement of rational thought.

[And to some men God gives] also Mental Substance. And Mental Substance is indivisible and changeless, never departing from its changelessness.

EXCERPT XVI

From the teachings of Hermes to Ammon.

The soul then is an incorporeal substance; and even when it is in a body, it does not depart from its own substantiality. For it is found to be self-moved not in something, nor in relation to something, nor for the sake of something. For it is prior in its power, and that which is prior is not in need of the things which are posterior.

That in which things are is place and time; <for it is the place and time that> physical movement goes on; and that for the sake of which these things exist is body. It is for the sake of body that time and place and physical movement exist; for bodies could not be constructed if there were no place for them, and bodies could not change if there were not time and physical movement.

Place exists for the sake of body; for it receives into itself the changes of the body, and so prevents the thing which is changing from being destroyed. The body, when it changes, is transformed into something different, and ceases to be in the state in which it was before, but it does not cease to be a body; and when it has changed into something different, it is in the state which belongs to that different thing. The body then changes merely in condition; for the body, *qua* body, persists, but the particular condition in which it was before does not persist.

*   *   *   *   *

It is for the sake of body then that place and time and physical movement exist.

And to each of these things is assigned its own peculiar property. The peculiar property of place is receptiveness; that of time is interval and number; [that of time is numbered]. But the peculiar property of soul is that sort of movement which belongs to intelligible substance.

EXCERPT XVII

From the teachings of Hermes.

Soul then, Ammon, is a substance which is self-determining in the beginning; but when it has chosen that course of life which is dependent on Destiny, and it takes on as an appendage something irrational, which is similar to matter.

... repugnance and desire. And repugnance, if it has formed a habit of will according to the reasoning of the soul, becomes courage, and is not led astray by cowardice. And desire, if it has formed a habit of will according to the reasoning of the soul, becomes temperance, and is not moved by pleasure. And when repugnance and desire have agreed together, and have formed a habit of will that is well-balanced, and both of them cleave to the reasoning of the soul, then justice comes into being; for their well-balanced habit of will takes from repugnance its excess, and raises to equality that which is lacking in desire. And repugnance and desire are commanded by the <intelligent> substance; this takes the lead, like a commander, and the reason accompanies it, like a counsellor.

The reason then belongs to the intelligent substance; <and opinion> a copy of reasoning, dim in comparison with reasoning, as is an echo in comparison with a voice, and the brightness of the moon in comparison with that of the sun, but clear in comparison with the irrational.

EXCERPT XVIII

From the teachings of Hermes.

Whence it [,the irrational part of the soul,] both exceeds and falls short, and is at variance with itself. It becomes worse when it is separated from the discursive thought; but when it follows and obeys the discursive thought, it shares with the reason [in its discursive thoughts].

But we have power to choose; for it is in our power to choose the better, and likewise to choose the worse—. [Yet men's evil actions are involuntary]; for the soul, when it cleaves to evil [bodily or material] things, draws near to corporeal nature, and for this reason the man who has chosen the worse is under the dominion of Destiny.

The intelligent substance in us is [the only thing in us that is] self-determining. The intelligent substance remains ever in the same state without change, not partaking of the nature of the things which come into being, and therefore Destiny has no hold on it.

...But Nature has co-ordinated <the irrational part of the soul> with the things that come into being; and the soul, when it has taken part with these things, takes part also in the Destiny by which they are governed.

EXCERPT XIX

From the teachings of Hermes.

The soul then [when it is by itself, is intelligent substance (i.e. pure mind); —When it is joined to a body, it draws to itself from the structure of the body something which is irrational]; but when it has been released from the physical body, it abides by itself in the intelligible world.

[The soul rules over the irrational thing which is joined to it, bringing into that thing a movement similar to the soul's own thought, and giving life to it when it comes into life; For it is a peculiar property of soul, that it gives to other things something similar to its own [substantive existence].

There are then two kinds of life and two kinds of movement, one that is according to true being, and another that is according to nature. And the life which is according to true being is self-determining, but the other is under compulsion; for everything that is moved is subject to the compulsion applied to it by that which moves it.

[When the soul's movement is the kind of movement which corresponds to true being, the soul is moved by love of "intelligible substance" (i.e. by desire for that which truly is,—the incorporeal and divine)] not partaking of the physical body. For if ..., it has neither reason nor intelligence. For all bodies are devoid of intelligence; but when a body has received a portion of true being, it becomes a living creature that has in it the breath of life.

The vital spirit is that part of the body to which belongs sensation; the reason is that part of the intelligent substance which has understanding. With the reason coexists knowledge of ...; with the vital spirit coexists opinion. The reason contemplates the <real> but the vital spirit discerns appearances. The vital spirit is parcelled out among the organs of sense; there is a part of it that sees, a part that hears, a part that smells, a part that tastes, and a part that feels by touch. This vital spirit if, —, discerns things rightly; but if not, it merely receives illusory impressions.

For the vital spirit gets the force with which it works from the Kosmos by which it is environed [i.e. the atmosphere]; but the soul gets from itself the force with which it works.

EXCERPT XX

From the teachings of Hermes.

The soul then is an incorporeal substance; For if the body has not soul, it will no longer be real. For all bodies need life to make them real, and life resides in soul.

For in the case of everything which comes into being, the coming-to-be must be followed by destruction. For that which comes into being <is of a certain size when it first comes to be, and having come to be, it increases>, the increase is followed by diminution, and the diminution by destruction.

But if a body has a portion of soul, then it is alive, and shares with the soul in the possession of reality. And that which is the cause of reality to another thing must itself be real in the highest degree. By 'reality' I here mean participation in life.

Now man is called 'a living being' because he is alive, and 'rational' because he has intelligence, and 'mortal' because of his body. The soul then, retaining unchanged its power of conferring life, confers on man intelligent life. For how could one say that man is a living being, if there were not a really existing thing that confers life on him? Nor could one say that man is rational, if there were not a really existing thing that confers on him intelligent life.

But the intellect is not fully developed in all men, because in some men the composition of the body <is not so contempered as to hit the mean.> For if there is an excess of the hot element in the composition of the body, the man is rendered light-minded and fervid; if there is an excess of the cold element, he is rendered dull and sluggish. For nature contempers the composition of the body according to [the influence of the stars]; and the soul, taking over the body as made by nature, thereupon confers life on the body which nature has made.

The contemperation of bodies is of three kinds, namely, that in which the hot element preponderates, that in which the cold element preponderates, and that which is in the mean; and nature contempers them according to the star <or planet> which has got control over the mixing of these elements.

Nature then makes the contemperation of the body resemble the ...of the stars; ...so that they are mutually affected....

EXCERPT XXI

From the teachings of Hermes.

The Pre-existent then is beyond all existent things, being prior even to the things which really exist. For — the term 'substantive existence', employed as all-inclusive, is applicable both to the objects of thought and to the objects of sense... the things which really exist, and which are regarded by thought as existing of themselves. But the objects of sense are contrary to the objects of thought, and exist in the other way; for they are not existent of themselves... The world of nature is an existent object of sense, and contains within itself all objects of sense.

Intermediate between the objects of thought and the objects of sense are the objects of opinion; and of these, some partake of the objects of thought, but others do not.

...of the gods apprehensible by sense; and these gods are images of the gods apprehensible only by thought. The Sun, for instance, is an image of the Maker who is above the heavens; for even as that supreme Maker made the whole universe, so the Sun makes the animals and the plants.

EXCERPT XXII

From The discourse of Hermes which is entitled APHRODITE.

How does it come about that children resemble their parents? I will explain this. When [nature operating in the father's body] stores up semen that is foamed forth from productive blood, it comes to pass that there is exhaled from the whole body a certain substance <viz. the 'vital spirit' which is the living and active ingredient in the semen> [and this substance is vitalised] by the working of a divine force, inasmuch as it is a human being that is being brought into existence. And it is to be presumed that the same thing takes place in the case of the woman also. When then the efflux from the man is prepotent, and its vigour is not impaired, the child that is produced will be like its father; and in the same way, if the conditions are reversed, the child will be like its mother. And if there is such a prepotency in respect of some part of the body, the child comes to resemble the father or the mother in that part... and sometimes even to remote generations... to compare the child with the form of its father... of that Decanus who had to do with the hour in which the woman was bearing the child.

EXCERPT XXIII

From the holy book of Hermes Trismegistus
which is entitled KORE KOSMU <viz. Eye-pupil of the
Universe>.

Isis. Give heed, my son Horus; for you shall hear secret doctrine, of which our fore-father Kamephis was the first teacher. It so befell that Hermes heard this teaching from Kamephis, the eldest of all our race; I heard it from Hermes the writer of records, at the time when he [initiated me in the black <great?> rites]; and you shall hear it now from me.

Having thus spoken, Isis first poured forth for Horus a sweet draught of ambrosia, such a draught as the souls are wont to receive; and thereupon she thus began her most holy discourse:

Inasmuch as heaven with its many circles, my son Horus, is placed above all the world of things below, [and the whole universe is not in any of its regions deprived of <left unprovided with> any of the things it needs], it must be that all the world which lies below has been set in order and filled with contents by the things which are placed above; for the things below have not power to set in order the world above. The weaker mysteries <things?> then must yield to the stronger; and the system of things on high is stronger than the things below, and is wholly steadfast, and cannot be apprehended by the thoughts of mortal men.

Thereupon men moaned, being afraid, the beautiful and everlasting duration of the things above. For it was to see the beauty of the sky when it was flooded with light by the Sun, and the well-nigh equal majesty of the night, torch-lit with light less than the Sun's, yet bright, when in their turn the other holy Powers moved along their paths in heaven with ordered movements in fixed periods of time, and by certain secret effluences wrought order and growth in the things below. And thus arose fears upon fears, and ceaseless questionings.

And as long as the Craftsman who made the universe willed not to be known, all was wrapped in ignorance. But when he determined to reveal himself, he breathed into certain godlike men a passionate desire to know him, and bestowed on their minds a radiance ampler than that which they already had within their breasts, that so they might first will to seek the yet unknown God, and then have power to find him. But this, Horus my wondrous son, it would not have been possible for men of mortal breed to do, if there had not arisen one whose soul was responsive to the influence of the holy Powers of heaven. And such a man was Hermes, he who won knowledge of all. Hermes saw all things, and understood what he saw, and had power to explain to others what he understood— [yet he did not make the truth known without reserve] for what he had discovered he inscribed on tablets, and hid securely what he had inscribed, leaving the larger part untold, that all later ages of the world might seek it.

And Hermes, having been bidden to attend on the gods to whom he was akin was about to ascend to the stars; but to him succeeded Tat, who was his son, and therewith inheritor of the knowledge which Hermes had acquired; and not long after, Asclepius, also named Imuthes, the son of Ptah, who is also named Hephaistos, and all those other men who, by the will of that Providence which reigns over all, were destined to search out with the utmost exactness the truths of the heavenly doctrine. But Hermes [when he was about to be released from the body] did not transmit the doctrine in its full completeness even to his own son, because Tat was still in his early youth. And thus did Hermes speak: 'I, even I, have beheld with the all-seeing eyes of mind the unseen things of ...; and as I examined them, there came to me by slow degrees, but came in very deed, accurate knowledge of the truth. [That knowledge I have set down in writing; And now, I must] deposit hard by the secret things of Osiris these holy symbols of the cosmic elements <i.e. the books of Hermes written in hieroglyphics> and after speaking over them a prayer, depart to heaven.'

It is not fitting, my son, that I should leave this report unfinished; I must tell you all that Hermes said when he was depositing his books. Thus did he speak: 'Ye holy books, which have been written by my perishable hands, but have been anointed with the drug of imperishability by Him who is master over all, remain ye undecaying through all ages, and be ye unseen and undiscovered by all men who shall go to and fro on the plains of this land, until the time when Heaven, grown old, shall beget organisms <i.e. men composed of soul and body> worthy of you.' Having spoken this prayer over the works of his hands Hermes was received into the sanctuary of the everlasting zones.

*   *   *   *   *

... the Sole Ruler summoned a council of the gods. The gods came, and He spoke, and said: 'Ye gods, all ye whose being has been made imperishable, ye whose lot it is to bear sway over the great world for ever, and who will never grow weary of transmitting the universe from hand to hand among you; how long shall this our sovereign rule remain unrecognised? How long shall we leave this conglomerate mass inert? Let it seem to those of after times an incredible tale that there has been a Chaos. Set your hands to mighty works. Let each of you for his own part bring something into being; and I myself will be the first to begin.' He spoke, and forthwith the hitherto homogeneous mass was separated into two parts; and ...

And thereafter, He gazed into the space around, and spoke again, saying 'Let heaven be filled with stars'. God spoke, and it was so....

But during no small interval of time the world below, my son, was inert, and remained barren; until those very gods who had already been bidden to go their rounds in heaven approached him who is King of all, and told him of the stillness of the things below, and said that these things also ought to be set in order. 'We pray thee then', said they, 'to look into this, and find out what is lacking to the things that now are and shall be hereafter; for this is no one's task save thine alone.'

When they had thus spoken, God smiled, and bade Nature be; and there came forth from his voice a Being in woman's form, right lovely, at the sight of whom the gods were smitten with amazement; and God the Forefather bestowed on her the name of Nature. And he conferred on Nature the government of all things in the world below, and bade her be productive of all manner of seeds. And Nature communed with herself, and saw that she must not disobey her Father's bidding; and [so she brought into being the seeds of all kinds of plants]. And God filled his august hands with the abundance of seeds which Nature supplied, and gripping the handfuls firmly, said 'Take them, thou holy Earth, take them, all-honoured one, thou that art destined to be mother of all things; and henceforward be not thou thought to come short of anything'. 'And saying this, God opened his hands, and flung forth all that was in them—.'

Thus it was that heaven came to be seen above, equipped with all its holy Powers,' and the earth below, equipped with all the goodly things that appertain to it. For even those things which mortals deem foul are goodly in God's sight, because they have been made subject to God's laws. And God was glad when he beheld his works and saw that they were now in motion.

And God was no longer willing that the region next below heaven should be inert, but thought good to fill this region also with living beings, that the intermediate space might not remain devoid of movement; and so he began to ply handicraft for this purpose, using substances suitable for the accomplishment of the work. He took of his own life-breath as much as would suffice, and blended it with intelligent fire, and mingled the blend with certain other materials unknown to men; and having fused together these ingredients, with utterance of certain secret spells, thereon he thoroughly stirred the whole mixture, until there bubbled up upon the surface of the mass a substance finer and purer than the things of which it was composed. This substance was transparent; none but the Craftsman himself could see it. And when it was wrought up to completion, and was neither liquefied by burning heat nor solidified by cold, but had a certain consistency peculiar to itself, God named it 'soul-stuff'. And out of this scum he wrought into existence many myriads of souls, moulding to his purpose in right order and due measure the stuff which formed on the surface of the mixture, and therewith speaking the fitting spell, that nothing might—

But the souls necessarily differed one from another, because the froth which exhaled from the mass when it was stirred together was not all of one quality. The first portion of it was more perfect than the second, and altogether purer; and the second portion was much inferior to the first, but far superior to the third; and so it went on, until the whole number of the different grades amounted to sixty. But God made a law by which he ordained that all the souls alike should be everlasting, inasmuch as they were all made of one substance, the composition of which was known to him alone. And he assigned to the souls divisions of space on high, one to each grade of souls; 'that they might make the cylinder revolve' according to a fixed order and a fitting arrangement, and might give joy to their Father [by hymns of praise].

Thereupon God took his stand in the beauteous vault of the aether, and summoned to him the tribes of souls that were now in being, and said, 'Ye souls, fair children of my anxious thought, whom I have brought to birth with my own hands, and whom I now station in the intermediate region of the universe, hearken to these my laws, and meddle with no place save that which is assigned to you by my decree. If you are steadfast in obedience, heaven shall be your reward; you shall be placed among the stars, and shall sit on thrones that are charged with potent forces. But if by any rash deed you transgress my ordinances, then, by this holy mixture out of which I brought you into being, and by these my soul-making hands, I swear that full soon will I construct bonds for your chastisement <i.e. I will make bodies for you and you will be chastised by incarnation>.

Having thus spoken, God mixed together the two remaining elements, water and earth, and breathed into them a certain life-giving substance, and spoke over them certain secret spells, potent indeed, but not so potent as those which he had uttered before. These things he stirred well together; and when the scum which floated on the surface of the mixture had become translucent, he took this scum, and out of it he fashioned the vital spirits of the animals. But the residue of the mixture he handed over to the souls that had by this time made progress, those souls that had ascended to the places near the stars, and had been given a new name, and were called 'holy daemons'; and he said to them, 'My children, offspring of my being, take the residue left over from my handiwork, and let each of you fashion something, relying on his own ability; and I will set before you as models these things which I have made'. And having taken [the vital spirits of the animals, which were by this time] well and fairly [finished, and set them before the souls] and then he withdrew, after 2 promising to join to the visible works of their hands the invisible vital-spirits, and to give to each of the creatures that should be made power to generate others like to itself, in order that the souls might not thereafter be obliged to make anything else beside what they made at first.—

Horus. *Tell me then, mother, what did the souls make?*—*And Isis said: When the souls, my son Horus, had received the mingled mass, they first examined it, and sought to find out of what ingredients it was compounded; but this it was not easy for them to discover. Thereupon they feared they might incur the Father's anger for having tried to find out; and they betook themselves to doing the work they had been bidden to do. Out of the upper part of the stuff, which was of very light consistency, they fashioned the race of birds; and out of the part which was less light, the race of fishes. And when the mixture had become half-solid, and was now heavy, they fashioned out of it the race of quadrupeds; and when what was left of it had grown cold, and was quite solidified, the souls made of it yet another sort of creatures, the breed of creeping things.*

—And God arranged the Zodiac in accord with the movings of nature; and having bestowed on it powers of all-various working, he bade it be productive of all the animals that were to be in all time to come.

But the souls, my son, thinking that they had now done something great, began to array themselves in presumptuous audacity, and transgress God's commands; for they sought to vie with the gods in heaven, claiming nobility equal to theirs, in that the souls themselves had been made by the same Maker. And so they now began to overstep the bounds of their own divisions of the atmosphere; for they would not any longer abide in one place, but were ever on the move, and thought it death <i.e. intolerable> to stay in one abode.

But when the souls did thus, my son, the Lord of all (so Hermes said when he told the tale to me) failed not to mark it; and he sought a way to punish them. And so the Ruler and Master of all thought good to fabricate the human organism, to the intent that in it the race of souls might through all time suffer punishment. 'And thereon', said Hermes, 'he sent for me, and said, "Thou soul of my soul, and mind of my holy mind, [make bodies out of which the souls may be imprisoned].

<This passage probably comes from another document> And God said, 'How long shall the world below be gloomy to look on How long shall the things that have been made remain with none to praise them? Come now, summon to me forthwith all the gods in heaven.' And when they had come in obedience to his command, 'Look down', said God, 'on the earth and all things there below, [and see how] —. And the gods quickly understood what their Sovereign wished to do; and when he spoke of the making of man, they agreed. And God asked each of them in turn, 'What can you provide for the men that are about to be made' Then the Sun said, 'I will shine [upon them in the day-time' The Moon promised to give light after the Sun had run his diurnal course; and she said also that she had already given birth to Silence and Sleep. Kronos <Saturn> announced that he had already become father of Penal Justice and Necessity. Zeus <Jupiter> said, 'In order that the tribe that is about to be may not be utterly destroyed by wars, I have already begotten Peace for them'. Ares <Mars> said he was already father of Struggle, Anger, and Strife. Aphrodite <Ve-

nus> delayed not, but said, 'And I, Master, will attach to them Love and Pleasure and Laughter'. And the Father was glad, my son, at what Aphrodite said. 'And I', said Hermes <Mercury>, 'will make mankind intelligent; I will confer wisdom on them, and make known to them the truth. I will never cease to benefit thereby the life of mortal men; and then above all will I benefit each one of them, when the force of nature working in him is in accord with the movement of the stars above.' And the Master was glad when he heard these words; and he gave command that mankind should come into being.

'And I', said Hermes, 'sought to find out what material I was to use; and I called on the Sole Ruler, and he commanded the souls to hand over to me the residue of the mixture. But when I received it, I found that it was quite dried up. I therefore used much water for mixing with it; and when I had thereby renewed the liquid consistency of the stuff, I fashioned bodies out of it. And the work of my hands was fair to view, and I was glad when I looked on it. And I called on the Sole Ruler to inspect it; and he saw it, and was glad; and he gave order that the souls should be embodied.'

Then first did the souls learn that they were sentenced; and gloomy were their looks. I will tell you what the souls said; listen, my glorious son. When they were about to be shut up in the bodies, some of them wailed and moaned, just that and nothing more; but some there were that struggled against their doom, even as beasts of noble temper, when they are caught by the crafty tricks of cruel men, and dragged away from the wild land that is their home, strive to fight against those who have mastered them.' And another shrieked, and again and again turning his eyes now upward and now downward, said, 'O thou Heaven, source of our being, and ye bright-shining stars, and never-failing light of sun and moon; and ye, aether and air, and holy life-breath of Him who rules alone, ye that have shared our home; how cruel it is that we are being torn away from things so great and splendid! —We are to be expelled from the holy atmosphere, and a place nigh to the vault of heaven, and from the blissful life we lived there, and to be imprisoned in habitations mean and base as these. Poor wretches that we are, what hard necessities await us! What hateful things we shall have to do, in order to supply the needs of this body that must so soon perish! Our eyes will have little room to take things in; we shall see things only by means of the fluid which these orbs contain; and when we see Heaven, our own fore-father contracted to small compass <i.e. an image small enough to fit into the eye>, we shall never cease to moan. And even if we see, we shall not see outright; for alas, we have been condemned to darkness. And when we hear the winds, our kinsmen, blowing in the air, deeply shall we grieve that we are not breathing in union with them. For dwelling-place, instead of this world on high, there awaits us a man's heart, a thing of little bulk. Unhappy we! What have we done to deserve such punishments as these? O Master, thou that art our Father and our Maker, why hast thou so soon ceased to care for the works of thy hands? Even yet hold us of some account, though it be but little. Ordain some limits to our punishment; and if [the sentence is irrevocable], make us forget what bliss we have lost, and into what an evil world we have come down, and so release us from our sorrow.'

Thus spoke the souls, my son Horus; and they obtained that which they sought. For the Sole Ruler came, and took his seat on the throne of truth, and spoke in answer to their prayer, saying: 'Ye souls, all ye that do obeisance to my unaging sovereignty, you have learnt, methinks, that it is by reason of the deeds which you have done before that you have to endure this punishment. For you know that, as long as you were sinless, you dwelt in the places nigh to heaven; but now that blame has come upon you, you have been condemned to imprisonment in the organs of mortal bodies, and must yourselves dwell in the region assigned to them. And in that region Desire and Necessity will be your masters; for it is they that, after me, are masters and captains of all things below. Howbeit, not at random have I ordained the changes of your state; but as your condition will be changed for the worse if you do aught unseemly, so will it be changed for the better if you resolve on action worthy of your origin. I myself will keep watch on you; and if the charges against you shall be but slight, you shall be released from the deadly bondage of the flesh, and, freed from sorrow, shall greet again your home above. But if you shall be found guilty of any greater sins, in that case, when you quit your bodily frames, you shall not thereafter dwell in [heaven], nor yet in human bodies, but you shall be transferred into the bodies of beasts, and shall thenceforth continue to wander upon earth.'

Having said this, my son Horus, God gave [bodies] to all the souls; and then he spoke again, and said, 'The destruction of your bodies then will be the starting-point for a rebirth, and their dissolution, a renewal of your former happiness. But your minds will be blinded, so that you will think the contrary, and will regard the punishment <i.e. life in the body> as a boon, and the change to a better state as a degradation and an outrage. But the more righteous among you, those who look forward to the change—'

<This passage is probably an insertion> *[Souls of the noblest kind,] when they enter human bodies, become righteous kings, founders of cities, and law-givers, genuine philosophers, true diviners, trustworthy prophets, skilled musicians, sage astronomers <or astrologers>, men that find sure omens in the flight of birds, priests exact in the rites of sacrifice, and all kinds of men that are of high worth in any sort of work. When such souls enter the bodies of birds, they become eagles; because eagles neither drive away other creatures of their kind nor devour them, and do not seek to wrong any other sort of animal that is weaker than themselves; for eagles are most righteous by nature. When they enter the bodies of quadrupeds, they become lions; for the lion is a strong beast, and one that trains itself to imitate with its mortal body the immortal nature of the gods, inasmuch as lions are never tired, and never sleep. When they enter the bodies of reptiles, they become dragons; for the dragon is a powerful animal, and long lived; and it is harmless, and so friendly to man, that some dragons are even tamed by men; it has no venom; and it renews its youth when it has grown old, resembling the gods in this. And among the fishes, such souls are dolphins; for dolphins take pity on men who fall into the sea; they convey the man to land if he is still alive, and they never even touch him if he is dead, though the race of fishes is voracious beyond all others.*

And having thus spoken, God vanished from their sight.

<This passage is a later insertion> *When these things had come to pass as I have told you, my son Horus, there arose from the earth a mighty spirit, named Momus, who had a body of enormous bulk, and*

a mind of surpassing power. This spirit was clothed in a body of manly form; he was comely and stately to look on, but exceeding fierce and terrible. And as soon as he saw the souls entering into their bodily frames, he asked (though he well knew the answer to his question), 'What are these creatures called, Hermes, you record-writer of the gods' 'They are called men,' *said Hermes. Then Momus said, 'Hermes, you are doing a rash thing in making man; for he is like to be a creature that sees with inquisitive eyes, and hears things he has no right to hear, and indulges greedily his sense of taste, and makes voluptuous use of his sense of smell, and misuses to all extremes his sense of touch. Tell me, you that are the author of his being, is it your settled purpose to leave him free from care, this being that is going to look with audacious gaze upon the beauteous mysteries of nature? Is it your will to let him be exempt from sorrow, this man that is going to send forth his designing thoughts to the very ends of the earth? And if so, will not men put forth audacious hands against the elements? They will dig up roots of plants, and investigate the properties of stones. They will dissect the lower animals,—yes, and one another also,—seeking to find out how they have come to be alive, and what manner of thing is hidden within — . They will cut down the woods of their native land and sail across the sea to seek what lies beyond it. They will dig mines, and search into the uttermost darkness of the depths of the earth. And all this might be borne, but they will do yet more: they will press on to the world above, seeking to discover by observation the laws of movement of the heavens. Are they then to meet with no impediment? Shall they never be overpowered by the cruel stings of fear, and shall they luxuriate in a life exempt from cares? Teach them henceforth to [keep their designs within the limits of what is fitting for them]. [Make them — ,] that they may fail to get the things they hoped for, and be subdued by the pangs of grief. Let their presumptuous eagerness be disappointed of its expectations. Let their souls be a prey to a succession of varying hopes, sometimes fulfilled and at other times frustrated, so that even the sweetness of attainment may be but a bait to lure the wretches on to more unmitigated miseries. [Let them be scorched by the flame of desire, that they may so lose heart, and be the more severely punished.'*

Hermes was pleased by what Momus said; for it was said in friendliness to him. 'Momus' said he, ' —and I will devise a secret engine, <viz the stars> linked to unerring and inevitable fate, by which all things in men's lives, from their birth to their final destruc-

tion, shall of necessity be brought into subjection; and all other things on earth likewise shall be controlled by the working of this engine.' So said Hermes to Momus; and he did even as he had said. And when the engine began to work, the keen-eyed goddess Adrasteia took her stand above to supervise the whole, having in her hands the confirmation of all that was wrought by the working of the engine.

And when these things had come to pass, and the souls had been embodied. [Are you grieved, my son Horus, when you hear this? Are you dismayed when your mother describes to you the miseries by which unhappy man was oppressed? You must hear something yet more terrible.]

For when the souls had but recently been imprisoned, they began to quarrel among themselves; and the stronger men used the weaker as tools, and made them attack each other, and array themselves in hostile ranks, and make war on one another. And the strong [tortured] and slew the powerless; and they enslaved the living, and cast out the dead unburied.

But when the mischief had grown great, the Elements were indignant, and resolved to make petition to God, who rules alone, concerning the savage conduct of mankind. And they approached their Maker, and addressed him as follows.

Fire was permitted to speak first, and said, 'Master, and Fabricator of this new universe, thou whose name is revered among the gods and hidden from men, how long is it thy purpose to leave the life of mortals godless? These men do not let me render the services for which my nature fits me; they put a false and unmeet stamp on my imperishable being. I am polluted, Master, and by men's audacity I am forced to consume human flesh. Reveal thyself at once to the world that needs thee, and put an end to the savagery of human life. Let men be taught to fear the penal justice of the gods, and then no man will sin. Bestow peace on mankind, and thereby fill the world with goodly hopes; and let them learn to give thanks to thee for thy benefits, that so I, the Fire, may render service at their sacrifices, and send up fragrant vapours to thee from the altar-hearth.'

Then spoke Air, and said, 'I too, Master, am made turbid by the reek which rises from the corpses, so that I breed sickness, and have ceased to be wholesome; and when I look down from above, I see such things as ought never to be seen '.

Next, my magnanimous son, Water was given leave to speak, and spoke thus: 'O Father, self-begotten, and Maker of Nature, that power which generates all things to give thee pleasure, it is high time for thee to give command that my streams be kept pure; for the rivers and seas are ever washing off the defilement of the slayers, and receiving the corpses of the slain.'

Next Earth stood forth, in bitter grief; and [when she was given leave to plead] my glorious son, she thus began: 'O King and Father, President of the over-arching spheres of heaven, and Governor of us, the Elements, that stand before thee, us out of whom all things get their beginning, and into whom they are resolved again when they cease to be, and reach their end, paying a debt that must be paid; thou didst make Earth more highly honoured than the other Elements; for it is I that, as thou hast commanded, both bring forth all things and receive them back into me. But now, I am dishonoured; [trouble] has risen up against me from mankind. Having naught to fear, they commit all manner of crimes; slaughtered by every sort of cruel device, men fall dead on my plains, O Lord, and I am soaked through and through with the juices of rotting corpses. Henceforward, Lord, since I am forced to contain beings unworthy of me, I wish to contain, together with all the things which I bring forth, God also. How long shall thy terrestrial world, peopled with mortals, have no God? Bestow upon Earth, if not thy very self,—that I ask not, for I could not endure to contain thee,—yet at least some holy efflux from thee.'

Thus spoke the Elements; and God filled the universe with the sound of his holy voice, and said, 'Go your ways, my holy children, that are worthy of your great Father; make no attempt to violate my laws, and leave not my universe bereft of your services. Another shall now come down to dwell among you, an efflux of my being, who shall keep holy watch on men's deeds. He shall be judge of the living,—a judge that none can deceive,— and a terrible king of the dead; and every man shall meet with such retribution as his deeds deserve.' Thereon the

Elements ceased from their entreating, and kept silence; and at
their Master's bidding, each of them continued to wield the
power committed to him.—

Thereupon Horus said: Tell me then, mother, how did Earth
attain to the happy lot of receiving the efflux of God ?—And Isis
answered: Mighty Horus, do not ask me to describe to you the
origin of the stock whence you are sprung; for it is not permitted
to inquire into the birth of gods. This only I may tell you, that
God who rules alone, the Fabricator of the universe, bestowed
on the earth for a little time your great father Osiris and the
great goddess Isis, that they might give the world the help it so
much needed.

It was they that filled human life with that which is divine
<i.e. religion>, and thereby put a stop to the savagery of mutual
slaughter.

It was they that established upon earth rites of worship
which correspond exactly to the holy Powers in heaven.

It was they that consecrated temples and instituted sacrifices
to the gods that were their ancestors, and gave to mortal men
the boons of food and shelter.

<This passage is almost certainly out of place>'They', said
Hermes, 'will get knowledge of all my hidden writings, and discern
their meaning;' and some of those writings they will keep to themselves, but such of them as tend to the benefit of mortal men, they will
inscribe on slabs and obelisks.'

It was they that introduced into men's life that mighty god,
the Oath-god, to be the founder of pledges and good faith;
whereby they filled the world with law-abidingness and justice.

It was they that, noting how corpses decay, taught men the
fitting way to swathe the bodies of those who have ceased to
live.

They sought to discover the cause of death; and they found
out that the life-breath, which has entered from without into
men's bodily frames, is apt to return to the place from which it
came, and [if a man runs short of it he swoons, but if he runs
entirely out of it he dies].

It was they that, having learnt from Hermes that the atmosphere had been filled with daemons, inscribed [forms of words invoking the daemons] on hidden slabs of stone.

It was they that, having learnt God's secret law-givings, became law-givers for mankind.

It was they that devised the [initiation and training] of the prophet-priests, to the end that these might nurture men's souls with philosophy, and save their bodies by healing art when they are sick.

When we had done all this, my son, Osiris and I, perceiving that the world had been filled with blessings by the gods who dwell in heaven, asked leave to return to our home above. But we were not permitted to return until we had invoked the Sole Ruler with a hymn, so that the atmosphere might be filled with [the sound of our song of praise] and we ourselves might be well received above when we ascended.—

Mother, said Horus, grant to me that I too may learn that hymn.—And Isis said, Hearken, my son. <Here followed the hymn>

EXCERPT XXIV

In the same book.

Isis. ' But if you wish to ask any further question, my magnanimous son, ask on.'—' My honoured mother,' said Horus, 'I wish to know what is the origin of kingly souls.'—And Isis said, 'My son Horus, the distinction by which kingly souls are marked out is as follows. There are in the universe four regions, which are subject to law that cannot be transgressed, and to kingly presidency; namely, heaven, the aether, the air, and the earth. Above, my son, in heaven, dwell gods, over whom, as over all else likewise, rules the Maker of the universe; in the aether dwell stars, over whom rules that great luminary, the Sun; in the air dwell souls, over whom rules the Moon; and upon earth dwell men, over whom rules he who is king for the time being; for the gods, my son, cause to be born at the right time a man that is worthy to govern upon earth. The other rulers are effluxes of Him who is king in heaven; and among them, he who is nearer to Him is more kingly than the others. The Sun, inasmuch as he is nearer to God, is greater and mightier than the Moon; (and the Moon is mightier than the earthly king). He who is king on earth is the last of the four rulers, but the first of men. As long as he is on earth, he has no part in true deity; but as compared with other men, he has in him something exceptional, which is like to God; for the soul which is sent down to dwell in him comes from a place which is situated above the places whence souls are sent down to dwell in other men <i.e. a higher stratum of the atmosphere>.

Now souls are sent down thence to reign as kings, my son, for these two reasons. Souls that have well and blamelessly run their appointed race, and are about to be transmuted into gods, are sent down to earth in order that, by reigning here as kings, they may be trained to use the powers which are given to gods; and souls that are already godlike, and have in some little thing transgressed God's ordinances, are sent down to be kings on earth in order that they may undergo some punishment in being incarnated, and yet may not suffer in like measure with the rest, but in their bondage may still retain the same preeminence which they enjoyed while they were free.

The differences in the characters of kings are not determined by the nature of their souls (for all kingly souls are godlike), but by that of the angels and daemons that have escorted the soul on its way down to earth. For souls that are of this quality, and come down to earth for this purpose, do not come down without escort and attendance; for the Justice that rules on high knows how to assign to each his due, even though they be exiled from the Happy Land. And so, my son Horus, when the angels and daemons who bring the kingly soul down from above are warlike, then that soul wages war; when they are peaceful, then it maintains peace; when they are disposed for judicial work, then it sits in judgment; when they are given to music, then it sings; when they are truth-lovers, then it pursues philosophy. For these souls, as of necessity, cling to the temper of the angels and daemons who bring them down to earth; for when they sink into the condition of man, they forget their own nature, and bethink them only of the disposition of those who have shut them up in the body.'

'Mother,' said Horus, 'you have full well explained these things to me; but you have not yet told me what is the origin of noble souls.'—Isis. ' Just as on earth, my son, there are certain grades of social standing which differ one from another, even so it is with the souls. For the souls also have certain places whence they come; and the soul which has come from a more glorious place is nobler than one that is not thus exalted. For just as among men the free man is held to be nobler than the slave, because that which is of superior and kingly nature necessarily enslaves that which is inferior, even so it is, my son, in the case of the souls.'—

Horus. 'Tell me, mother, what is the origin of male and female souls.'—Isis. 'The souls, my son Horus, are all of one nature, inasmuch as they all come from one place, that place where the Maker fashioned them; and they are neither male nor female; for the difference of sex arises in bodies, and not in incorporeal beings. And the reason why the souls of males are more robust, and those of females delicate, [is not the air, my son, in which the soul dwelt before it was embodied, but simply] the body itself, in which the soul is enwrapped. The body is a mixture of the elements, that is, of earth, water, air, and fire; and so, since the body of the female has in its composition an excess of the fluid element and the cold element, and a deficiency of the dry element and the hot element, the result is that the soul which is enclosed in a bodily frame of this nature is melting and voluptuous, just as in males one finds the reverse; for in males there is an excess of the dry element and the hot element, and a deficiency of the cold element and the fluid element, and hence it is that the souls in male bodies are rougher and more energetic.'—

Horus. 'Tell me, mother, what is the origin of intelligent souls?' —Isis replied, 'The organ of sight, my son, is wrapped in membranes; and when these membranes are dense and thick, the eye sees but dimly, but if they are rare and thin, it sees with the greatest keenness. And even so it is in the case of the soul. For the soul also has certain wrappings of its own, which are incorporeal, inasmuch as the soul itself is incorporeal. These wrappings are coats made of the air that is within us.' When these coats are thin and rare and transparent, then the soul is intelligent; but when on the other hand they are dense and thick and muddied, as the outer air is in stormy weather, then the soul cannot see far, but sees only what is close at hand.'—

And Horus said, 'Why is it then, mother, that the men who dwell beyond the borders of our most holy land <i.e. Egypt> are not so intelligent as our people are?'— 'The Earth', said Isis, 'lies in the middle of the universe, stretched on her back, as a human being might lie, facing toward heaven. She is parted out into as many different members as a man; and her head lies toward the South of the universe, her right shoulder toward the East and her left shoulder toward the West; her feet lie beneath the Great Bear, and her thighs are situated in the regions which follow next to the South of the Bear. Evidence of this may be seen in the fact that the men of the South, who dwell where the top of Earth's head lies, have the tops of their heads well developed, and have handsome hair; the men of the East are apt for battle, and are good bowmen, because in them the right hand is the stronger; the men of the West are —, and for the most part fight with the left hand; and those who live beneath the Bear have strong feet, and sturdy legs as well. And those who come next after them, and dwell a little farther from the North <that is Italy and Greece>, all these have comely thighs and well-shaped buttocks. Now all these parts of the earth are active in some respects, but sluggish in all else, and the men whom they produce are somewhat sluggish in intelligence. But the right holy land of our ancestors lies in the middle of the earth; and the middle of the human body is the sanctuary of the heart, and the heart is the head-quarters of the soul; and that my son, is the reason why the men of this land, while they have in equal measure all other things that all the rest possess, have this advantage over all other men, that they are more intelligent. It could not be otherwise, seeing that they are born and bred upon Earth's heart.

And there is another reason also. The South, my son, being receptive of the clouds which are formed by condensation from the atmosphere,—. Indeed, it is said to be in consequence of the conveyance of the clouds to the southern region when they have thus been formed, that our river <i.e. the Nile> flows from that quarter, the [clouds] being there broken up [in rain]. Now wherever a cloud arrives, it makes the air below it misty, and fills it with smoke, so to speak; and smoke or mist is an obstruction not only to the eyes, but also to the mind. And the East, my glorious son, is troubled and overheated by the rising of the sun in close proximity to it; and likewise its opposite, the West, is affected in the same way at the sun's setting; and thus both the East and the West cause the intelligence of the men born in those regions to be wanting in clearness. And the North, with the cold that belongs to it by nature, freezes the minds as well as the bodies of the men who live beneath the northern sky. But the country which lies in the middle is undisturbed, and is consequently superior both in itself and in the men born in it; for in virtue of the continual serenity of its climate, it produces men of high intelligence. And it disciplines and educates men of other races also; for it is the only land that is victorious over all competitors, and having won the victory, it bestows on its defeated rivals the gift of its own knowledge, as a king might send a good satrap to govern a conquered province.'—

Horus. 'Explain to me this also, my lady mother; why is it that in long diseases, though the man is still alive, the reason and the soul itself is sometimes disabled ?'—Isis replied, 'Among animals, my son, there are some that have an affinity to fire, some to water, some to air, some to earth, and some to two or three of these elements; and again, some of them are alien to fire, some to water, some to earth, some to air, some to two of the elements, and some to three. For instance, the locust, my son, shuns fire, and so does every kind of fly; the eagle, the falcon, and all high-flying birds shun water; fishes shun air and earth; and snakes avoid pure air. And on the other hand, snakes and all creeping things love earth; all animals that swim love water; the birds love the air ; and fire is loved by all creatures that fly high and spend their lives near the sun <e.g. by eagles>. Every soul therefore, as long as it is in the body, is weighed down and oppressed by these four elements. For this reason then the soul does not enjoy perfect happiness here on earth, but is perturbed, inasmuch as it is divine by nature and is hemmed in by the elements; and it is intelligent to some extent, but not so intelligent as it would have been if it were not bound up with the body. But if the body is storm-tossed and perturbed by disease or —, then the soul too is tossed upon the waves, like a man that has fallen into the deep sea, and is swept along unresisting.'

EXCERPT XXV

Written by Hermes: a discourse of Isis to Horus.

'Wondrously', said Horus, 'have you, my mighty mother Isis, described to me in all details the wondrous making of souls by God, and my wonder ceases not; but you have not yet told me where the souls go when they are released from their bodies. I desire therefore to be initiated in this doctrine also, and to give thanks for that to you alone, my immortal mother.' —And Isis said, 'Give heed, my son; for this inquiry is most needful; and I, who am myself participant in the being of the Immortals, and have journeyed through the Plain of Truth, will describe to you in all particulars the things that are. I begin by saying that [which is composite is broken up and destroyed, but that which is not composite is not destroyed but has a place to which it goes when it disappears from our sight].

But perhaps some one will say that when the souls go forth from their bodies, they are indistinguishably diffused in the air, and are dispersed throughout the boundless atmosphere, and that they cannot thereafter retain their identity and come back again to dwell in other bodies, nor yet return to the place from which they came before; just as it is impossible that the water [which is poured out from a vessel] should return to the same place from which it was taken, but it is mingled with all the mass of flowing water.

But in the case of the soul, high-minded Horus, it is not so. Water is a body, an irrational thing, composed of many ingredients crushed into fluidity; but the soul, my son, is a thing of peculiar nature, a thing that has been made by the hands and mind of God, and is guided [by God himself] on the way that leads to Mind. And that which consists of one thing only and not of many cannot be mingled with anything else. Hence it follows that the union of the soul with the body must have been effected by compulsion.

Souls, when they quit the body, are not all sent promiscuously to one and the same place; nor is each of them sent to some place at random and by chance; but each soul is sent to its own proper place. This you may clearly see from what befalls the soul even when it is still in the body, and is [weighed down] against its proper nature. Give heed, well-beloved Horus, to the similitude which I am about to set forth. Suppose that in one and the same enclosure there are shut up men, and eagles and doves and swans and hawks and swallows and sparrows and flies, and lions and leopards and wolves and dogs and hares and cows and sheep, and snakes, and some of the amphibious animals, such as seals and otters and tortoises and the crocodiles of our own country; and suppose, my son, that all these creatures are released from the enclosure at one moment. Will not the men be sure to betake themselves to market-places and houses, and the eagle to the upper air, which is its natural abode, and the doves to the lower air not far from earth, and the hawks to a higher region than the doves? Will not the swallows make their way to the dwellings of men, and the sparrows to the neighbourhood of fruit-trees, and the swans to places where they are free to sing? Will not the flies seek places close to the ground, only so far above it as the scent of men can rise? For the fly, my son, is peculiarly greedy for human flesh, and is a grovelling creature. Will not the lions and leopards betake themselves to the mountains, and the wolves to uninhabited places? And will not the dogs follow at men's heels, and hares go to coverts, and cows to farmsteads, and the sheep to the pastures? Will not the snakes creep into holes in the earth? And will not seals and tortoises and the like seek hollows and flowing waters, that they may neither be deprived of dry land nor suffer want of the water that is congenial to them? For each of the creatures is sent back to its own place by that thing within it by which its action is determined. And even so does every soul, whether incarnated as a man or dwelling on earth in some other shape, know whither it must go; unless indeed, my son, some follower of Typhon <i.e. the perverse opponent> were to step forth and tell us that it is possible for a bull to live in the deep sea, and a tortoise in the air. If then it is so with the souls when they are immersed in flesh and blood, and if they do nothing against God's ordering even when they are undergoing punishment,—for incarnation is a punishment inflicted on them,— will they not much more act thus when they are released from this punishment, and have obtained the liberty which belongs to them by nature?

—And the arrangement of the things above the earth is as follows. The space from the topmost height of heaven down to the moon is reserved for gods and stars, and for Providence <i.e. the divine power by which men are governed> in general; but the space from the moon down to us on earth, my son, is the dwelling-place of souls.

<This appears to be an extract from another document> Howbeit, the air has a movement of its own, which we are wont to call wind, a movement which serves for the refreshment of things on earth; about that I will speak later on. But the air in no way impedes the souls by its own movements; for while the air is in motion, souls are free to dart through it upward and downward, as it may chance, without any hindrance; they flow through it without mixing with it or adhering to it, just as water flows through oil.

And this space <viz the space between the lunar sphere and the earth>, my son, consists of four main regions, and sixty subdivisions. Of the four regions, the first extends upward from the earth, and contains four subdivisions; and so far up does the earth reach in some hilly and mountainous places; for such is the nature of the earth, that it cannot rise above the first region. The second region contains eight subdivisions; and in these eight subdivisions take place movements of winds. And where there is movement of wind, there birds can fly; but above this region, the air is not in motion, and does not bear the weight of any living creature. Howbeit, such is the power given by nature to the air of this second region, that it goes to and fro, together with the living creatures contained in it, not only in the eight subdivisions which properly belong to it, but also in the four which are adjacent to the earth; but the earth cannot rise into the eight subdivisions which belong to that windy air. The third region contains sixteen subdivisions, and is full of fine pure air. The fourth region contains thirty-two subdivisions; and in them is air which is fine and pure in the highest degree, and perfectly translucent. (—the sphere of the moon,) the boundary between the air and the heavens, which are fiery by nature.

This arrangement extends in a straight line from the top to the bottom of the atmosphere; there are four regions, and sixty subdivisions. And in these subdivisions, which are sixty in number, dwell the souls, each in that subdivision for which it is suited by its nature. The souls are all constituted alike, but they are not equal in rank; in proportion as one subdivision stands above another in distance from the earth, in the same proportion does a soul that is in the one subdivision surpass in eminence, my son, a soul that is in the other.

I will now begin afresh, most glorious Horus, and tell you in succession what souls go to each one of the subdivisions when they depart from life on earth. I will speak of the subdivisions in order, beginning with the highest, and ending with places close to earth.'

EXCERPT XXVI

Concerning the incarnation of souls, and their reincarnation in other bodies.

Isis. 'The space between earth and heaven is parted out into divisions, my son Horus, according to a system of measured arrangement. These divisions are variously named by our ancestors, some of whom call them 'zones', others 'firmaments', and others 'layers'. They are the haunts of the souls that have been released from their bodies, and likewise of the souls that have not yet been embodied. And each of the souls, my son, resides in one division or another according to its worth. Godlike and kingly souls dwell in the highest division of all; the souls that are of lowest rank, and all that are wont to grovel, dwell in the lowest division; and the souls of middle quality dwell in the middle division.

Those souls then, my son Horus, which are sent down to earth to bear rule there, are sent down from the highest zones; and when they are released from the body, they return to the same zones, or even to a place yet higher, excepting those of them that have done things unworthy of their own nature, and transgressed the commandments of God's law. These souls the Providence which rules above banishes to the lower divisions according to the measure of their sins, even as it raises up from lower to higher divisions souls that are inferior in power and dignity, [if they have lived good lives on earth].

    *   *   *   *   *

...For there are [in the world above two gods], who are attendants of the Providence that governs all. One of them is Keeper of souls; the other is Conductor of souls. The Keeper is he that has in his charge the unembodied souls; the Conductor is he that sends down to earth the souls that are from time to time embodied, and assigns to them their several places. And both he that keeps watch over the souls, and he that sends them forth, act in accordance with God's will.

[And in agreement with these, my son, and working in reciprocation as a counterpart to the administration of things in the world above, is Nature upon earth], who is the maker of the mortal frames, and fashioner of the vessels into which the souls are put. And Nature also has at her side two Powers at work, namely, Memory and Skill. The task of Memory is to take care that Nature adheres to the type that has been established from the first, and that the body which she fashions on earth is a copy of the pattern on high; and the task of Skill is to see that in each case the frame that is fashioned is conformable to the soul that comes down to be embodied in it,—to see that lively souls have lively bodies, and slow-moving souls slow-moving bodies; that energetic souls have energetic bodies, and sluggish souls sluggish bodies; that powerful souls have powerful bodies, and crafty souls crafty bodies; and in general, that every soul gets such a body as is suitable for it.

...For it is not without purpose that Nature has provided birds with plumage, and has given force to quadrupeds by arming some with horns, and some with teeth, and some with claws or hoofs. And to the reptiles she has given soft bodies, flexible and yielding; and that their pliancy may not make them utterly helpless, she has placed in the mouths of some of them a palisade of teeth, and has given strength to others by increasing their bulk. And the fishes, which are timid creatures, she has made to live in, that element in which fire cannot put in action either of its two powers; for in water fire neither shines nor burns; and every fish, swimming in water, flees whither it will, protected by its own timidity, and having the water for a shelter to hide it from sight. But rational animals <i.e. men> Nature has equipped with senses more perfect and more accurate than those which she has given to other creatures,

For the souls are shut up in bodies of this kind or that, each soul in a body that is like it; so that those souls which possess the faculty of discernment enter human bodies; those which are flighty enter bird-bodies; those which are [violent] enter quadruped bodies, for quadrupeds obey no law but that of force; those which are crafty enter reptile bodies, for reptiles never attack men face to face, but lie in ambush, and so strike them down; and those which are timid, and all souls that are unworthy to enjoy the other elements, enter fish-bodies.

But in each kind of living creatures may be found some that do not act according to their natural dispositions.'—'Tell me, mother,' said Horus, 'what do you mean by that?'—Isis replied, 'A man, my son, may transgress the law laid down by his power of discernment; (a bird may —;) a quadruped may avoid compulsion; a reptile may lose its craftiness; and a fish may rise above its timidity.

And it comes to pass, my son, that in every class of men there are found some souls that are kingly. For there are many kinds of kingship; there are kingships of [political power], and kingships of art and science, and of divers other things also.'—'Again I ask,' said Horus, 'what you mean?'—Isis. ' For instance, my son, your father Osiris is king of men that have passed away, and the ruler of each nation is a king of living men; and thrice-greatest Hermes is king of the art of teaching; and Asclepius the son of Hephaestus is king of the art of medicine. [And Osiris again is king of might and strength, and after him you yourself, my son; and Har-neb-eschenis is king of philosophy; and Asclepius again, he who is also called Imuthes, is king of the art of poetry.] For, to speak generally, you will find, my son, if you look into the matter, that there are many who rule as kings, and many departments over which they rule. But he who has mastery over all, my son, comes from the highest division of the atmosphere, and those who have mastery over this or that department [come from high up but below this highest sphere]. And it comes to pass that other souls also are found to differ in quality; some are fiery and some cold, some haughty and some meek, some skilful and some unskilful, some active and some inactive, and others differ in other ways. And these differences also result from the positions of the places whence the souls plunge down to be embodied. For those who have leapt down from a kingly zone reign upon earth as kings; those who have come from a zone of science and art are occupied with sciences and arts; those who have come from a zone of industry become workers, and provide food by their labour; and those who have come from a zone of inactivity live idle and desultory lives. For the sources of all earthly things, my son, are on high; those sources pour forth [their influences] upon us by fixed measure and weight; and there is nothing that has not come down from above.

And all things go back again to the place whence they have come down.'—Horus.' What do you mean by that, mother? Give me an example.' Isis answered, 'A manifest sign of this return of things to their source has been placed in living beings by most holy Nature. Our life-breath, which we draw from above out of the air, we send up again to the place whence we received it. We have in us bellows-like organs, my son, by which this work is done; and when these organs have closed the apertures through which the life-breath is taken in, then we ourselves abide no longer here below, but have gone up on high.'

Of the arrangement of the things above, and of their descent to earth, I have now said enough. But there are added to us, my glorious son, other qualities also, which result from the proportions in which things are combined in the mingled mass of the body.—' But tell me, mother,' said Horus, 'what is this "mingled mass"?'—Isis. 'It is a combination and mixture of the four elements; and from it there is exhaled a vapour, which envelops the soul, and is diffused in the body, imparting to both something of its own quality; and thus are produced both the differences between one soul and another, and the differences between one body and another. If there is an excess of fire in the composition of the body, in that case the soul, being hot by nature and having more heat added to it, makes the living creature more active and spirited. If there is an excess of air, in that case the creature comes to be light and flighty and unsteady in soul and body alike. If there is an excess of water, the result is that the creature's soul flows freely and diffuses itself readily, and is highly capable of flinging itself on things and cleaving to them, because water has the power of associating with things. For water unites with all things; and when there is much water, and it envelops a thing, then it dissolves that thing into itself; but when there is only a little water, and it sinks into the thing, then it is transmuted into that with which it is mingled. And such bodies, being flaccid and spongy, are not tightly knitted together; a little thing is enough to cause their dissolution. If there is an excess of the earthy element, in that case the result is that the creature's soul is dull, because, though the soul itself is a thing of rare consistency, it cannot easily get free, but is hampered by the density of [the vapour exhaled from the mingled mass of the body]; and the body is solid, but inert and heavy, and cannot be put in motion by the will without a strong effort. But if all the four elements are combined together in fit proportions, then the creature is so made as to be ardent in action, light of movement, ... in ... , and solid in structure. For the earthy element is that which makes the body solid; the watery element is that in it which makes it diffuse itself so as to unite with things; the airy element is that in us which causes movement; and all these are roused to action by the fire in us.

<This paragraph must have been written by someone else>
All creatures then that have had assigned to them large portions of fire and air, and small portions of water and earth, have become birds; and they live their lives on high, in the region of those elements of which they are chiefly made. All those that have had put into them much fire, a little air and a moderate portion of water and of earth, have become men. And in man, the excess of the hot element has been turned into intelligence. For the mind in us is a hot thing; it has no power to burn, but it penetrates all things. All creatures that have in their composition much water, much earth, and a little air and fire, have become four-footed beasts; and the presence of the hot element in them makes them more pugnacious than the other animals. All those that have had put into them much earth and water, a moderate portion of air, and no fire, have become reptiles. The absence of fire causes them to be lacking in boldness and openness; the excess of water makes them soft and supple; the excess of earth makes them heavy and sluggish; and the fact that they have some air in them makes them [capable of moving quickly if at any time they have to move]. All those that have in them much of the fluid element, a little of the dry element, no fire, and no air, have

become fishes. The absence of fire and air makes them timid, and apt to dive into the depths; and the excess of the fluid element and the presence in them of some earth cause them to live in water that has some earth dissolved in it, by reason of their affinity to these two elements.

*   *   *   *   *

And this also I tell you, my well-beloved son, that as long as the mingled mass of the body keeps its own quality unchanged,— as long as the fire in it receives no access of heat, the air no access of anything of airy nature, the water no access of fluid, and the earthy element no access of density,—so long the creature is in health; but when it does not keep unchanged the original proportions of its several elements, but one of them is either increased or diminished,—I do not mean an increase or diminution caused by the operation of the environment, nor by that change in bodies which takes place in the course of growth, but an increase or diminution that results from an alteration in the mixing of the elements of which the body is composed,—when, I say, the hot element, or one of the other elements, is increased or diminished, then the creature is diseased.

Now just as the vapour that is produced by the first coming together and mixing of the elements in the body, whatever the quality of that vapour may be, mingles with the soul and assimilates it to itself, even so [every alteration in the quality of the vapour causes a corresponding alteration in the quality of the soul]. As long as the soul continues to be in its original condition, it maintains its good order unimpaired; but when either the mixed mass as a whole, or some one part of it, receives, by subsequent addition from without, a portion of one of the elements larger than that which was originally assigned to it, then there is an alteration in the vapour thence produced, and the altered vapour alters the condition of the soul.'

EXCERPT XXVII

Written by Hermes: an extract from the Discourse of Isis to Horus.

For a refutation, great king, when it has been recognised, brings him who has been refuted into [knowledge] of things which he did not know before.

EXCERPT XXIII

Hermes, when some one asked him what God is, said: 'The Maker of the universe, Mind most wise, and everlasting'.

EXCERPT XXIX
[Written by Hermes.]

There are seven wandering stars which circle at the threshold of Olympus, and among them ever revolves unending Time. The seven are these; night-shining Moon, and sullen Kronos <Saturn>, and glad Sun, and the Lady of Paphos <Venus>, and bold Ares <Mars>, and swift-winged Hermes <Mercury>, and Zeus <Jupiter>, first author of all births, from whom Nature has sprung. To those same stars is assigned the race of men; and we have in us Moon, Zeus, Ares, the Lady of Paphos, Kronos, Sun, and Hermes. Wherefore it is our lot to draw in from the aetherial life-breath <i.e. from the aether, which is the life-breath of the universe> tears, laughter, wrath, birth, speech, sleep, desire. Tears are Kronos; birth is Zeus; speech is Hermes; anger is Ares; the Moon is sleep; Aphrodite is desire; and the Sun is laughter, for by him laugh all mortal minds, and the boundless universe.

FRAGMENTS

1. The soul, when it has quitted the body, does not flow back into the soul of the universe, but remains separate, that it may be called to account by the Father for the deeds which it has done in the body.

2. There is one God; he is beyond comprehension and beyond appraisement.

3. God is called Master and Father.—God is one. And he that is one is nameless; for he does not need a name, since he is alone.

4. God is without father and without mother; for he has been generated by none but himself.

5. There have been very few men that have had perfect knowledge. Among those few are my kinsmen Uranos, Kronos, and Hermes.

6. The world has been made by God's providence.

7. That which is mortal cannot draw near to that which is immortal, nor that which is for a time to that which is everlasting, nor that which is corruptible to that which is incorruptible.

8. Man has been made by God in the image of God. God has fashioned with consummate skill each member of man's body; every one of the members is perfectly adapted both for use and for beauty.

9. The ruler of the daemons.

10. For piety is knowledge of God.

11. And the cause of this is the will of Him who is without beginning, whose name cannot be spoken by human lips.

12. For there is, my son, a secret doctrine, full of holy wisdom, concerning Him who alone is lord of all and ..., whom to declare is beyond the power of man.

13. God is His own father and his own mother.

14. Seeing God.

15. ... Out of those two things, the immortal and the mortal, God made this one thing, man, making him in one respect mortal and in another respect immortal. And him God took and placed between that which is divine and immortal and that which is mortal and mutable, that he might behold the things of heaven with wondering reverence,' (and tend the things of earth).

16. Man has two souls. One of them comes from the first Intelligible, and partakes of the power of the Demiurgus; the other soul is put into the man by the revolution of the heavenly bodies, and into this latter soul enters subsequently the soul which is able to see God.

17. The divine Good is ... God; the good of man is union with God.

18. Materiality is brought into existence out of substantiality.

19. Those men who are devoid of mind are merely led along in the train of Destiny. They have no conception of anything incorporeal, and they do not rightly understand the meaning of Destiny, that very power by which they are led; they

complain of the bodily discipline which she imposes, and they do not recognize any other kind of happiness than that which she confers.

20. Philosophers are above Destiny; for they find no joy in the happiness she gives, since they hold pleasures in subjection; and they are not harmed by the ills she inflicts, because they dwell at all times in the immaterial world.

21. He who has learnt to know himself ought not to set right by means of magic anything that is thought to be amiss, nor to use force to overcome necessity,' but rather to let necessity go its own way according to its nature. A man ought to seek to know himself and God and hold his passions in subjection, and to let Destiny deal as she wills with the clay which belongs to her, that is, with his body. And if a man thinks thus and behaves thus, ...

22. *Ephraim Syrus, Refutations of Mani, Aararcion, and Bardaisan,* edited and translated by C. W. Mitchell, A. A. Bevan, and F. C. Burkitt, vol. ii, p. xcix.
'Hermes taught that there was a Bowl, filled with whatever it was filled with, and that there are Souls excited by desire, and they come down beside it, and, when they have come close to it, in it and by reason of it they forget their own place.... Hermes teaches that the souls desired the Bowl.'

23. *From the third of the Discourses of Hermes to Asclepius.*
For it is not possible for the uninitiated to have such holy secrets told to them. But hearken ye with attentive mind. There was and ever is one thing alone, even Mind, the source of intellectual light; and beside the unity of this one thing, there was nothing else in being. This Mind, ever existing in itself, ever encompasses all things with its own light and spirit. There is no god, nor angel, nor daemon, nor any other being, that is outside of Him; for He is Lord and Father of all ..., and all things are in Him and subject to Him.

24. *From the third of the Discourses of Hermes to Asclepius.*
     If it had not been ordained by the providence of Him who is
     Lord of all that I should reveal this doctrine, ye would not
     have been possessed by such passionate desire to seek the
     truth concerning this; but as it is, ...   Hearken ye to that
     which I have yet to tell. Of this spirit, concerning which I
     have many times spoken before, all things have need; for ...
     it gives life and sustenance to all things. It is dependent on
     the holy source, ... being ever the cause of light(?)) and life to
     all things, inasmuch as it is the one thing that is fecund.

25. If any man then has an incorporeal eye, let him go forth from
     the body to behold the Beautiful, let him fly up and float
     aloft, not seeking to see shape or colour, but rather that by
     which these things are made, that which is quiet and calm,
     stable and change less,... that which is one, that which issues
     from itself and is contained in itself, that which is like noth-
     ing but itself.

26. Say not then, in your thought concerning Him who alone is
     good, that anything is impossible; for to Him belongs all
     power. And think not that He is in anything, nor again that
     He is outside of anything; for He is limitless himself, and is
     the limit of all things; He is encompassed by nothing, and
     encompasses all things. ... For in what do bodies differ from
     that which is incorporeal, and things which have come into
     being from that which is without beginning? Is not the
     difference this, that the one is self-determining, and those
     other things are subject to necessity? ..., but the things
     below, being imperfect, are perishable.

27. For God's Word, who is all-accomplishing and fecund and
     creative, went forth, and flinging himself upon the water,
     which was a thing of fecund nature, made the water preg-
     nant.

28. ...; for it has over it as ruler the creative Word of the Master of all. That Word is, next after Him, the supreme Power, a Power ungenerated, boundless, that has stooped forth from Him; and the Word presides over and governs the things that have been made through him.

29. But tell me, great Agathodaimon, why was he called by this name by the Lord of all? I have already told you; did you not understand? The nature of His intellectual Word is generative. You may call him what you will, provided that you understand this, that he is perfect and issues from one that is perfect, and that he works perfect goods, and makes and vivifies all things. Since then he is of such a nature, he is rightly called by this name.

30. *From the first of the Explanatory Discourses of Hermes to Tat.*
The Word of the Maker, my son, is everlasting, self-moved, without increase or diminution, immutable, incorruptible, ...; he is ever like to himself and equal to himself, equable, stable, well-ordered; after the supreme God he stands alone.

31. *From one of the Discourses of Hermes to Asclepius.*
And Osiris said, 'Tell me next, most great Agathodaimon, how did all the land come forth? ' And the great Agathodaimon said, 'It came forth by [separation] and drying up, as I told you. For when the many waters were bidden by the [Lord of all] to go back into themselves, then the land came forth. At first it was muddy and quivering; but afterwards, when the sun shone forth, and scorched and dried it without cease, the land was firmly fixed amid the waters, being encompassed by the water. And Osiris said, 'Tell me, most great Agathodaimon, [whence did this great sun come forth?' And the great Agathodaimon said, 'Osiris,] do you wish me to describe the origin of the sun? The sun came forth by the providence of Him who is Master of all'.

32. The Maker and Lord of all spoke thus, 'Let earth be' [ ]; and straightway earth came into being, and so began the making of the world.

33. Front the first of the Explanatory Discourses of Hermes to
Tat.

And straightway the Lord of all spoke with his own holy and
creative speech, and said, 'Let the sun be'; and even as He
spoke, Nature drew to herself with her own breath the fire,
which is of upward-tending nature, that fire, I mean, which
is unmixed and most luminous and most active and most
fecund, and raised it up aloft from the water.

34. God said to the beings that He had made: 'And on you that
are subject to me I will impose as an irresistible constraint
this commandment that has been given you by my speech;
this you shall have as your law.'

35. For God, as being perfect <perhaps skillful> and wise,
imposed order on disorder, ... ' that so the things of mind, as
being prior and mightier, might preside and hold the first
place, and the things perceptible by sense, as being secondary, might be placed under them. And so that which is
downward-tending and heavy has in it a wise Word; and
this Word is of creative nature, being fecund and life-giving.

36. We shall know both the God who is preconceived and the
second God, <i.e. Kosmos> who, by the will of the first God,
is like him in all else, but fall short of him in two respects,
namely, in that he is in a body, and in that he is visible.

37. Shahrastani (*Haarbrucker* ii, p. 8 1).

'Concerning Adsimun (Agathodaimon), the philosophers
hand down the tradition that he said "that the first principles
were five, namely, the Creator, Reason, Soul, Space, and
[Void] <perhaps rather time>, and that the composite things
came into being thereafter". But this is not reported of
Hermes'.

APPENDIX

CORPUS HERMETICUM

Corpus Hermeticum is the name given by recent commentators to a collection of about seventeen distinct documents, which first makes its appearance (as a collection) in manuscripts of the fourteenth century. In the MSS. the collection as a whole bears no title, but each of the several documents contained in it has a separate heading of its own. The heading of the first document is Ερμου τρισμεγιστου Ποιμανδρης; and Ficinus, who published a Latin translation of the first fourteen documents in 1471, made the mistake of supposing that heading to be meant for a title of the whole collection. Turnebus, who printed the *editio princeps* of the Greek text (1554), followed Ficinus in this mistake, and entitled *Corp. IXIV Mercurii Trismegisti Poemander,* Similarly, Flussas (1574) gives to *Corp. I-XIV,* together with a *'Caput XV'* made up of Hermetic excerpts from elsewhere, the title *Mercurii Trismegisti Pimandras,* distinguishing the several documents as *'Caput I', 'Caput II',* &c. (He appends ' *Caput* XVI ' under the different title *Aesculapii ad Ammonem.)* The blunder was corrected by Patrizzi (1591), who uses the name *Poemander* rightly to denote *Libellus* I; but Parthey (1854) reverted to the old mistake, giving the title *Hermetis Trismegisti Poemander* to his edition of *Corp. I-XIV,* and calling the several documents *cap. 1, cap. 2,* &c. This is much as if one were to call the New Testament as a whole 'the Gospel according to St. Matthew', and refer to the Epistle to the Romans, for instance, as 'the sixth chapter of Matthew'. The documents of the *Corpus* differ from one another in the same sort of way as the various writings of the New Testament; it is certain from internal evidence that most of them, if not all, were written by different authors; and there is nothing to show that the majority of the writers had read *Corp.* I, or had ever heard of the name *Poimandres.*

As to the numbering of the documents, there is much discrepancy and confusion. The variations are shown in the appended table.

By separating the two parts of XI and the two parts of XII, I have increased the number of distinct documents in the *Corpus* from seventeen to nineteen; and if I had been starting afresh, I should have numbered then consecutively from I to XIX. But in order to avoid confusion of references, I have thought it best to retain the numbering of Flussas and Parthey in respect of *Libelli* I-XIV, and that of Flussas and Reitzenstein in respect of XVI, and to follow Reitzenstein in calling the last two documents XVII and XVIII. The 'Caput XV' of Flussas is not a part of the *Corpus;* there is therefore no *Libellus* XV in the present edition.

The manuscripts of the *Corpus* have been carefully investigated by Reitzenstein, to whom I owe most of the information given in the following list. But to the fifteen MSS. mentioned and described by him *(Poim.* pp. 323 ff.) must be added three Oxford MSS. (Bodl. 3388, which I call Q; Bodl. 8827, which I call R; and Bodl. 3037, which I call S), of the existence of which he appears to have been unaware. All the manuscripts reproduce, with slight variations, the text of a common archetype, which was full of corruptions. The first task of an editor is to reconstruct the text of the lost archetype; his second and more difficult task is to infer from this what the author of each document wrote; his third task is to find out what the author meant. And in cases in which it is impossible to recover the precise words which the author wrote, it may still be possible to guess his meaning.

LIST OF MSS. OF THE CORPUS

A: *Laurentianus* 71, 33; 14th cent.; contains *Corp.* IXIV.

This manuscript was brought from Macedonia to Cosimo de' Medici at Florence, and was by him handed over to Marsiglio Ficino, who made from it the Latin translation which he published in 1471.

From 'a twin-brother of A' (Reitz.) are derived the following three MSS.:

Ottobonianus Graec. 153, 15th cent.

Coislinianus 332, 15th cent.

Parisinus 2518, written by Vergicius, 16th cent.

B: *Pansinus Graec.* I220; middle of the 14th cent.; contains *Corp.* I-XVIII

There are numerous corrections by one or more later hands (B); but it appears that these corrections are for the most part conjectural, and not derived from another MS.

C: *Vaticanus Graec.* 237; 14th cent.; contains *Corp.* I-XVIII.

Closely connected with C are:
Parisinus Graec. 2007, I6th cent.
Ottobonianus Graec. I77, I6th cent.

D: *Vindobonensis phil.* 102; I5th cent.; contains *Corp.* I-XVIII. The printed text of Turnebus is a reproduction of a MS. nearly related to D; so that his edition may be treated as equivalent to a MS. of this family.
Palatinus Graec. 53, I5th or 16th cent., was found by Reitzenstein to be closely connected with D.

M: *Vaticanus Graec.* 951; I4th cent.; contains *Corp.* I-XVIII.

Q: *Bodleianus* 3388 (Arch. Seld. B 58); 15th cent. The text breaks off at the foot of fol. 62 b, in *Corp.* XIII. I4; and the following leaves, which presumably contained the rest of the *Corpus* down to the end of XVIII, have been lost. Q is closely connected with D.
Bodleianus I6987 (d'Orville IO9, Auct. X, I. 4. 7); 16th cent.; contains *Corp.* I-XVIII. This MS. is a faithful transcript of Q. There are numerous corrections by a different hand; the corrector must have used another MS.

R: *Bodleianus* 8827 (Misc. 131, Auct. F, infr. 2, 2); 16th cent.: contains *Corp.* I-XVIII.
In *Corp.* I-XIV, R is derived from a MS. hardly distinguishable from A. (In this part of R, there are numerous corrections by a different hand; these corrections must have been taken from another MS.) The writing of *Corp.* XVI-XVIII is smaller, but similar in character to that of I-XIV, and both parts of the MS. may have been written by the same hand. The text of XVI-XVIII appears to be derived from a MS. closely related to D. (See the readings of R given in the footnotes to *Corp.* XVI-XVIII.)

S: *Bodleianus* 3037 (Misc. Gr. 36, Auct. E 2. 8): 16th cent. The text of S breaks off in *Corp.* IX. 10, and the rest is lost; but the prefixed *Index capitum* gives the headings of all the documents in the *Corpus*, including XVI-XVIII. S is closely connected with C.

Reitzenstein mentions three other MSS., viz.: *Parisinus Graec.* I297; 16th cent.; contains *Corp.* I-XIV; 'much touched up, often agrees with B.' *Vaticanus Graec. 914;* end of I5th cent.; contains *Corp.* I. 1-28. *Parisinus Graec. suppl.* 395; I7th cent.; contains *Corp. I.* 1-21. But these three are of no importance.

It is possible that there may be in existence some MSS. of the *Corpus* which have not yet been discovered; but it is not likely that any future discovery will make any appreciable addition to the material already at our disposal. The known MSS. are more than sufficient to enable us to reconstruct the lost archetype from which they are all derived; the more serious difficulties begin when we try to correct by conjecture the corrupt text of that archetype. Reitzenstein considers that, when the relations of the MSS. to one another and to the printed texts have once been ascertained, an editor need concern himself only with the readings of A, C, and M, and can safely disregard the rest. I have not done precisely that; but I hope that what I have done in this matter does not fall very far short of that which he thinks requisite. In *Corp.* I and XIII, I have given the readings of the MSS. used by Reitzenstein (viz. ABCDM), and of the printed text of Turnebus, and added those of Q. In *Corp.* II-XI, I have given the readings of A, Q, and Turn.; and in II-IX. 10, I have added those of S, using S as a substitute for C, with which it is closely connected. In *Corp.* XII and XIV, not having a collation of A in my hands, I have used R as a substitute for A (to which R, as tested in *Corp.* I and XIII, closely adheres), and have given the readings of Q, R, and Turn. in XII, and those of R and Turn. in XIV. And in Corp. XVI XVIII, I have given the readings of the MSS. used by Reitzenstein (viz. BCDM), and those of Turn., and have added those of R (which, in this part of the *Corpus*, agrees closely with D). It would have been more entirely satisfactory if I could have added the readings of C and M in II-XI, and those of A, C, and M in XII and XIV; but I see no reason to think that, if I had postponed the completion of my work on the text till I could go to Italy to get those readings, the results would have been of sufficient importance to compensate for the delay. The manuscripts differ but slightly from one another and from the text of Turnebus; and it is unlikely that, if I had had before me a complete *conspectus* of the readings of all existing MSS., I should have arrived at a different conclusion as to the meaning of a single clause in the whole *Corpus*.

When and by whom was the archetype written? Reitzenstein *(Poim.*, pp 211, 319, 325 f.) says that a damaged manuscript of the *Corpus* was rediscovered in the eleventh century, and came into the hands of Michael Psellus, the great reviver of Platonic studies in Byzantium (c. A.D. I050); that Psellus wrote or got someone to write a copy of that manuscript; and that the copy written by Psellus, or under his direction, was the archetype from which our MSS. are derived. And he thinks it probable that the traditional text contains glosses and interpolations added by Psellus, and that, in *Corp.* XVIII especially, Psellus filled gaps in the text by inserting conjectural supplements. But what evidence is there that Psellus took the part assigned to him by Reitzenstein, or any part at all, in the transmission of the *Corpus?*

In support of his statements, Reitzenstein puts forward only the two following facts. (I) In *Corp.*I. 18, there is inserted in the text of Cod. M an anonymous *scholion*, in which it is pointed out that ' this 'goes" (i. e. the author of *Corp. I*, who is assumed to be Hermes) must have been acquainted with the Mosaic account of the Creation. And in the margin of Cod. B, this same *scholion* is written by a later hand (B), with the superscription του ψελλου (2) In *Cod.* M (which contains several different and unconnected works), the *Corpus Hermeticum* is immediately preceded by two copies of a treatise of Psellus on the *Chaldaean Oracles*, and the second of these two copies is written by the same hand as the *Corpus Hermeticum*.

The second fact is negligible. It does not follow, because two works which appear side by side in a *Codex* of the fourteenth century were written by the same hand in that *Codex*, that the archetype of the one had been written by the hand of the man (of the eleventh century) who was the author of the other, or had ever been in that man's possession.

It seems then that the only evidence that Psellus had a hand in the transmission of the *Corpus* is the fact that a *scholion* on *Corp.* I. 18 is ascribed to Psellus by an unknown person who revised *Cod.* B. Assuming the truth of this ascription. how much can be inferred from it? It necessarily follows that Psellus had read and reflected on *Corp. I*; and as this *libellus is* not known to have been anywhere in existence in the middle ages except as a part of the *Corpus Hermeticum*, it is probable (but not certain) that Psellus had in his hands a MS. of the whole *Corpus;* that he wrote in the margin of that MS. his *scholion* on I. 18; and that from that MS. were derived both the M-text of the *Corpus,* and the unknown MS. from which the reviser of *Cod.* B got the *scholion.* But it does not follow that Psellus transcribed the *Corpus* with his own hand, or had it transcribed for him, and that all our MSS. are derived from that transcription. And still less does it follow that he added to the corruption of the text by inserting glosses, supplements, or conjectures of his own.

If we take it as established that Psellus had in his hands a MS. of the *Corpus,* it is a legitimate hypothesis that that MS. was the archetype of all our MSS.; and considering the leading part which he is known to have taken in the revival of Platonic studies, it is perhaps more likely that it was so than that it was not so. But as far as I have been able to ascertain, it is a hypothesis only, and not a proven fact.

What was the history of the text before the time of Psellus? Some help towards answering this question may be got from the fact that excerpts from three of the *libelli* of which the *Corpus* is made up occur in the *Anthologium* of Stobaeus (c. A. D. 500). The text of these pieces as given by Stobaeus differs from that of the *Corpus* archetype in many details; but there are some corruptions which are common to Stobaeus and the *Corpus,* and must therefore have got into the text of these three *libelli* before A. D. 500.

At what date was the collection of documents which we call the *Corpus* put together? As far as I know, there is no absolutely cogent proof that it was in existence before the fourteenth century, in which our earliest MSS. were written. But as there must have been a lapse of time between the writing of the Corpus-archetype and the loss of some of its leaves, and a further lapse of time between the loss of the leaves and the writing of our MSS., it may be considered almost certain that the collection as a whole existed at least as early as the twelfth century. Moreover, it is probable that the *Corpus* as a whole was known to Psellus, and consequently, that the *libelli* of which it is composed had been brought together by about A.D. 1050. That, however, is the earliest date at which any trace of it can be found.

The *Corpus* was almost certainly known to the author of the *Hermippus,* as he shows knowledge of five at least of the *libelli* contained in it, and in some of his borrowings from them, reproduces the corruptions of our *Corpus*-text. But the date of the Hermippus is unknown; it may have been written as late as the eleventh century, or even later.

Fulgentius Mythographus (c. A. D. 500) refers to *Libellus I,* and quotes a phrase from it; but that is no proof that the collection of libelli which we call the *Corpus Hermeticum* existed in his time.

Stobaeus prefixes to his excerpts from *Libellus* X the heading 'Hermes to Tat' and to those from *Libellus II* the heading 'Hermes to Asclepius'. (Of his two excerpts from *Libellus IV,* the first has no heading, and the second is headed simply Hermes'.) It is to be inferred from this that he found *Libellus* X (and presumably *Libellus* IV also) in a book entitled 'The discourses of Hermes to Tat', and *Libellus* II in a book entitled 'The discourses of Hermes to Asclepius '. He shows no knowledge of any collection resembling our *Corpus,* which contains discourses addressed to Tat together with others addressed to Asclepius. Nor is any knowledge of the *Corpus* as a whole shown by Lactantius or Cyril, though both of them quote from or refer to some of the libelli included in it.

The alchemist Zosimus (soon after A. D. 300) had read *Libellus I and Libellus* IV; 3 but there is no evidence that he had read them in the *Corpus.*

It is possible then that the *Corpus* was first compiled in the time of Psellus; and it is not impossible that Psellus himself was its compiler. On the other hand, it is also possible that this collection of Hermetic documents had been made several centuries before the date of Psellus, and even that, though unknown to Stobaeus, Cyril, and Lactantius, it was already in existence in their time, and had come into being almost immediately after the composition of the latest of the *libelli* contained in it. In short, the *Corpus* may have been put together at any time between A.D. 300 and 1050. Or again, it may not have been put together at any one time, or by any one person, but may have been formed gradually, by appending to *Corp. I* a series of other *libelli* (or small groups of *libelli*) in succession, and at various dates.

Whence were the individual *libelli* taken? To this question also no definite answer can be given. The several *libelli* may have been taken directly from the collections of Hermetica known to Stobaeus (the *'Discourses of Hermes to Tat'*, &c.); though in that case, it is not clear for what reasons the man or men who put them into the *Corpus* selected some of the *libelli* contained in those collections, and rejected others. But it is possible that some of the Hermetic *libelli* included in the collections used by Stobaeus were also in circulation singly; and there may have been others which had never been included in them, but stood alone. If so, a compiler of the *Corpus* may have added each *libellus* in turn to his own collection as he happened to meet with it.

In some of the MSS., the *Corpus* is divided into two distinct parts, the first part (*Corp. I-XIV*) being thought to contain the teachings of Hermes, and the second (*Corp. XVI-XVIII*), the teachings of Asclepius. It is probably a result of this distinction that *Libelli* XVI-XVIII were omitted in A; the transcriber copied only 'the teachings of Hermes', and did not go onto copy 'the teachings of Asclepius', which he considered to be a different work. But we do not know whether this division existed from the first, or was subsequently introduced by some redactor or copyist. As a matter of fact, *Corp.* XVI, in which the teacher is Asclepius, and the surviving fragment of *Corp.* XVII, in which the teacher is Tat, are similar in general character to the majority of the preceding *libelli*; and must have come from similar sources; while *Corp.* XVIII, which the transcribers apparently assumed to be a speech (or two speeches) delivered by Asclepius, has in reality no connection either with Hermes or with his pupils.

At any rate, it seems to have been by deliberate intention that the three *libelli* in which Hermes does not appear either as teacher or as pupil were placed together, and put at the end of the collection. But in *Corp.* IXIV, there are few traces of designed arrangement. It is true that *libellus* I, in which a man (assumed by the transcribers to be Hermes) is taught by God, and sets forth to teach to mankind the *gnosis* which God has taught him, is well suited for its place at the beginning; and the documents which follow may have been regarded as specimens of that teaching of which *Libellus* I describes the origin. But in II-XIV, there is no internal connection between adjacent documents, and the order in which these *libelli* stand in the *Corpus* appears to be merely accidental.

THE LATIN ASCLEPIUS

THE ASCLEPIUS has come down to us in the form of a Latin dialogue attributed to Apuleius. This Latin dialogue is a translation of a Greek original, which was known to Lactantius and others, but is now lost.

The manuscript tradition of the Latin text has been thoroughly investigated by P. Thomas; and the results of his researches are incorporated in the text which he has published in his edition of the philosophic writings of Apuleius (*Apulei opera quae supersunt vol. III, De philosophia libri; rec. P. Thomas*, Teubner, Lips. I908). Thomas's edition supersedes all earlier publications of the text; and I have used it as my sole authority for the readings of the manuscripts.

Thomas classifies the more important manuscripts in two groups, as follows:

I. Codices melioris notae:

(1) B = Bruxellensis I0054-I0056; written early in the eleventh century. Collated by Thomas. This MS. is very decidedly superior to all the rest. The hands of several correctors can be distinguished. One of these, B 2, who made his corrections at or near the end of the eleventh century, seems to have been a well-instructed man. In a few instances he alone gives what is certainly or probably the true reading; but Thomas concludes that his emendations are merely conjectural. The other correctors of B contribute nothing of value.

(2) M = Monacensis 621; twelfth century. Collated by Goldbacher for his edition of Apuleius, 1876, and again by Thomas.

(3) V = Vaticanus 3385; twelfth century. The text of the *Asclepius* contained in this MS. has not yet been collated. But as

V very closely resembles M (being, in Goldbacher's opinion, a more carelessly written copy of the same original from which M was copied), it is not likely that its collation will add largely to the material at our disposal for textual restoration. M and V are closely related to B; but Thomas thinks it probable that they were copied, not directly from B, but from a corrected copy of B.

(4) G = Gudianus I68 Bibliothecae Guelferbytanae; thirteenth century. Collated by Goldbacher.

II. Codices deteriores:

Collated by Goldbacher:

(1) P = Parisinus 6634; twelfth century.

(2) L = Laurentianus plut. LXXVI cod. 36; twelfth or thirteenth century.

(3) F = Florentinus, olim Marcianus 284; twelfth century.

Besides these two groups, Thomas mentions a MS. in the British Museum (Add. 11983, twelfth century), which he has found to be of very little value; and a large number of 'interpolated MSS.', which he has deliberately disregarded.

Thomas has reconstructed the text of the archetype from which our MSS. are derived. But that is only the first stage on the road to the discovery of the Hermetic teacher's meaning. The text of the archetype itself was corrupt; and even if we could restore the Latin to the exact form in which it came from the hand of its first writer, we should still be far from the completion of our task. We have to do with a Latin translation of a Greek document. The Greek text was probably already damaged when it came into the translator's hands; the translator was very imperfectly qualified for his work, and it is certain that he has frequently blundered. Our first business is to work back to the Latin text as the translator wrote it; but having done this, we have still to guess what was the Greek which the translator had before him, and thence to infer the meaning which the writer of the lost original intended to convey. Thomas has brought together the results of the previous work of other scholars in the emendation of the text, and has added much of his own that is of high value; but he has still left much to be done. Not only have both the Greek original and the Latin translation been damaged by errors of transcription; but it is evident that either the original or the translation has been mutilated in a quite exceptional way. Some passages have been lost, some have been misplaced, and many words, phrases, and sentences have been transposed from a context in which they made sense to a context in which they make nonsense. If the Latin text had once existed in an intelligible and clearly written form, it is difficult to imagine any process by which it could have been reduced to its present state. The ordinary causes of corruption do not suffice to explain its condition. The facts might perhaps be accounted for by assuming that the translator never wrote out a fair copy of his work, but left it full of erasures and corrections, with words and phrases, representing his second thoughts, scribbled in wherever he could find room for them; and that this confused mass of words was afterwards copied out by some one who mechanically wrote down what he saw before him, without regard for the meaning.

The text which results from my attempts to restore the original order of the words is still very faulty, and I hope that it will be further emended by others; but in spite of the many problems which remain unsolved, I think that it is near enough to the original to enable us to recover the thoughts of the writer (or writers) of the Greek treatise in the main, though not in every detail.

In the English translation which faces the Latin text, I have aimed at expressing what I suppose to have been the meaning of the original Greek, rather than the meaning—or, too frequently, the absence of meaning—of the Latin.

The component parts of the ASCLEPIUS.

It appears from internal evidence that the dialogue has been made up by putting together three distinct and unconnected documents—which I have named respectively 'Asclepius I (De homine)', 'Asclepius II (De origine mali)', and ' Asclepius III (De cultu deorum)'—and adding a 'prologus' and an 'epilogus'.

The contents of ASCLEPIUS 1. That part of the traditional text which I call *Ascl. I (viz.* chs. 2-14 a) is a well-constructed whole, the parts of which are arranged and linked together with some skill. It is a treatise *'de tota summitate'* (ch. 7C)—concerning

Deus, Mundus, and *Homo,* and their interrelations;—but the writer deals with this all-embracing subject from a definite point of view, and according to a definite plan. Throughout the discussion, *Man* is the central figure; and the teacher nowhere loses sight of his practical aim— that of urging men to live the life to which, as men, they are called. To this end he describes man's origin and nature (partly cosmic and partly supracosmic), and his station among and relations to beings of other grades; the twofold function assigned to him in accordance with his twofold nature; and the destiny which awaits him according as he fulfils his function or neglects it. The subdivisions in the treatment of the theme are clearly marked, and yet are so connected that we pass on from each to the next without a break. There are two subordinate topics on which the writer has a special message to deliver, viz. the call to renounce possessions, and the mischief of a certain method of philosophic teaching. But each of these topics is introduced without breach of continuity. The renunciation of possessions is spoken of as a thing required with a view to the fulfilment of man's function; and the corruption of philosophy is coupled with the love of possessions, as one of the hindrances to the realization of man's high destiny. Thus the concluding paragraph, on philosophy, is made to arise naturally out of the main subject; and so the discourse ends appropriately with a description of that teaching which the writer holds to be the true philosophy, and of which the treatise itself is a specimen.

Asclepius I, then, is a well ordered whole, complete in itself. There can, I think, be little doubt that the Greek original of Ascl. I at first existed as a separate document, of the same type as the *Hermes to Asclepius* libelli preserved in the *Corpus;* and it may be presumed that it once formed part of the collection of discourses known to Stobaeus.

The sources of ASCL. I.

In this treatise, as in most of the *Hermetica,* there is little novelty or originality in the doctrines taught; and the discourse of Hermes contains few statements to which parallels cannot be found in earlier Greek writings. Yet the teaching of Ascl. I is not a mere repetition of traditional formulae; the writer's words ring true, and are alive with genuine feeling. If he has adopted his beliefs from others, they are none the less his own.

The influence of Plato is manifest throughout. The fundamental articles of the writer's creed—the doctrine of a supracosmic God, who is the maker and ruler of the universe, and that of a supracosmic element in the human soul—have been transmitted to him from Plato; and verbal echoes of phrases used by Plato may be recognized (see for instance the reminiscences of the *Timaeus* in ch. 8). But there is ample evidence of dependence on Greek writers of later date than Plato. The terms hule and qualitas, as employed in Ascl. I, did not come into use until after Plato's time. The cosmology of chs. 2-6 is largely Stoic. The notion of a lower and mortal soul which is either composed of fire and air, or inseparably connected with those elements, must have been arrived at by a blending of Platonism with Stoic physics.

The writer of Ascl. I says that man has been embodied on earth 'in order that he may tend the things of earth'; and it is in the treatment of this theme, if anywhere, that he shows independence. The earliest Pagan writer in whom I have found this thought expressed is Cicero; and he probably got it from Posidonius. In this part of Ascl. I, therefore, the influence of Posidonius may be suspected.

The modification of a fundamentally Platonic system of thought by an intermixture of Stoic physics, such as we find in this document as well as in most of the other *Hermetica*, must have been derived from Antiochus and Posidonius, or from writers subsequent to them and influenced by them.

There seems to be nothing distinctively Egyptian in the doctrine of Ascl. I. The religious fervour of the writer is characteristic of his Egyptian nationality; but there is nothing in his dogmas that cannot be derived from Greek philosophy.

There are several phrases which show some resemblance to passages in the first two chapters of Genesis. There is, then, a possibility that the writer was to some slight extent affected by Jewish influence; but as each of these thoughts may very well have been suggested in some other way, it remains a possibility only.

The writer uses the term ο κυριος as a name or title of the supreme God (ch. 8). Is this to be regarded as a result of Jewish influence? The word κυριος (with a dependent genitive) was applied to Zeus by Pindar, and according to Liddell and Scott, κυριος occurs 'in inscriptions, as a name of divers gods, Zeus, Hermes, Kronos, &c., vide C. I. Index III; so Kuria of Artemis, &c., ib.' But it was not commonly used by Greek philosophic writers with reference to the supreme God. There is no instance of this use of it in Diels Fr. Vorsokr., in Plato, in Aristotle, or in Diels Doxogr.1 But it was employed by the translators of the LXX as a rendering of the Hebrew name of God; and where it is similarly used by Pagan writers, it may have been taken over by them from Hellenistic Jews. It occurs frequently in the books of magic; e.g. the god is addressed as Kurie in Dieterich Mithrasliturgie, pp. 8, 1O (thrice), 14 (twice), and Dieterich Abraxas, p. I77, &c. Its use in such cases is comparable to that of the Hebrew names employed in magic invocations.

I have failed to find the slightest trace of Christian influence in Ascl. 1.

Date of the Greek original of Ascl. I.

The only definite terminus a quo is that which is given by the fact that the writer mixes Stoic physics with his Platonism. This sort of syncretism began in the time of Antiochus and Posidonius, i.e. in the first half of the first century B.C. It is therefore certain that the treatise cannot have been written before I00 B. C. But it was probably not written until much later.

A terminus ante quem may, perhaps, be inferred from the absence of any recognition of the existence of Christianity. The attitude of the writer of Ascl. I presents in this respect a contrast to that of the writer of Ascl. III. The latter, writing about A. D. 270 (see below), regards the advance of Christianity with horror and dismay; it is already clear to him that the Christians will soon get the upper hand, and that the Pagan cults will be abolished. But the writer of Ascl. I, when he asks himself what is the most serious obstacle in the path of those who seek salvation, finds it in the fact that certain Pagan teachers attach too much importance to the study of mathematics. If he had been aware that the very existence of his religion was threatened by the spread of Christianity, he could hardly have omitted to mention at this point a danger in comparison with which the error of which he speaks would have seemed to him a negligible trifle. This seems a sufficient reason for putting the

date of Ascl. I earlier than that of Ascl. III. Ascl. I was probably
written at a time when Christianity was not yet strong or
aggressive enough to cause grave alarm or distress to the adherents of the old religions; Ascl. III was written at a time when it
had already become apparent to the writer, not only that a
danger was impending, but that the total extinction of Pagan
religion was inevitable. For reasons given below, I think that a
man in the situation of the writer of Ascl. I would not have been
likely to ignore this danger at any time later than A.D. 260. We
may therefore fix on 100 B.C. and A.D. 260 as the extreme limits
between which the date of Ascl. I must be placed; and we might
with strong probability restrict the range somewhat more nar-
rowly, and say that the date must lie between 50 B.C. and A.D.
250.

I can find no internal evidence which would enable us to fix
the date of Ascl. I more exactly; but on the ground of considera-
tions which apply to the *Hermetica* in general, I am inclined to
think that this libellus is not likely to have been written before
the second century A. D.; and perhaps we should not be far
wrong in conjecturing that the writer was a contemporary of
Clement, who was teaching in Alexandria between A. D. 190
and 200.

The circumstances of the writer.

The author of Ascl. I was probably an Egyptian by race. He
can hardly have been a priest; for he takes no interest in theurgic
ritual; and the worship of 'daemons' (i.e. temple-gods) is, in his
eyes, a comparatively low form of religion, though better than
none. It may be inferred that he had not been trained in the
schools of the Egyptian priests, but had received a Hellenic
education in Alexandria. Perhaps he had attended the lectures
of one of the professional teachers of Platonism in that city, and
is speaking from his own experience when he complains that
such teachers put difficulties in the way of a seeker after God by
including in their curriculum a compulsory course of mathematics. But in spite of these difficulties, he succeeded in learning as much of Greek philosophy as he needed for his purpose;
and we may suppose that he afterwards retired to some more
secluded place, where he could live the contemplative life in
companionship with a small group of congenial spirits, at first,

perhaps, as a pupil of some older teacher of the gnosis, and afterwards as a teacher in his turn. The instruction in these little communities must have been chiefly oral, and carried on, for the most part, by means of colloquies between the master and a single pupil at a time; and when one of the teachers committed his thoughts to writing, no doubt he reproduced, in the form of imaginary dialogues between Hermes and Tat or Asclepius, the method and contents of his own talks with this or that disciple.

If the writer of Ascl. I practised what he preached he must have renounced all private possessions; and it almost necessarily follows from this that the brotherhood to which he belonged, and of which he was perhaps the head, held property in common, and that the produce of their labours was thrown into a common stock, from which the wants of all the members were supplied. They must have divided their time between cultus terrenorum and *cultus caelestium*; that is, they must have been occupied partly in tilling the piece of land which they owned collectively, and partly in adoration of the di caelestes (especially in the form of hymn singing), and in drawing near to the supreme God by private prayer and meditation, and by such talk between teacher and pupil as is exemplified in our *Hermetica*. They felt that, in living such a life as this, they were doing the work which God had sent them down to earth to do; and they looked forward with trustful hope to the time when they would be 'released from the bonds of mortality', and, by God's grace, permitted to return to their true home above.

Asclepius II.

That part of the composite dialogue which I call Ascl. II deals with the origin of evil; the writer seeks to account for the existence of evil by attributing it to the operation of hule. This discussion is not in any way connected either with the contents of Ascl. I or with those of Ascl. III; and the dualism of Ascl. II is irreconcilable with the monism of Ascl. I and Ascl. III. There can, therefore, be little doubt that the Greek original of Ascl. II was in existence before it was made use of to form a part of the Asclepius. It appears to be complete in itself; but whether it was an independent *libellus*,' or a piece extracted by the compiler of the Asclepius from a longer document, we have no means of knowing.

There is no indication of any definite date for the Greek original of Ascl. II. We may suppose it to have been written in the same period as the Greek originals of Ascl. I and Ascl. III, i.e. probably about A.D. 150-270; and this supposition is to some extent confirmed by the resemblance between the teaching of Ascl. II and that of Numenius and Hermogenes (A. D. 150-200) on the same subject.

The contents of ASCLEPIUS III.

That part of the traditional text which I have named Ascl. III presents, at first sight, a mere chaos of passages not only unconnected with Ascl. I and Ascl. II, but also unconnected with one another. But this confusion may be in part, if not wholly, a result of the mutilated and disordered state in which the Latin text has come down to us; and it seems probable that the Greek original of Ascl. III existed as a single document before the composite dialogue was compiled.

It appears that a number of passages were somehow severed from their context, but were preserved as detached fragments; and that these fragments were collected into two blocks, which have been inserted into the text at the two places at which we find them. I have transposed these passages to what I conjecture to have been tbeir original positions.

Even in that part of the text which is undoubtedly continuous there is a lack of orderly and systematic arrangement; the writer seems to stray at random from one topic to another, as each in succession happens to occur to him. (In this respect, Ascl. III stands in marked contrast to Ascl. I.) The treatise as a whole has little unity; and it is difficult to describe its subject in a single phrase. But every part of it contributes in some way to the exposition of what the writer holds to be the true religion; and in some parts at least he is occupied in explaining what gods are to be worshipped, and how men ought to worship them. In the Prophecy he laments the impending abandonment of the old cults; his repeated assertion that men make gods is a defiant justification of the usages of Pagan worship in the face of Christian hostility; and the passage on time and eternity leads up to a mention of that vision of the Eternal in which all worship culminates. Perhaps then the loosely connected discus-

sions of which Ascl. III is composed may be fairly compre-
hended under the title De cultu deorum.

The sources of ASCLEPIUS III.

The influence of Plato is manifest throughout. The fundamental conceptions of the writer—that of a supracosmic God,
and that of an incorporeal νους—are derived from Plato. The
notion of eternity is Platonic; and the use of the word aeternitas
(aion) to express this notion comes from the Timaeus.

To Stoic influence must be ascribed the use of the term
spiritus (pneuma). The definition of vox (φονη) is Stoic. In the
words *quod dicitur extra mundum*, the writer refers to the Stoic
doctrine of a void outside the Kosmos. The statement that no
two individuals are alike is derived from the Stoics of the
second century B. C., who maintained this doctrine in opposi-
tion to the Academics; and the astral explanation of individual
differences would hardly have been found in the writings of
any Stoic earlier than Posidonius.

In the account of the life after death, the assumption that all
souls alike, on their separation from the body, ascend into the
atmosphere is of Stoic origin; and the division of the atmosphere into two distinct strata, and the purgation of impure
souls in the lower stratum, are derived from Posidonius.

The statement that νους is *divina pars mundi,* is due to the
influence of Stoic materialism, but may perhaps have been
transmitted to the writer by the Peripatetic Critolaus and the
Platonist Antiochus. The remarks on circular movement may
perhaps have been derived from Aristotle.

The views expressed in connexion with the statement that
man makes gods are Egyptian rather than Hellenic. In these
passages, the writer formulates certain beliefs of his country-
men; he is here speaking of things familiar to him by direct and
personal knowledge, and has no occasion to borrow from earlier writers.

The notion of a system of departmental gods, and the names
Zeus, Heimarmene, indicate a Stoic source; but the terms *Decani,
Horoscopi,* and *Pantomorphos* are derived rather from the astral
religion of Hellenistic Egypt.

The form of the Prophecy, may have been suggested by
earlier apocalypses, Egyptian or Jewish; but its contents, so far
as it refers to contemporary events, must be original.

Analogies to Jewish teaching may be found in the exaltation of human procreation, in the statement that man is made *ex parte corruptiore mundi et ex divina*, ch. 22 (cf. Gen. ii. 7, and in the application of the term *summus* to the supreme God (*summus qui dicitur deus*,); but there is no proof that the writer was in any way affected by Jewish influences.

There is not the slightest reason to think that any part of the doctrine of Ascl. III has been derived from Christian sources. On the other hand, the writer's attitude is to a large extent determined by his repugnance to Christianity. This repugnance finds direct expression in the Prophecy, and underlies his treatment of the topics of god-making and procreation.

THE *HERMETICA* IN THE *ANTHOLOGIUM* OF *STOBAEUS*

JOANNES STOBAEUS, at some date not far from A. D. 500, compiled a large collection of extracts from Pagan Greek writers. The collection was divided into four books, and was entitled σκλογων, αποφθεγματων, υποθηκων βιβλια τεσσαρα. It seems to have been made up by putting together the contents of earlier collections of extracts, and adding to them passages extracted by Stobaeus himself from books which he had read. He arranged the extracts in chapters according to subjects, and placed at the head of each chapter a superscription stating the subject of the extracts contained in it.

Photius (c. A. D. 850) read this *anthologium* in a copy differing little from the original as written by Stobaeus; and in his *Btbbiotheca*, p. II2a, I6ff., he describes it as a work in two volumes (τευχη) consisting of four books (βιβλια) and gives the superscriptions of the 208 chapters into which the four books were divided.

Our MSS. of Stobaeus are derived from an archetype closely resembling the MS. used by Photius, if not from that very MS. But at some time not far from A. D. 1000, the two volumes of which the archetype consisted were separated; the two parts passed into different hands, and thenceforward, each of them was copied and recopied separately. Hence the first part (Bks.

I and II) has come down to us in one set of MSS., and the second part (Bks. III and IV) in another set of MSS. The two parts consequently came to be edited separately, as if they were two different works; and the editors gave to Bks. I and II the title *Eclogae physicae et ethicae,* and to Bks. III and IV the title *Florilegium.* Either the term *Eclogae* or the term *Florilegium* might serve as a title for the whole (each extract, whether in Bks. I and II or in Bks. III and IV, is an *ecloga,* and tbe four Books are collectively a *florilegium);* but the assignment of the title *Eclogae* to one part of the collection and the title *Florilegium* to the other is arbitrary and groundless, and Wachsmuth and Hense, the latest editors, have rightly rejected these titles. In their edition, what had hitherto been called *Stob. Ecl.* is called *Stobaei Anthologii libri duo priores,* and what had hitherto been called *Stob. Floril.* is called *Stobaei Anthologii libri duo posteriores;* and their correction will doubtless be henceforth accepted by all scholars.

After the separation of the two parts of the *Anthologium,* the first part (Bks. I and II) was reduced to smaller compass by an epitomator, who had a preference for philosophical writings. He copied out almost in full Bk. I, chs. I30; but from that point onward as far as his handiwork can be traced (i.e. down to Bk. II, ch. 9), he omitted nearly all extracts except those from Plato, Aristotle, Archytas, Porphyry, and (fortunately for our present purpose) Hermes. The last part of his *epitome* (Bk. II, chs. I0-46) is lost. It is only this mutilated *epitome* of Bks. I and II, and not the full text of these two books as read by Photius, that has come down to us in the MSS. of Stobaeus. Some of the missing passages have, however, been recovered from a *gnomologium,* partially preserved in a cod. Laurentianus (fourteenth century), the compiler of which borrowed largely from the four Books of Stobaeus at a time when they were still complete; and from that source Wachsmuth has been able to print the text of Stob., Bk. II, chs. 15, 31, 33, and 46.

Stobaeus seems to have got his *Hermetica* from (I) a collection of Ερμου λογοι προς Τατ; (2) a collection of Ερμου λογοι προς Ασκληπιον ; (3) a collection of Ερμου λογοι προς Αμμονα; and (4) a collection of 'Ερμου λογοι Ισιδος προσ Ωορν. The total number of Hermetic excerpts in his *Antholopium* is forty-two, if we include *Exc.* [XXVIII] and [XXIX], and count as separate excerpts the two parts of Stob. I. 4I. I (which I call *Exc.* II B and *Exc.*

XI), and the two parts of Stob. I. 4I. 6 (which I call *Exc. IV* B and *Exc.* III). Of these, ten are taken from *libelli* which have been preserved in the *Corpus Hermeticum* (Corp. II, IV, and X); and one (Stob. 4. 52. 47) is an extract from the Greek original of the Latin *Asclepius.* The remaining thirty-one are given in the present edition as Excerpts I, IIA, IIB, III, IVA, IVB, V—[XXIX]. I have arranged and numbered them, grouping together the *Hermes to Tat* Excerpts (IXI), the *Hermes to Ammon* Excerpts (XIIXVII), the Excerpts in which there is no indication of the pupil's name (XVIII-XXII), and the *Isis to Horus* Excerpts (XXIII-XXVII); and I have divided the longer Excerpts into numbered sections.

Twenty-seven of these 'Excerpts', as well as all the ten extracts from *libelli* which are extant in the *Corpus*, occur in Stob. Bk. I, and two *(Exc. I* and *Exc.* XVIII) in what remains of Stob. Bk. II. There are only two Hermetic extracts *(Exc.* II A and *Exc.* XXVII) in Stob. Bk. III, and only one (the extract from the original of *Ascl. Lat.)* in Stob. Bk. IV. But by an accident which must have happened before the separation of the two parts of the *Anthologium,* the leaf of Bk. II on which *Exc. I* was written in the archetype was, together with two other leaves, shifted from its place, and inserted in Bk. IV; and the contents of these three leaves have consequently been transmitted as part of the text of Bk. IV. For the text of *Exc. I* therefore we are dependent on the MSS. of Bks. III and IV (the so-called *Florilegium),* and not on the MSS. of Bks. I and II (the so-called *Eclogae).* Wachsmuth has now restored these misplaced passages to their original positions in Bk. II, chs. I, 4, and 2.

Of the MSS. which contain the extant remains of Stob. Bks. I and II, two only need be taken into account, as all the other MSS. are derived from them. These two are

cod. Farnesinus (F), fourteenth century; cod. Parisinus (P), fifteenth century.

F and P then are our only sources for the text of all the Hermetic extracts except four. F is much the better of the two; but the evidence of P also is of some value. There are in P numerous corrections by two or three later hands; but these corrections (marked p2) are conjectural.

The other four Hermetic extracts (viz. *Excerpts I,* IIA, XXVII, and the fragment of the Greek original of *Ascl. Lat.)* have come down to us in the MSS. of Stob. Bks. III and IV. Of these, the earliest and best is cod. Vindobonensis (S), written soon after A.D. IOOO. The *editio princeps* of Bks. III and IV by Trincavelli (Tr.) faithfully reproduces the text of a cod. Marcianus (fifteenth or sixteenth century) closely related to S, if not wholly derived from it, and is useful chiefly as a substitute for certain missing parts of S. There are two other MSS. which are of some value, as representing a text of different descent, viz. cod. Escurialensis (M), *c.* A.D, IIOO, and cod. Parisinus (A), fourteenth century. Hense has also made use of the cod. Laurentianus (L) mentioned above, which contains extracts from Stob. Bks. III and IV as well as from Stob. Bks. I and II, and of another *gnomologium,* preserved in cod. Bruxellensis (Br.), fourteenth or fifteenth century, which likewise contains borrowings from Stob. Thus our sources for these four Hermetic extracts are S (with Tr.) and MA, supplemented by L and Br.

The chief printed editions of Stobaeus are the following:—

Bks. I and II: Canter *(ed. princeps),* Antwerp, 1575; Heeren, 1792-I80I; Gaisford, 1850; Meineke, I860-3; and Wachsmuth, Berlin, I884.

Bks. III and IV: Trincavelli *(ed. princeps),* Venice, I535-6; Gesner, 1st edition I543, 2nd ed. I549, 3rd ed. I559; Gaisford, I822; Meineke, I860-3; and Hense, Berlin, I894-I9I2.

Wachsmuth and Hense have investigated the MSS. far more thoroughly than any of the previous editors; and the edition of the *Anthologium* of Stobaeus which they have produced by their combined labours supersedes all earlier publications of the text Their edition is my sole authority for the readings of the MSS. in the Hermetic extracts.

The task which Wachsmuth and Hense have set themselves in their edition, and which they may be considered to have accomplished, as far as its accomplishment is possible, is that of restoring the text of the *Anthologium* as written by Stobaeus. There remains the further task of emending the more or less corrupt text of each extract as read by Stobaeus, and so recovering, as nearly as may be, the original text of the passage as written by its author. For the performance of this task also, Wachsmuth and Hense have given valuable help; but much remains to be done; and it is this that, as far as the Hermetic extracts are concerned, I have aimed at doing in the present edition. Starting from the text of the archetype of the Stobaeus MSS., as reconstructed by Wachsmuth and Hense, I have tried to discover or guess, firstly, what words the author of each Hermetic passage wrote, and secondly, what he meant by the words he wrote. When one has concluded that a phrase is corrupt, the best way to deal with it is usually to attack the second of these two problems first; i. e. to infer from the context, and from parallels in other writings, what the author must have meant, and thence, if possible, to infer what words he used to express his meaning. In a matter of this kind, complete success is unattainable; but there is much that can be done, and it is to be hoped that the process of recovering the thoughts of the Hermetic writers, to which I have tried to contribute, will be taken up and carried farther by others.

TESTIMONIA

THE earliest evidence for the existence of writings of similar character to our religious and philosophic Hermetica is that of Athenagoras, A. D. 17 780. But that evidence is not quite free from doubt; for the statement which Athenagoras apparently ascribes to Hermes, viz. that he was descended from 'gods' who were men (i. e. from men who were held to have become gods after death), might have occurred in any sort of document the teaching of which was attributed to Hermes, e. g. in a dialogue dealing with astrology or magic.

Tertullian, *De an.* 33, quotes a passage from a writing of the same kind as our *Hermetica*. His obscure style makes it difficult to be sure what he means in the three passages in which he mentions Hermes Trismegistus without quoting him; but it may be inferred from *Adv. Valentin.* 15 and *De an.* 2 that he knew of writings of which Hermes was supposed to have been the author, and which contained doctrines resembling those of Greek philosophers, and especially those of Plato. His evidence proves then that in A. D. 207-13 some *Hermetica* similar to ours were in existence, and were accessible to Christian readers; but it does not prove that at that time any of the extant *Hermetica* had yet been written.

In the writings of Clement of Alexandria, there is no mention of any Greek *Hermetica*. What is to be inferred from this fact? Large parts of Clement's *Stromateis* are occupied with discussions of the relation between Greek philosophy and 'barbarian' philosophy (by which he usually means the teaching of Moses and the Hebrew prophets). He seeks to prove that the Greek philosophers were later in date than the Hebrew writers, and 'stole' from them. If he had known our *Hermetica,* and believed them to contain the teachings of an ancient Egyptian sage, he could not possibly have omitted to speak of them in the course of these discussions. He could not have failed to notice the resemblance between the Hermetic doctrines and those of Plato; and he would have said, as others did, 'Plato borrowed from Hermes'. His silence concerning the Greek *Hermetica* can therefore be accounted for only by assuming either that they were not yet in existence; or that they were in existence but unknown to him; or that he knew them, but knew them to be of recent date, and therefore had no more reason to speak of them than of other recent writings. Now the hypothesis that no such writings were yet in existence is excluded by the evidence of Clement's contemporary, Tertullian, who quotes from a philosophic *Hermeticum;* and if writings of this character were known to Tertullian, it is most unlikely that they were unknown to Clement, whose work as a teacher in Alexandria must have brought him into contact with thinkers of all kinds that were to be found in Egypt, Pagans as well as Christians. It is therefore probable that Clement knew of the existence of some Greek *Hermetica* of the same character as ours, but knew them to have been composed by men of his own time, and therefore to have no bearing on the question what sort of doctrines were taught in Egypt before the beginnings of Greek philosophy.

Arguments *ex silentio* are often of little weight; but in the case of Clement, the force of this argument will, I think, be evident to any one who reads the following passages. *Strom.* I. 15. 66-73 (a long list of Greek philosophers who were either barbarian by race or pupils of barbarian teachers). *Strom.* I. 21. 134 (an item in a long list of Pagan prophets):αλλα και των παρ Αιγυπτιοις ανθρωπων ποτε, γενομενων δε ανθρωπινη δοξη θεων, Ερμης τε ο Θηβαιος και Ασκληπιος ο Μεμφιτης. Strom. *5. 5. 29:* Και ολως ο Πυθαγορας και οι απ αυτου συν και Πλατωνι μαλιστα των αλλων φιλοσοφων σφοδρα τω νομοθετη ωμιλησαν (i. e. read the Books of Moses), ωσ εστιν εξ αυτων συμβαλεσθαι των δογματων. Why did not Clement mention the much more evident resemblance between the doctrines of Plato and the Greek *Hermetica? Strom.* 5. 12. 78: Clement quotes Pl. *Tim.* 28 C (τον γαρ πατερα... εξειμειν αδυνατον), and says that Plato got this thought from *Exod. xix,* where it is shown that God is aoratoV kai arrhtoV; and he compares some verses of Orpheus, who, he says, got the same truth from the same source. Why did he not rather adduce Herm. *ap.* Stob. *Exc.* I (which is much more like the passage in Plato), if it was known to him? *Strom.* 6. 4 358: ευροιμεν δ αν και αλλο ματυριον εισ βεβαιωσιν του τα καλλιστα των δογματων τουσ αριστους των φιλοσοφων παρ ημων (i.e. from our Hebrew Scriptures) σφετερισαμενους ως ιδια αυχειν το και παρα των αλλων βαρβαρων (i.e. from others besides the Hebrews) απηνθισθαι των εις εκαστην αιαιρεσιν συντεινοντων τινα, μαλιστα δε Αιγυπτιων τα τε αλλα και το περι την μετενσωματωσιν τησ ψυχης δογμα. μετιασι γαρ οικειαν τινα φιλοσοφιαν Αιγυπτιοι αυτικα τουτο εμφαινει μαλιστα η ιεροπτεπης συτων θρησκεια. (Here follows a list of the different orders of Egyptian priests, and of the subjects dealt with in the 'Books of Hermes' which priests of the several orders were required to study.) δυο μεν ουν και τεσσαρακοντα αι πανυ αναγκαιαι τω Ερμη γεγονασι βιβλοι ων τας μεν τριακοντα εξ, την μασαν Αιγυπτιων περιεχουσας φιλοσοφιαν, οι προειρημενοι (πριεστσ) εκμανθανουσι, τας δε λοιπασ εξ οι παστοφοροι, ιατρικας ουσασ ... και τα μεν Αιγυπτιων, ωσ εν βραξει φαναι, τοιαυτα Ινδων δε η φιλοσοφια κ.τ.λ. Clement evidently means by 'Books of Hermes' books written in the Egyptian language, and ascribed to Thoth, which were used in the schools of the priests. He must have got the list of books, directly or indirectly, from a native Egyptian; and he knew nothing about their contents, beyond the meagre information which he gives at second hand. If he had believed any Greek *Hermetica* known to him to be translations or paraphrases of ancient and genuine 'books of Hermes', he would necessarily have referred to them here, as the best evidence accessible to him and his readers concerning the character of the 'Egyptian philosophy', instead of talking of the books studied by the priests, books which he could not read, and about which he knew very little.

We must conclude then that Clement either did not know of any Greek *Hermetica* such as ours, or else, as seems more likely, knew of some such writings (not necessarily any of those which have come down to us), but knew that they were of recent date, and that their contents could not be rightly attributed to the ancient teacher Hermes.

Did Origen (A. D. 185-255) know any philosophic or religious *Hermetica?* No quotations from or references to Hermetic documents have been found in his writings. Origen, like his teacher and predecessor Clement, repeatedly asserts that Moses and the Hebrew prophets were prior in time to the Greek philosophers, and says that, as far as there was any borrowing, it must have been the Greeks that borrowed from the Hebrews; but he does not discuss this question at length and in detail, as Clement does; and I do not know of any passages in Origen's works in which the course of his argument is such that, if he had known any Greek *Hermetica* and thought the teachings contained in them to be Egyptian and of ancient date, it would have been *necessary* for him to speak of them.

It may however be said of Origen, with even more confidence than of Clement, that if any such writings were current in his time, he must have been aware of their existence. Origen was born and brought up in Alexandria, and lived and taught there as head of the Catechetical School (with some intermissions) from A. D. 203 to 230, after which he migrated to Palestine. He had a wide and thorough knowledge of Pagan philosophic writings, and especially of those of the Platonists, down to and including Numenius. Some have thought that he was for a time a pupil of Ammonius Saccas, and a fellow-pupil with Plotinus (who was junior to him by about eighteen years). Statements to that effect seem to have arisen out of a confusion between the Christian Origen and a Pagan Platonist of the same name. But be that as it may, the fact remains that he was living in Egypt at the same time as Ammonius Saccas and Plotinus; that he *may* have been personally acquainted with one or both of them; and that he *must* have got his Platonism from the same sources that they did, or from similar sources. Among the sources from which he got it, were any *Hermetica* included? That question we have no means of answering. There are in his writings many passages which, in the thoughts expressed, closely resemble passages in our *Hermetica*; but I have found no instances of verbal resemblance of a kind that could be held to prove direct borrowing; and the resemblances in thought prove nothing more than that both Origen and the Hermetists were familiar with Platonism.

In any case, Origen's writings are of special significance for the study of the *Hermetica*, because he lived at the very time during which we have reason to think that most of the earlier of our extant *Hermetica* were written. He was a Platonist as well as a Christian. The Platonism that is to be found in his writings is intermixed with allegorical interpretations of Bible texts, but it can, for the most part, be disentangled from them without much difficulty; and we have it in a specimen of the kind of Platonism that was current in Egypt at that time, i.e. after Numenius, and before the publication of the teachings of Plotinus.

The date of the sentence concerning Hermes in Cyprian (?) *Quod idola* is so uncertain, that no inference can safely be drawn from it.

The author of the *Cohortatio ad Graecos* (probably A. D. 260-302) quotes Herm. *ap.* Stob. *Exc.* I; and if the conjecture 'Αψαθου δαιμονος φορ Ακμωνος is accepted, he also knew a Hermetic dialogue in which Agathos Daimon was the teacher.

The earliest Pagan *testimonium* is that of Porphyry, who, in his *Letter to Anebo*, written in the latter part of the third century, said that he had met with some philosophic *Hermetica* (*Abammonis resp.* 8. 4a: εν τοις συγγραμματιν οις λεγεις περιτετχηκεναι... τα μεν γαρ φερομενα ως Ερμου κ.τ.λ.).

It might perhaps be argued that the Greek *Hermetica* may have been for some considerable time kept secret (as is enjoined in some of them), that is, may have been passed from hand to hand within the small groups of men for whose instruction they were written, but concealed from all others; and that they may therefore have been in existence long before they became known to outsiders. But that seems improbable. Among 'seekers after God', such as were the authors of our *Hermetica* and their pupils, conversions to Christianity must have been frequent; and a Hermetist who had become a Christian would no longer have any motive for concealing the writings which he had previously held sacred. There was therefore nothing to prevent these documents from becoming widely known soon after they were written.

We find then that the external evidence agrees with and confirms the conclusion to which the internal evidence points, namely, that most of the extant *Hermetica* were written in the course of the third century after Christ, and that few of them, if any, can have been written long before A.D. 200.

That most of them, if not all, were in existence at the end of the third century, is proved by the evidence of Lactantius.

The treatise of Lactantius *De opificio dei*, his larger work *Divinae institutiones*, and his treatise *De ira dei* were written between A.D. 303 and 3II. The contents of the *Divinae institutiones* are repeated in an abridged form, with some variations and additions. in the *Epitome div. inst.*, which was written by Lactantius some years later, perhaps about A. D. 315. For the text of Lactantius, my authority is Brandt's edition, *Corp. scripl. eccl. Lat. vol. xix* (I890) and vol. xxvii (1893-7).

In the *De opif dei* (*c.* A.D. 304), there is no mention of Hermes. In *Div. inst.* 2. I0. I4f., speaking of the making of the human body by God, Lactantius mentions Hermes, together with the Stoics and Cicero, as having dealt with the subject, and adds, 'I pass over this topic now, because I have recently written a book (Viz. the *De opif. dei*) about it '. But he does not there say that he made use of any Hermetic document when he was writing the *De opif dei*; and it is possible that the Hermetic passage (probably *Corp.* V. 6) to which he refers in *Div. inst. l. c.* was not known to him until after the *De opif. dei* was finished.

Brandt, *Über die Quellen von Lactanz' Schrift De opificio dei* (*Wiener Studien* I3, I89I, pp. 255-92), tries to prove that one of the two main sources of the *De opif dei* was a Hermetic document— probably, he thinks, the *Aphrodite,* of which Herm. *ap.* Stob. *Exc.* XXII is a fragment. His argument may be summarized as follows: 'Lactantius, throughout *De opif: dei* cc. 2-I3, insists on the *beauty* of man's bodily structure even more than on its *utility.* Now that is exceptional; in most other writings on the same topic (e.g. in Cic. *Nat. deor.* 2. I33-53) the utility of the bodily organs is spoken of, but not their beauty. Lactantius must therefore have drawn from a source other than Cicero and

Varro, and other than the Stoic writings of which Cicero and Varro made use. And as Lactantius in *Div. inst.* 2. I0. I3 says that Hermes had dealt with the subject, the peculiar source from which Lactantius drew in the *De opif: dei* must have been a *Hermeticum*. In that *Hermeticum*, beauty must have been spoken of side by side with utility. The only extant Hermetic passage in which the construction of the human body by God is dealt with is *Corp.* V. 6; and that', says Brandt (mistakenly, as it seems to me), 'cannot be the passage referred to in *Div. inst. l. c.*, because it speaks only of the beauty of the bodily organs, and not of their utility. The *Hermeticum* of which Lactantius made use in the *De opif dei* must therefore have been a *libellus* which is now lost; and it may very likely have been the *Aphrodite*. From it are derived those parts of the *De opif. dei* in which either the utility and the beauty of the bodily organs are spoken of together, or their beauty is spoken of alone; viz. *cap.* 2~ *cap.* 5. I3, nearly the whole of *cap.* 7, much in *cap.* 8. I-8, much in *cap.* I0, and most of *cap.* I3.'

If that were established, it might be said that a large part of the contents of a lost Hermetic *libellus* has been preserved in the *De oplf. dei*. But Brandt's argument does not appear to me to be convincing. Beauty as well as utility is spoken of in this connection by Minucius Felix, *Octavius* I7. II: 'formae nostrae pulchritudo deum fatetur artificem: . . . nihil in homine membrorum est, quod non et necessitatis causa sit et decoris.' The passages of Lact. *De opif dei* which Brandt thinks to be of Hermetic origin are an expansion of that statement. Minucius Felix shows no knowledge of Hermetic writings. His *Octavius* was certainly known to Lactantius; and the passages in the *De opif dei* of which Brandt speaks may have been suggested to Lactantius either by that passage of Minucius Felix, or by some Stoic treatise which was known to both of them. We must conclude then that there is no evidence that anything in the *De opif. dei* of Lactantius comes from a Hermetic source. But Hermes is many times spoken of and quoted in the *Div. inst.*, and is once referred to in the *De ira dei*.

Lactantius knew of 'many' writings ascribed to Hermes that were of the same character as our *Hermetica* ('libros, et quidem multos, ad cognitionem divinarum rerum pertinentes', *Div. inst.* I. 6. 4). He had read the Greek original of *Ascl. Lat.*, which he calls Λογος τελειος; and as he refers to three different parts of it *(Ascl. Lat.* I. 8; III. 24b-26a; *Epilogus* 4I a under that same title—*Div. inst.* 4. 6. 4; 7. I8. 4; 6. 25. I) there can be no doubt that the compilation of that composite dialogue was already completed, and that it was known to him in a form differing little from that in which it has come down to us in the Latin translation. There is positive proof that he knew also *Corp.* XII. ii *(Div. inst.* 6. 25. IO), *Corp. XVI (Div. inst.* 2. I5. 7), Herm. *ap.* Stob. *Exc. I (Epit.* 4. 5 and *De ira dei* II. II), and *Exc.* II A *(Div. inst.* 2. I2. 5); and there is probably, if not certainly, a reference to *Corp.* V in *Div. inst.* 2. IO. 14. It is possible, but not certain, that *Corp.* X *is* referred to in *Div. inst.* I. II. 6I and *Corp.* IX in *Div. inst.* 2. I5. 6. Lactantius also quotes or refers to several passages in Hermetic writings which were known to him but are not now extant *(Div. inst.* I. 6. 4; 4. 7. 3; 7.I3. 3; 1. 7. 2; 4. 8. 5; 7. 9. II).

It may be inferred then from the evidence of Lactantius that nearly all the extant *Hermetica,* as well as a considerable number of Hermetic *libelli* that are now lost, were written before A.D. 311 at the latest, and probably before A. D. 300.

From the time of Lactantius onward, the existence of religious or philosophic *Hermetica,* and the resemblance of the doctrines taught in them to those of Platonism, were widely known among the Christians In the course of the Arian controversy of the fourth century, disputants on both sides referred to these documents. (See Marcellus of Ancyra and Ps.Anthimus.) They were read by Didymus (A. D. 380-93), and by Cyril of Alexandria (A. D. 435-4I). Augustine (A. D. 413-26) read *Ascl. Lat.* in the translation which has come down to us, but does not appear to have read any other *Hermetica.* He did not read Greek; and the Λογος τελειος was probably the only *Hermeticum* that had in his time been translated into Latin. Lactantius, Augustine, and Cyril took for granted the antiquity and authenticity of the *Hermetica;* and it does not appear that any doubt on that point arose among Christians thenceforward down to the time of Casaubon.

The Pagan Neoplatonists paid little attention to the *Hermetica* Porphyry spoke of them in his *Letter to Anebo,* but there is no reference to them in any of his extant writings. The author of *Abammonis responsum* shows knowledge of them in his reply to Porphyry. Iamblichus is said by Proclus *In Tim.* II7 D to have cited a statement of 'Hermes'; and Proclus makes use of that statement to show that a certain doctrine was taught by 'the tradition of the Egyptians '. But with these exceptions, the *Hermetica* are ignored in Neoplatonic literature. Seeing that the doctrines set forth in the Hermetic writings are closely connected with those taught by Plotinus and his successors, we might have expected the Neoplatonists to be keenly interested in these documents. Why did they neglect them, and prefer to accept as inspired scriptures the *Oracula Chaldaica* and the *Orphica*, which would seem to us far less suitable for their purpose? Probably because they knew that the attribution of the *Hermetica* to the ancient prophet Hermes was an error. Porphyry uas too good a scholar and critic to be misled in this matter; he must have seen them to be what in fact they are, namely, documents written by Egyptian Platonists in his own time, or very shortly before it. The author of *Abammonis resp.* knew at least that they were not written by Hermes (that is implied by his phrase τα φερομενα ως Ερμου, 8. 4 a, which he may have taken over from Porphyry); though he mistakenly thought that they correctly reproduced the meaning of doctrines taught in books written by ancient Egyptian priests. The later Neoplatonists, if they were aware that the *Hermetica* were of recent date, would have little reason to refer to them; for all that was acceptable to them in the teaching of the *Hermetica* was to be found more fully worked out in Plotinus.

Some of our *Hermetica* were known to the alchemist Zosimus (A.D. 300-50?). Stobaeus, *c.* A.D. 500, had access to the whole mass of *Hermetica,* and made copious extracts from them. About the same time Fulgentius happened to meet with *Corp.* I; and the Λογοσ τελειος, and at least one other *Hermeticum* were read by Lydus, *c.* A. D. 550. From that time onward the Greek *Hermetica* seem to have been little known and seldom read, until they were brought to light again in the revival of learning which took place at Constantinople under the lead of Psellus. In that interval (A,D, 550-I050) most of them perished; and (apart from extracts and quoted fragments) those only survived which were, at some date unknown to us, put together to form the *Corpus Hermeticum.* The Latin *Asclepius* may have owed its preservation to the fact that it was mistakenly ascribed to Apuleius, and handed down together with his writings.

But while the reputation of Hermes as a philosopher and teacher of religion dwindled in Europe, it lasted on undiminished in another region. The centre in which it most strongly maintained itself, and from which it spread afresh, was Harran, an important city in northern Mesopotamia, situated on the main road between Babylonia and the West. When Christianity, in the course of the fourth century, became the dominant religion in the neighbouring regions of the Roman empire, the majority of the Harranians refused to be converted, and continued to worship in their heathen temples as before; so that Harran came to be spoken of by Christians as a 'city of Pagans'. When Syria and Mesopotamia were invaded and conquered by the Arabs (A. D. 633-43), a large part of the Harranians were still Pagans; and under Moslem rule they adhered to their religion with the same pertinacity. We hear little of them for nearly two centuries; but they emerge into light again in the reign of the Abbasid caliph al-Ma'mun (son of Harun ar-Rashid). In A.D. 830, al-Mamun, setting out from Bagdad, his capital, on a campaign against the Byzantines, passed through Harran, and noticing, among those who there presented themselves before him, some people strangely dressed, asked them, 'To which of the peoples protected by law do you belong?' They answered, 'We are Harranians'. 'Are you Christians?' 'No.' 'Jews?' 'No.' 'Magians?' 'No.' 'Have you a holy scripture or a prophet?' To this question they gave an evasive answer. 'You are infidels and idolaters then', said the caliph, 'and it is permitted to shed your blood. If you have not, by the time when I return from my campaign, become either Moslems or adherents of one of the religions recognized in the Koran, I will extirpate you to a man. Under this threat, many of them, in outward profession at least, went over to Islam, and others to Christianity. But some of them held out, and consulted a Moslem jurist, who, in return for a large fee, gave them this advice: 'When al-Mamun comes back, say to him, "We are Sabians"; for that is the name of a religion of which God speaks in the Koran.' Al-Mamun never came back (he died two or three years later, while still at war); but the Harranian Pagans acted on the advice of the jurist. They called themselves Sabians, and were thenceforward officially recognized by the Moslem government as entitled to toleration under that name.'

But in order to make good their claim to this legal status, it was necessary for them not merely to call themselves by a new name, but also to put forward a Book on which it could be said that their religion was based, and a Prophet or Prophets to whom the contents of that Book had been revealed. The sacred books of the sect which had hitherto been denoted by the name Sabians were probably unknown and inaccessible at Harran; and if they had been known there, it would have been evident that those books had nothing to do with the religion of the Harranians. It was thereforenecessary to choose some other writings, which would serve the purpose better.

Now the religion of the Pagan Harranians of the ninth century was the indigenous religion of heathen Syria, more or less modified by Hellenic and perhaps by Persian and other influences. For the mass of the people, religion must have been, there as elsewhere, a matter of cult far more than of doctrine. Of the local cults of Harran some descriptions have come down to us in Arabic writings; but these are mostly vague and meagre, and some of the more definite statements are evidently due either to gross misunderstanding or to malicious invention. We learn from them, however, that there was at Harran a temple of the Moon-god Sin, and that among the deities worshipped by the Harranians the seven planet-gods were prominent; and there are also descriptions of a cult which seems to show some resemblances to Mithraism.

But there were among the Pagans of Harran learned men who were well acquainted with Greek philosophy; and in those times Greek philosophy meant a religious philosophy founded on Plato and Aristotle—that is, in one word, Neoplatonism. The religion of these men must have been related to that of the uneducated mass of worshippers of Sin and the planet-gods in the same sort of way that the religion of Iamblichus was related to that of uneducated Pagans in the Roman empire. And when the Pagan Harranians were required, on pain of death or merciless persecution, to name a Book on which their religion was based, it would necessarily fall to the learned men among them to find an answer to the question, and to speak on behalf of the whole body. They might have said with some truth that their religion (i.e. the philosophic religion of these learned men themselves, though not the religion of the mass of Pagans) was based on Plato's Dialogues; but they preferred to name what were believed to be the more ancient writings from which Plato had derived his wisdom—that is, the Greek *Hermetica*. 'Our Scriptures', they must have said to the Moslem officials, are the Hermetic writings; and our Prophets are those whose teaching is recorded in those writings, namely, Hermes Trismegistus, and his teacher Agathos Daimon.'

The Moslems did not set any fixed limit to the number of 'prophets' acknowledged by them (among those whom they recognised as prophets were Adam, Seth, Enoch, Noah, Abraham, &c., and we are told by one authority that the total number of prophets amounted to 313, Chw. i. 626); and there might be no great difficulty in adding two more to the list; but it would be easier to get these two accepted if they could be identified with prophets already well known to Mohammedans. It was probably for this reason, and at the suggestion of Harranians, that Agathodaimon came to be identified with Seth son of Adam, and Hermes with Idris, whom Moslems held to be identical with Enoch (*Koran* 19. 57 and 21. 85).

The fact that the Harranian Pagans, when required to name a Scripture, chose the *Hermetica*, proves that in A.D. 830 a collection of *Hermetica* was known and read in Syria; and the fact that they named Agathodaimon as a prophet together with Hermes proves that their collection included some dialogues (now lost, and known to us only by a few fragments and references), in which Hermes was the pupil, and Agathos Daimon the teacher. It may be inferred from the occurrence of the names Tat, Asclepius, and Ammon in conjunction with that of Hermes in Arabic writings, that these Harranians had in their possession Hermetic *libelli* in which the pupils were so named; and among these were presumably some that are now lost, as well as those which have come down to us.

In the ninth century, Hermetic documents were most likely known to some scholars at Harran in the original Greek; but the *Hermetica* had probably been translated into Syriac long before that time, and were doubtless usually read in Syriac by Harranians and their neighbours at Edessa and elsewhere.

From that time onward, for about two centuries (A. D. 850-1050), we hear much of the Harranian Pagans. Some of them rose to positions of high eminence, and played an important part in the intellectual life of Bagdad.

The most famous of them is Thabit ibn Qurra, who was born A.D. 835, and died *c.* A.D. 901. During the earlier part of his life he resided in Harran, as a money-changer. But shortly before A.D. 872, there was a schism in the comnunity of 'Sabians', as the Harranian Pagans were now called; Thabit's party was defeated, and he was expelled, and forced to leave the city. After some years he settled at Bagdad, was introduced to the caliph, and attained to high favour at court; and he got the government to recognize him and his companions as a separate and independent community of 'Sabians', with a head of its own. Most of the learned men of Harran probably migrated to Bagdad and joined him. The community thus established at Bagdad must have been a sort of school of Pagan Neoplatonism, in some respects analogous to the school of Pagan Neoplatonism which had flourished at Athens until suppressed by Justinian about 350 years before. But there were doubtless considerable differences; and one of the differences was this, that whereas the Neoplatonists of Athens had ignored the *Hermetica*, the Harranian Neoplatonists of Bagdad recognized the *Hermetica* as their 'Scripture', and regarded the Hermetic teaching as the source whence their philosophy was derived.

Thabit lived on at Bagdad, occupied in teaching and writing, till his death about A. D. 901. We are told that towards the end of his life he was forced to become a Mohammedan; but his sons remained Pagans, and the Pagan community which he had founded in Bagdad continued its activities after his death.

Thabit's work as a writer extended over a wide range of subjects. He is spoken of as highly distinguished in mathematics, astronomy, logic, and medicine, as well as in philosophy. His mother tongue was Syriac, but he knew also the Greek and Arabic languages. Barhebraeus says that Thabit wrote about I50 works (translations included?) in Arabic, and I6 in Syriac. He translated Greek writings, and corrected earlier translations made by others; and according to an Arabic writer, it was said that 'no one would have been able to get any benefit from the philosophic writings of the Greeks, if they had not had Thabit's translations'. Among his writings on philosophy and logic were the following: a *Tractatus de argumento Socrati ascripto;* a

Tractatus de solutione mysteriorum in Platonis Republica obviorum;
a translation of part of Proclus's commentary on the *Aurea
carmina* of Pythagoras; an *Isagoge in logicam;* commentaries on
Aristotle's Περι ερμηνειας, and a part of Aristotle's Φυσικη
ακροασις; extracts from Arist. *Cat., Anal. prior.,* and Περι ερμ.
But he was, like the Neoplatonists of Athens, interested in
Pagan cults (more especially, perhaps, but not exclusively, the
local cults of Harran), as well as in philosophy; and under this
head may be placed the following titles given in the list of his
writings: *Liber de lege et canonibus* (ceremonial law and ritual?)
*ethnicorum; Liber de sepultura mortuorum; Liber de confirmatione
religionis ethnicorum; Liber de munditie et immunditie; Liber de
animalibus sacrificio aptis; Liber de horis precum; Liber de lectionibus
recitandis ad singulas septem planetas accommodatis; Liber de
poenitentia et deprecatione; Liber de religione Sabiorum; Liber de
legibus* (ceremonial regulations?) *Hermetis, et de orationibus*
(prayers) *quibus utuntur ethnici.* From one of these books (perhaps the *Liber de confirmatione religionis ethnicorum)* must have
been taken the following passage, quoted from Thabit by Barhebraeus: 'We are the heirs and propagators of Paganism.... Happy
is he who, for the sake of Paganism, bears the burden (of
persecution?) with firm hope. Who else have civilized the world,
and built the cities, if not the nobles and kings of Paganism ?
Who else have set in order the harbours and the rivers? And
who else have taught the hidden wisdom? To whom else has
the Deity revealed itself, given oracles, and told about the
future, if not to the famous men among the Pagans? The Pagans
have made known all this. They have discovered the art of
healing the soul; they have also made known the art of healing
the body. They have filled the earth with settled forms of
government, and with wisdom, which is the highest good.
Without Paganism the world would be empty and miserable.'
   Thabit seems to have also dabbled in the 'occult' sciences; he
paid some attention to astrology, and he wrote a commentary
on a 'Book of Hermes' concerning *doctrina litterarum et nominum—*
probably a treatise dealing with the cryptic significance or
magic efficacy of letters of the alphabet. It is very likely that he
knew other books also on such subjects (e.g. on astrology) that
were ascribed to Hermes, and assumed them to have been
written by the same Hermes that he believed to be the author of

the teachings recorded in the religious and philosophic *Hermetica*.

Thabit's son Sinan was a physician of high repute, and held by official appointment the position of head of the medical profession in Bagdad. Masudi says that Sinan had a thorough knowledge of mathematics, astronomy, logic, metaphysic, and the philosophic systems of Socrates, Plato, and Aristotle.

Chwolsohn (i. 577 sqq.) enumerates twenty-seven other 'Sabians' (i.e. Harranian Pagans) whose names have been preserved. One of them, al-Battani (A.D. 877-918), was a famous astronomer and mathematician, known as Albategnus in medieval Europe.

It appears that the 'Sabians' lived on at Bagdad, and continued to be known there as a separate sect, for about 150 years after the death of Thabit (A. D. 900-1050). At that time the 'Golden Age' of the great caliphs (al-Mansur, ar-Rashid, and al-Mamun, A. D. 754-833) was past, and the vast empire over which they had ruled had fallen to pieces. The decline may be said to have begun in the reign of Mutawakkil, c. A.D. 850. There was a period of confusion, in the course of which caliphs at Bagdad were helpless in the hands of Turkish praetorians, and provincial governors made themselves independent and established local dynasties. But shortly before A.D. 950 one of these local rulers, a son of Buwayh, who had got possession of a large part of Persia, made himself master of Bagdad; and thenceforward (until the coming of the Seljuks in 1055) the Buwayhids governed there as 'Mayors of the Palace', and the caliphs, reduced to impotence, retained only a shadowy dignity as pontiffs. Thus during the greater part of the century A.D. 950-1050 Bagdad was under a tolerably firm and settled government, and though shorn of much of its earlier glory, was still the chief city of a considerable dominion (Mesopotamia, Iraq, and western Persia).

During these political changes, students pursued their work without intermission, some at Bagdad, and others at the place of residence of this or that local dynast; and it was not until after the political decline had begun that Arabic learning reached its highest level.

In the intellectual activity of A. D. 900-1050 the Sabians of Bagdad took their part. During that time, or at least during the

earlier part of it, there was still under Moslem rule much freedom of thought; and non-Moslems, though subject to occasional illusage or annoyance, were often well received at court,
and found the highest careers open to them. But from about
A.D. 1050 we hear no more of these Sabians; and their disap-
pearance is probably to be accounted for as the result of a
gradual increase in the strictness with which Mohammedan
orthodoxy was enforced.

Among 'the two and seventy jarring sects' of Islam, there
were, and had been from the first, two main tendencies in
conflict. There was a school of theologians (the 'orthodox' theologians as they may be called) who relied wholly and solely on
the authority of revelation—i.e. on what God had revealed to
Mohammed—and refused to diverge from this or go beyond it;
and opposed to them there was a school of 'liberal' theologians,
who, while accepting the authority of the Koran, claimed a right
to the use of human reason in the interpretation of the sacred
text, and exercised that right to a varying extent. In the ninth
century, when the Arabs had got access to Greek learning, there
arose, side by side with the two schools of theologians, a third
school, that of the 'philosophers' Philosophy meant, for the
Arabs, not a search for truth in any direction, but adherence to
those philosophic doctrines which they had learnt from the
Greeks—that is, to Neoplatonism; so that the 'philosophers'
were, in fact, a sect among other sects. They were professedly
Mohammedans (differing in this from the Sabians, who were
not Mohammedans in any sense), and they did not openly reject
the Koran; but they disregarded it as far as they could with
safety, and when obliged to take notice of it, contrived some
sort of compromise between their Neoplatonic doctrines and
those of Moslem theology. Meanwhile, the liberal theologians
also read the philosophic writings, and got from them arguments which they employed in their controversies with the
more rigidly orthodox. Thus the 'orthodox theologians' and the
'philosophers' came to stand opposed to one another as the two
extremes, while the 'liberal theologians' held an intermediate
position between them.

Under the great caliphs, the liberal theologians had, on the
whole, the upper hand, and men of all ways of thinking could
express their opinions openly. But as time went on, the ortho-

dox party grew in strength, and asserted itself more and more. The tenets of this party, or of a comparatively moderate section of it, were formulated by al-Ashari (who died A. D. 935, i. e. about half a century after the founding of the Sabian community in Bagdad); and his followers, known as 'the Asharites', carried on the struggle until they brought it to a victorious conclusion. From the school of the Asharites issued Ghazali (A.D. I058-IIII),who 'crushed the philosophers', and finally established the system of Mohammedan orthodoxy which has, in the main, been in force from his time down to our own day.

Thus, about A. D. I050 the forces hostile to freedom of thought were already prevailing. Men such as the Sabians of whom I have been speaking could no longer venture to speak out; they could escape ill-treatment only by remaining in obscurity; and they were probably soon absorbed into the mass of orthodox Moslems.

Now the time at which the Sabians disappear at Bagdad (c. A.D. 1050) is just about the time at which documents of the *Corpus Hermeticum*, after an interval of five centuries during which nothing has been heard of them in Europe, reappear at Constantinople, in the hands of Psellus. Is there not something more than chance in this? It may be that one of the Sabians of Bagdad, finding that his position under Moslem rule was becoming unendurable, migrated to Constantinople, and brought in his baggage a bundle of Greek *Hermetica*—and that our *Corpus* is that bundle. If so, the line along which the *libelli* of the *Corpus* have been transmitted to us from Egypt runs through Harran and Bagdad. This is merely an unproved hypothesis; but it is one that agrees well with the facts known to us. The Pagans of Harran almost certainly possessed the whole collection of *Hermetica* (including many documents that are not now extant) in Greek, at the time when they adopted these writings as their Scriptures, in A.D. 830; and there can be little doubt that Thabit, who was a good Greek scholar, still had a copy of them in Greek at the end of the ninth century. During the 150 years which had since elapsed, knowledge of Greek must have almost, if not quite, died out at Bagdad, and the *Hermetica* must have been now read only, or almost only, in Syriac or Arabic translations. But a man such as the Sabian I am supposing would, even if he did not himself know the Greek language, have good reason to preserve with care, and to take with him when he migrated to a place where Greek was spoken, any portions of his Scriptures, in the original Greek, that had chanced to escape destruction and to come into his hands; and it is just such a chance collection of specimens that we have in the *Corpus*.

Moreover, if we choose to indulge in yet further conjectures, there is nothing to prevent us from supposing that it was the arrival in Constantinople of a few such Sabian Neoplatonists from Bagdad, and the writings which they brought with them, that first started that revival of Platonic study in which Psellus took the leading part. This would be very much like what took place four centuries later, when Neoplatonism, conveyed by Greeks who migrated westward, passed on from Constantinople to Florence, and again carried with it the *Corpus Hermeticum*.

It is almost surprising that no extracts or quotations from the *Hermetica* (except the insignificant scrap which I call Fragment 37) have been found in Arabic writings. Possibly some such passages may yet be discovered. There may be in existence unpublished MSS. containing treatises on philosopbic or religious subjects, written by Thabit b. Qurra or by other Sabians of Bagdad; and it might be expected that these men would sometimes quote from the documents which were regarded as their Scriptures.

AlKindi (who died about A. D. 873, i.e. before the Sabian community in Bagdad was founded) said that he had seen a book 'the teaching of which is accepted by' the Pagans of Harran, and which consisted of treatises 'which Hermes wrote for his son' (i.e. a collection of *Hermes to Tat* documents); but he does not quote from these documents, and he tells us little about their contents, except that they teach 'the unity of God'.

Shahrastani(A.D. II53), Katibi (A.D. I276), and other Arabic writers give summaries of the philosophic teaching of the Harranian Sabians; and the contents of these summaries are probably derived (either directly or through Moslem intermediaries) from some of the writings of Thabit and his associates. The doctrines which these Arabic writers ascribe to the Harranian Sabians are for the most part such as are to be found in our *Hermetica*, or might have been found in *Hermetica* now lost; but we have no means of knowing whether the Sabian writers got them from the *Hermetica,* or from Platonic sources of the same kind as those from which the Hermetists drew.

Among the Arabic writers whose *Testimonia* are known to me, the only one who shows any considerable knowledge of the contents of the Greek *Hermetica* is the mystic Suhrawardi (A.D. II9I). This man says he 'finds himself in agreement' with Hermes as well as with Plato; and this implies that he knew writings which contained philosophic or religious teachings ascribed to Hermes, and saw that these teachings resembled those of Plato. He says 'it can be proved' of Hermes (as well as of Plato) that he 'saw the spiritual world'; and he must have found his proof of this in passages of the *Hermetica* in which Hermes speaks of 'seeing' God or things incorporeal 'with the eye of the mind'. He says that Hermes (as well as Pythagoras, Plato, and others) taught 'transmigration of souls', and the doctrine 'that the spheres of heaven give forth sounds'; these statements must be based on particular passages in the *Hermetica.*

It appears then that Suhrawardi had the same sort of knowledge of the philosophic *Hermetica* that he had of the writings of Plato, and of the doctrines ascribed to Pythagoras by Greek tradition; and hence it may be inferred that he had either himself read some of the *Hermetica* (in a Syriac or Arabic translation), or got information about their contents from the writings of Sabians or Moslems who had read them. We know from Barhebraeus *(Testim.)* that a Syriac translation of a collection of *Hermes to Tat* dialogues was extant in and after Suhrawardi's time.

The statements of Arabic writers concerning Hermes show that, down to the twelfth century and later, his name was widely known among them, and was held in high repute as that of a teacher of philosophic religion, but they add nothing to our knowledge of the Greek *Hermetica.* There has come down to us, however, one document which may be called an Arabic *Hermeticum;* namely, *Hermes de castigatione animae,* a translation of which is given at the end of the *Testimonia.* There are many passages in it which contain teaching that closely resembles that of some of the Greek *Hermetica.* It seems probable that most of these passages are extracts from the writings of men who knew the Greek *Hermetica* (or Syriac or Arabic translations of them), and that some of them have been translated, with little alteration, from Greek originals. It is possible that some of these Greek originals were *Hermetica*; but it cannot be said with certainty of any passage in the *Castig. an.* that it is a translation of a Greek *Hermeticum*.

A collection of 'Sayings of Hermes ' is given by Honein ibn Ishaq, *Dicta philosophorum* (Loewenthal, 1896). This book contains a *gnomologium* in which are reported *dicta* of several sages (Socrates, Plato, Aristotle, &c.), one of whom is Hermes. Among the thirty-six sayings ascribed by him to Hermes are the following: 'Desire is slavery; renunciation is freedom.' 'He who publicly reprimands any one deserves blame and contempt.' 'Let nothing of the advantages which the Creator has given you be small in your eyes, that you may not lose that which is already given.' 'Leave the liar and his company, for you get nothing that is of use from him; he is like the mirage in the desert, which shines, but does no quench your thirst.' 'He who scorns another on account of his sins finds no forgiveness.' ' For the merciful, the repentance of the offender is a sufficient advocate.' 'Death is like an arrow (that is already) in flight, and your life lasts only until it reaches you.' 'The height of magnanimity is to be merciful to fools.' Gnomic sayings such as these have nothing to do with the Greek *Hermetica*. It is evident that the name Hermes has here been employed at random, and it is a mere chance that these sayings are ascribed to him, and not to Socrates or some other sage. This document therefore is, for our present purpose, significant only as showing that in the ninth century Hermes was, in the circle to which Honein belonged, reputed a 'wise man' in the same sense as the chief Greek philosophers.

Bardenhewer, in his introduction to the *Castig. an.* says that there is an unpublished writing of Mubashshiri b. Fatik *(Cat. bibl. Acad. Lugd.Bat.* iii, p. 342) which contains a *collectio acute dictorum* (doubtless a *gnomologium* resembling that of Honein), and in which *Hermes gravem agit personam;* and that there are other similar and partly identical Arabic collections of gnomic sayings.

The Orion Mystery

are the pyramids a map of Heaven?

Robert Bauval
&
Adrian Gilbert

At last the solution to the mystery of the pyramids! Robert Bauval and Adrian Gilbert have joined forces to present to the lay reader the latest, exciting findings concerning the star cult of Ancient Egypt. Even more startling they have discovered a hidden "message" left in the Pyramid Texts by the ancients which sheds a completely new light on the significance of the Giza pyramids. This new material, which is the result of twelve years of painstaking research backed up by published papers in the highly respected Journal of Egyptology at Oxford, presents at long last the real, "astronomical" time-message inherent in the plan of the Giza pyramids. Using the pyramid texts, the plan has been decoded and explains the significance of the pyramids.

"Let me say that I found your astronomical observations very interesting...I am very much in agreement with your contentions that the stars in Orion's Belt were an important element in the orientation of the Great Pyramid. I think that you have made out a very convincing case that the two other pyramids at Giza were influenced by it..." (Letter to Robert Bauval from Professor I.E.S. Edwards, Keeper of Egyptian Antiquities at the British Museum 1955 to 1974, and acclaimed author of The Pyramids of Giza. (Penguin Books)

Available from all good bookshops
ISBN 1-873616-07-4 ppr £10.95
ISBN 1-873616-08-2 cloth £19.95

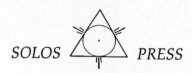

SOLOS PRESS